*Customs
and Traditions
of the
Canadian
Armed Forces*

Customs and Traditions of the Canadian Armed Forces

by E.C. Russell

DENEAU
PUBLISHERS
& COMPANY LTD.

in co-operation with the
Department of National Defence
and the Canadian Government Publishing Centre,
Supply and Services Canada

ISBN: 0-88879-026-0 (hardbound)
ISBN: 0-88879-027-9 (softbound)
© Minister of Supply and Services Canada, 1980

Second printing, May 1981
Deneau Publishers & Company Ltd.
281 Lisgar Street, Ottawa, Canada

Canadian Cataloguing in Publication Data

Russell, Edward C., 1913-
    Customs and traditions of the Canadian Armed Forces
Includes bibliographical references and index.
ISBN 0-88879-026-0 bd. ISBN 0-88879-027-9 pa.
1. Military ceremonies, honors, and salutes—Canada.
2. Canada. Armed Forces—Military life.
I. Canada. Dept. of the Secretary of State.
II. Title.
U773.R87 355.1'00971 C80-090012-X

PRINTED IN CANADA

This modern tendency to scorn and ignore tradition and to sacrifice it to administrative convenience is one that wise men will resist in all branches of life, but more especially in our military life.

Field Marshal Lord Wavell:
Address to the officers of
the Black Watch
(Royal Highland Regiment) of Canada,
Montreal, 1949.

Contents

Illustrations

Colour of Air Command

Squadron standard of 400 Squadron

Black and white photographs

Foreword

As nations go, Canada is a young country. Her armed forces, therefore, relatively speaking, are mere striplings in point of time. Yet, in the century and a bit since Confederation, through war and peace, the Canadian Forces have won respect the world over. Canadians, often called an "unmilitary" people and seldom known for excessive demonstrativeness, have come to regard the forces with esteem and, indeed, affection. Reduced to simplest terms, when they were needed, they were there, ready. Whatever the task or the magnitude of the sacrifice, the forces have acquitted themselves with spirit and a professionalism second to none.

In the course of these pages, the author has gathered the threads of Service beliefs, ideas and attitudes, coloured them with scenes of historical experience and achievement, and woven these threads into a rich and bright-hued fabric called custom and tradition in the Canadian Forces. This book, therefore, though not a history, is an important milestone in the development of the forces.

Many books have been written describing and interpreting the histories of the Royal Canadian Navy, the Canadian Army and the Royal Canadian Air Force. It is too soon to attempt to do the same for the eleven-year-old unified force. But this volume is a timely one. For the first time, the customs and traditions currently observed in the forces have been recorded and their importance in the preservation of high morale and what might be called the "spirit of the Service," described. It is my expectation that this work will contribute in a substantial way to better understanding amongst our sailors, soldiers and airmen, and the people of this wonderful land.

R. H. Falls
Admiral
Chief of the Defence Staff

National Defence Headquarters
Ottawa, Ontario
4 December 1979

Preface

On 1 February 1968, the three former Services, which had been for four years proceeding through various stages of integration, became a single, unified Service called the Canadian Armed Forces (more often called, simply, the Canadian Forces). Overnight, the legal entities known as the Royal Canadian Navy, the Canadian Army and the Royal Canadian Air Force ceased to exist in favour of the new single force. In the near-decade since that day, many of the wrinkles in the new all-green fabric have been ironed out, producing an even more smooth and efficient product.

However, in such a drastic reorganization of a centuries-old system, which in the past had served so well, it was recognized by the defence staff that there was a danger of creating a vacuum in a realm of the old Services — customs and traditions — unless positive steps were taken to inform the officers, men and women of the meaning and value of this aspect of their heritage. This book is the result of one of those steps.

At the outset, it was readily apparent that in treating such a vast subject, the major challenge would be the setting of limits. While history is an indispensable tool in discussing the origins of custom and tradition, there was to be no attempt to present the history of the Canadian Forces or its units. Fundamental to the work would be a discussion of customs and traditions as they exist and are observed today. It was also decided that areas such as dress distinctions and unit badges, though related to the subject of this study, are too extensive for the present volume, and guidance to the reader as to where such material may be found should be provided in footnote form.

On the matter of documentation, it was felt that the casual reader could readily disregard the footnotes, but that the serious student might profit from full citations throughout the work. Full chapter notes are listed at the end of this text.

Most works of this kind in the past have been designed primarily for the commissioned officer. The treatment here is hoped to be of interest to all ranks and the public at large.

In the researching and writing of this work, I have been most fortunate in the assistance I have received. In their wisdom, senior officers in National Defence Headquarters made it my good fortune to be attached to the Directorate of Ceremonial, whose director, Lieutenant-Colonel N. A. Buckingham (ret'd), and staff, have unstintingly shared their knowledge of my subject as well as clerical and stenographic help, in a truly cheerful, co-operative manner.

The task of researching this study would have been doubly difficult had I not had the fullest co-operation of the staffs of the Library of the Department of National Defence and the Directorate of History.

In addition to books and primary source documents, a very important, indeed indispensable, reservoir of source material is the current knowledge and living memory of Service people, active and retired. I am greatly indebted to the hundreds of people, from general officer to corporal, whom I have interviewed in establishments, units and ships, and to those who took the time and trouble to answer so fully my numerous written queries.

My obligations also include those patient, interested people who graciously read the manuscript at various stages of the writing and saved me from many a slip and error: Lieutenant-Colonel N.A. Buckingham (ret'd); Mr. P.A.C. Chaplin; Rear-Admiral J.A. Fulton; Colonel Strome Galloway; Major General G.A. MacKenzie; Lieutenant-General H. McLachlan; Captain (N) J. W. Russell; and Lieutenant Commander N.J. Russell (ret'd). However, in defence of my critics, I must record that errors of fact, inferences drawn and opinions expressed, are my own.

E. C. Russell
NDHQ Ottawa
1 January 1979

Introduction

Custom and tradition are part and parcel of our daily lives, civilian and military alike. They are very real aspects of life, yet they are rather nebulous terms. Custom and tradition are hard to define with any degree of preciseness; it is easier to say what they are not than what they are.

Custom may be said to be a long-established, continuing practice or observance, considered as an unwritten rule, and dependent for its continued reality and usage on long consent of a community. Many aspects of our social existence are governed or regulated by custom.

Tradition is not so much a practice, but a process of handing down, or passing from one to another, knowledge, beliefs, feelings, ways of thinking, manners or codes of behaviour, a philosophy of life or even a faith, without written instructions. Tradition employs symbolism, as it must, for human beings, save for the exceptionally articulate, find it difficult to express spiritual and abstract ideas in a few words. Long-held feelings and convictions, man has found, are much more effectively conveyed one to another embodied in a symbolic act or a phrase long understood and accepted. How better can one express one's love of country, respect for law and institutions, consideration for one's fellow citizens, and veneration of one's heritage, than by the physical stance and attitude taken when the national flag is hoisted or lowered?

But it must also be remembered that customs and traditions are not sacrosanct for all time. Like words of the language, they are living things; they come and go. For they reflect social conditions and moral values. They mirror political innovation and technological advance. They change. As Alfred Whitehead, the philosopher, put it, societies which cannot combine reverence for their symbolism with freedom of revision must ultimately decay. It is essential that outworn sentiment be quietly retired, and it will be, for the essence of custom and tradition is that they live by consent.

The rate of rapid change in modern society has of necessity resulted in the disappearance of countless minor customs within a generation. For example,

1

only a very few years ago, no commissioned officers would be seen in civilian clothes without a hat. How else would he give or return a salute without lifting his hat? But the trade of the hatter, like that of the milliner, has to a large degree disappeared. Again, he would not be seen in uniform camouflaged with burgeoning bags of groceries. But with the arrival of the supermarket, the discouragement of goods delivery, and the mass entry of wives into the outside working world, there is no practical alternative. Similarly, there was a time not too long ago when few commissioned officers would be seen riding a bicycle into barrack or dockyard, but wartime shortages of fuel and transportation soon changed the picture.

Some changes in customs in the Canadian Forces came about through the legislated unification of the Services. To many, it seems strange to see seagoing officers and men wearing moustaches contrary to the custom long held by the royal navies but fully in line with army and air force tradition. Yet the time-honoured naval hand salute, with the back of the hand visible, now applies to land and air personnel.

On a more serious note, one recalls the story of the mutiny in HMS *Bounty* in 1789, the eventual courts martial, and the anguished scene as the young midshipman learned his awful fate when he saw his dirk on the table pointing towards him. Right up to the unification of the Services in 1968 a regulation of the Royal Canadian Navy read:

If the Accused is an officer and has been found guilty, the Officer of the Court will, prior to the court reopening, have turned the Accused's sword towards him.[1]

Another custom that is not long gone was the auctioning of a deceased man's belongings and the paying of prices away beyond the value of the goods by his comrades in arms. This was an effort to cushion the financial blow to the man's wife and children before the days of Service pensions.

Perhaps people are more honest today. In any event, the coloured strand called the Rogue's Yarn once laid into naval cordage, to discourage theft and fencing, has disappeared, as has the Broad Arrow which marked the king's stores from the time of Henry VIII until 1949 in Canada, almost four centuries.[2]

Sometimes, words describing a custom remain part of the language, long after the custom itself has disappeared, for example, "drummed out." One of the last times that a soldier was tried, found guilty, and "drummed out" of the regiment to the tune of "The Rogue's March" and suffered the indignity of being booted out the barrack gate by the youngest drummer, was in 1867.[3]

Similarly, though the term "cashiering" is still fairly well-known, this ignominious form of dismissal of an officer has seldom been practised in recent years. An interesting case of such a sentence being inflicted was that of an officer of the 64th Regiment of Foot found guilty of drunkenness while responsible for prisoners of war at Melville Island, in the North-west Arm of Halifax harbour in 1813.[4]

Then there are those customs that start out in a more or less frivolous way, become firmly entrenched for a time, then quietly fade away. An example is the top button of the uniform jacket. During the Second World War, in the Royal Canadian Air Force, to leave the top button not done up was the mark of the fighter pilot. In a corvette or a frigate of the Royal Canadian Navy with perhaps six or seven lieutenants borne, including the captain, the top button of the naval officer's monkey jacket, left unsecured, identified "No. 1," the first lieutenant, that is, the executive officer or second-in-command. A very popular custom in the informal atmosphere of war, the unsecured top button could not stand up to the "good order and discipline" of peacetime.

On quite a different plane, it is unfortunate that in the minds of some outside the Service, there is confusion regarding military tradition. From time to time "the military mind" is castigated, and it is said that military people are hidebound, unbending traditionalists who look at defence problems today in terms of how the last war was fought. Such critics confuse and compound two quite separate areas of thought and endeavour.

No one in his right mind is going to be a party to strategic concepts, tactical thinking, or operational procedures that have no place in modern times. But this should not be confused with the traditional military appreciation of the solid value of the qualities we call patriotism, dedication, loyalty, honour, courage, and the resultant pride in one's unit and pride in the Service.[5] An eminent naval historian has said it most aptly:

> The planes, torpedoes, bombs and mines of the Navy may be likened to mushrooms in the meadow of its long story: but Tradition — what is expected of it and what it expects of itself — is a full-grown oak tree, still in its prime, still planted squarely in the middle of the field.[6]

Canadians in the past learned to their sorrow that sometimes a people must stand and fight for the principles they cherish. Essential characteristics of a military force charged with the defence of a people are the standards of training, the levels of discipline, and the quality of leadership, which together constitute professional competence. The goal, then, is to prepare the sailor, soldier and airman to face with confidence and spirit the stresses and demands of modern warfare. But there is one more ingredient in the mix that produces the first-class fighting man. It is morale. As Field Marshal Montgomery has said, the morale of the soldier is the most important single factor in war.

A Serviceman does, indeed, "march to a different drum." To succeed in action he must have courage and the mental and physical toughness essential to endurance. His training must give him the necessary skills, and confidence in his weapons. He must believe in his leaders, have trust in his comrades, and know what he is fighting for. His self-discipline must be such that he can and will obey orders implicitly under the most trying conditions, yet do so with imagination and resourcefulness, and if need be with independence. No matter how sophisticated the vehicle or the weapon, it is the spiritual well-being and professional competence of the individual fighting man that determines the decisive force in battle.

The history of our forces over the years gives ample confirmation that custom and tradition make a strong contribution to the building of high morale and sense of purpose by fostering that pride in the Service and in themselves that has so often inspired Canadians to press on in adversity and win through to victory.

1
The Salute

The salute is as old as history itself, for, essentially, it is at once a greeting and a mark of respect, and, as such, long pre-dates organized military forces. In whatever stratum of society, the characteristic that marks a gentleman or a lady is the respect he or she shows towards superiors, subordinates and peers alike. One way in which members of the Canadian Forces show such respect is in the pride and smartness with which they salute or pay compliments, a mark of good manners indispensable to Service discipline.

Like many other customs, saluting has something dynamic about it. Whether by hand, gun or ensign, it is full of life. Outward appearances change from time to time, but the symbolism, the feeling or message conveyed, remains constant. An eighteenth century author described the salute of his day in this quaint, but colourful, word-picture:

> Salute, in military matters, a discharge of artillery, or small arms, or both, in honour of some person of extraordinary quality. The colours likewise salute royal persons, and generals commanding in chief; which is done by lowering the point to the ground. In the field, when a regiment is to be reviewed by the king, or his general, the drums beat a march as he passes along the line, and the officers salute one after another, bowing their half-pikes or swords to the ground; then recover, and take off their hats. The ensigns salute all together, by lowering their colours.[1]

Salutes can be categorized as royal salutes, national salutes and personal salutes. Such marks of respect or paying of compliments are accorded in different ways, examples being: the hand salute; the sound of bugles or trumpets; piping the side on board ship; the playing of the national anthem and other musical salutes; parading guards and bands; the discharge of guns;

5

and the dipping of ensigns and lowering of colours. Each form of salute has a long tradition of its own.

The hand salute is the personal salute of officers and other ranks. It is a symbolic movement having several meanings. It is a greeting. It is a mark of mutual respect, trust and confidence. It is an act of courtesy and good manners. It is a mark of loyalty. It is a recognition of the authority vested in the queen's commission and the responsibility and status of the bearer of that commission; it also demonstrates the willingness, indeed the obligation, to accept direction. And there is no servility in the salute, no loss of dignity, for everyone in the Service has a superior and receives direction, right up to the chief of the defence staff and Her Majesty the Queen who exercise their various authorities by virtue of the powers vested in them by Act of Parliament.

The hand salute of the Canadian Forces is the naval salute in which the palm of the hand is turned slightly down and inwards, and is not seen, unlike the flat, open-palmed salute of the army and air force tradition. It was adopted at the time of the unification of the forces in 1968. Yet, historically, the hand salute was used in the British army long before it was in the Royal Navy.

There are several stories about the origin of the hand salute, but because of the long practice of this custom such beliefs can seldom be substantiated. Most contain the idea of showing friendly intention: the open right hand, the weapon hand, empty; the visor of the knight's helmet lifted to the open position, showing the face and demonstrating the voluntary vulnerability of the person saluting. However, in spite of the lack of hard evidence, it would seem reasonable to assume that the hand salute has evolved from the ancient gesture of greeting and mark of respect, the uncovering of the head, which, itself, probably originated in the days of chivalry.[2]

Previous to the middle of the eighteenth century, in the British army as well as on the continent, it seems quite clear that the personal salute was given by removing the hat. Indeed, this custom persisted in the Royal Navy well into the nineteenth century. But in the years between the Rising in Scotland (1745) and the American Revolution (1776), certain regiments of the British army sporadically introduced the hand salute of touching the head-dress. A regimental order of the Coldstream Guards in 1745 read: "The men ordered not to pull off their hats when they pass an officer, or speak to them, but only to clap up their hands to their hats, and bow as they pass by." This would seem a reasonable step when one considers the ornate design of the regimental headdresses of the period and the wear and tear involved in their continual removal.[3]

This would seem, too, to explain the difference between the army salute —

the flat, open palm and the simple touching of the elaborate hats of the time, and the naval salute — the turned down palm (said to be soiled with pitch) being the first movement of seizing the broad-brimmed tarpaulin hat of the sailor between thumb and forefinger for purposes of removal in saluting. Certainly, the naval hand salute, the one used today in the Canadian Forces, became official in the Royal Navy in 1890 and was clearly defined in article 145 of *King's Regulations & Admiralty Instructions* (1908) which applied to the newly established Royal Canadian Navy on its formation in 1910.[4]

Of course, the hand salute has a much wider application than the mark of respect given and returned by individual persons. There is the expression of loyalty when the national anthem is played; of respect for the flag and what it stands for, at colours and sunset; and for the queen's colour and the standards, colours and guidons of units.

One such observance is peculiar to shipboard life. It is customary for officers and men to salute when boarding and leaving the ship. In some navies, the person pauses at the ship's side, faces the stern (where the ensign and quarter-deck are located) and then salutes. Although this is not normal practice in HMC ships, the salute associated with stepping on to the quarter-deck is still a practice in Canadian ships of war.

The origin and precise meaning of the salute to the quarter-deck have long been debated. Some claim that it is a mark of respect for the place of command and the royal authority from which the command, the captain's commission, is derived. But many historians believe, though without solid evidence, that this salute has evolved from an obeisance paid to a shrine or crucifix which it is said was once housed aft, and may even be related to religious observances of pre-Christian times.

Certainly, there is abundant proof that, for centuries, the quarter-deck has been considered a territory almost hallowed in nature, respected as the place of honour in the ship, the seat of authority and command, an area of the upperdeck restricted to use by only certain members of the ship's company, and requiring a standard of dress and decorum not demanded for other parts of the ship.[5] Something of the aura of a respect approaching reverence peculiar to the quarter-deck may be seen in this excerpt from the writings of a sea officer nearly a century and a half ago:

Every person, not excepting the captain, when he puts his foot on this sacred spot, touches his hat ... So completely does this form grow into a habit, that in the darkest night, and when there may not be a single person near the hatchway, it is invariably attended to with the same precision.[6]

In HMC ships, what is deemed to be the forward limit of the quarter-deck is marked by a strip of brass fixed to the deck plating, forming a line across the ship's deck from side to side. This is a far cry from the quarter-deck of the old "wooden walls," elevated above the main deck and, yet again, above the half-deck. And it may be because of the radical changes in ship design that the ancient custom of saluting the quarter-deck is, in fact, waning. The locating of sonar detection gear, mortar wells and flight decks in the after part of the modern destroyer has probably doomed the spacious quarter-decks of yesteryear and, therefore, the activities and observances traditionally associated with them.

Finally, there is the hand salute which is given in certain units in commemoration of those who have gone before, an act which symbolizes what might be called the "spirit of the Regiment." Each day all ranks on first entering the armoury housing the Royal Montreal Regiment face and salute a tablet fixed to the wall which is dedicated to the regiment's fatal battle casualties. The same observance is made in the Belleville Armoury of the Hastings and Prince Edward Regiment where an eight foot square plaque in the form of a crown and shoulder flash, unveiled in 1965, is a reminder of those who have been transferred to the regiment's "White Battalion."[7] Similarly, all ranks who pass the plaque in the centre of the drill hall of Les Fusiliers Mont-Royal pause and salute the regimental dead who fell "au champ d'honneur."[8]

The cadets of the Royal Military College of Canada, Kingston, are reared in the same tradition. At the entrance to the college grounds is a massive gate of limestone and granite erected by the RMC Club, the foundation stone of which was laid in 1923 by the Governor-General, Viscount Byng of Vimy. On bronze tablets affixed to the gate are the names of the college's war dead. In keeping with the custom of the Service, all cadets salute the Royal Military College Memorial Arch.[9]

Closely related to the hand salute is the salute when armed with a rifle, the "present arms," and the first movement of the "present," the butt salute. Here again is the continuing theme of voluntary defencelessness to show friendly intent. In the position assumed by the sentry or guard the weapon is harmless.

An early instance of the present was the case of the Green Regiment, one of the regiments of the City of London Trained Bands or Militia, at the Restoration of 1660. This unit formed a guard of honour at Southwark Bridge for the return from exile of King Charles II. We are told that these troops "who by order of their Officer's, had presented to His Majesty as he passed the Butt end of their Musquets, gave and discharged a great many Vollies of shot" after the royal cortège had passed.[10]

Although there is no official Canadian Forces pattern sword, this weapon is still used on ceremonial occasions, and this despite the fact that the Royal Canadian Air Force discontinued the use of the sword in 1952. Swords are used by armed parties escorting the queen's and unit colours, and in change of command ceremonies. Sea officers still wear swords when making formal calls on dignitaries at ports-of-call.

As in other forms of salute, the sword, though drawn, is, in the final position, pointing to the ground, a friendly, as opposed to a hostile, gesture. This act symbolizes the trust in putting down one's guard. The guard, or that part of the sword protecting the hand, was in early times in the form of a cross, and still is in some patterns today. This has given rise to the long-held belief that the first movement, wherein the hilt is brought up to the chin, is a relic of the Crusader of medieval times and his custom of kissing the cross (hilt) immediately before going into combat.

The firing of gun salutes in honour of a royal or other distinguished personage, or in honour of a foreign state, or to mark a special occasion, is a very old custom. Gun salutes executed by the Canadian Forces today are fired from the guns of HMC ships, and by batteries of the Royal Regiment of Canadian Artillery at designated saluting stations from coast to coast.

This ancient custom seems first to have developed in ships at sea. In the days of sail, the guns ranged at their ports along the length of the gun decks were often kept fully shotted and charged, ready for action. Firing them in salute meant that for the considerable length of time it took to swab, re-load and run out the guns again, the ship was virtually defenceless, indicating friendly intent.

Some form of protocol measuring the degree of honour accorded by the number of rounds fired has always been observed. Many a gunner has passed marbles from one pocket to the other to make certain of avoiding insulting some lofty personage or causing an international incident! It is interesting to compare the language used in regulations today with those of nearly two centuries ago:

Military honours consisting of gun salutes . . . to distinguished personages . . . shall be classified as: . . . General Salutes in which the number of rounds fired depends on the occasion or the status of the personage being honoured . . . .[11]

When any Persons of Quality, or of a Publick Character, embark on board any of His Majesty's Ships, they may be saluted at their coming on board, and also at their departure, with the following Number of Guns.
viz.:

A Duke, or Ambassador with 15 Guns. Other Public Ministers, or Persons of Quality, with 11 guns or less, according to the Degree of their Quality.[12]

The point that intrigues most people regarding the gun salute is the fact that on most occasions the number of rounds fired, both long ago and in modern times, is an odd number: twenty-one guns for a royal salute and national salute, nineteen for an ambassador, seventeen for an admiral or a general, and so on. Here, again, much has been written about this interesting custom related as it is to ancient religious beliefs and old superstitions. Shakespeare was very much aware of this phenomenon, as shown in "The Merry Wives of Windsor," where he has Falstaff saying in regard to a third-time occurrence:

> I hope good luck lies in odd numbers . . . They say there is divinity in odd numbers . . .
> (Act V, Scene 1).

The fact is that, traditionally, odd numbers in the firing of salutes meant joyous occasions, and even numbers indicated death, though, of course, there have been exceptions. A seventeenth century writer had this to say:

> The odd number in ways of salute and ceremony is so observable at sea, that whensoever guns be given otherwise it is taken for an expression that either the Captain, or Master, or Master Gunner is dead in the voyage. . . . It is a general custom also (as aforesaid) upon the death either of the Captain, Master, Master-Gunner, or any chief officer, that when the corpse is thrown overboard to its sea grave, to ring the knell and farewell with some guns; the which (as aforenoted) are always to be of an even number.[13]

Just when the practice of firing gun salutes took on the status symbol system of number of rounds fired is not known. The evidence suggests the human frailty of one-upmanship was the villain. Certainly, as early as Elizabethan times, there were complaints about the expense of firing guns in salute in large numbers.[14] This led to various regulations designed to limit and define the number of rounds fired.

One of these was published in 1688 in London called "An Establishment Touching Salutes by Guns to be Henceforth Observed in His Majesty's Royal Navy." A scale of salutes to be accorded naval officers was laid down: for a captain, eleven guns; for a captain doing the duty of a commodore, thirteen guns; a rear-admiral, fifteen guns; a vice-admiral, seventeen guns; and an admiral, nineteen guns. No mention was made of the honours to be accorded royalty, but by regulation in 1731 the admiralty decreed that a royal salute was to be "such number of guns as the Chief Officer shall think proper, not exceeding 21 guns each ship." Thus, it would seem that the salute for the sovereign was perhaps a progression from that for an admiral.[15] But where the Lord High Admiral of England came into the picture was not mentioned.

A quite different form of salute is the dipping of the ensign. It evolved from the early custom of lowering topsails or, in small craft, letting fly the mainsheet. In spilling air out of the sail, the symbolic gesture of taking way off the vessel was achieved, indicating submission. This idea can be seen in an eighteenth century seaman's handbook: "To lower or strike the Flag, is to pull it down upon the Cap; and is either done in saluting with the utmost Respect, or in Token of yielding to an Enemy in Fight."[16]

In the British tradition the custom of dipping the ensign to a ship of the Royal Navy developed in the centuries between King John and Trafalgar, a period of six centuries. The English monarchs demonstrated their sovereignty over the "Narrow Seas" of the English Channel by demanding, and for the most part getting, this mark of respect for the British flag.[17]

Finally, the gun salute has for centuries had a part in expressing the joy of a people's thanksgiving, much in the same spirit as a Te Deum is sung in the churches for deliverance from catastrophe. Sometimes the guns roared out in the sheer joy of celebration.

One such occasion on the grand scale was the celebration of a small city, Norwich in East Anglia, when the Spanish Armada was destroyed in battle and storm in 1588.

On 22 September, the daye of giving God thanks for the overthrowe of the Spanyards, the great guns were firing salvoes in salute all day long, the town's soldiers let off their calivers and muskets in the meadows. The flags were hung out and to the accompaniment of drums, flutes and trumpets the waits [official bands of musicians maintained by a city or town] sang at the city cross.[18]

Many have seen the great cross illuminated against the night sky high on Mount Royal above the city of Montreal. But few relate that scene to one that occurred only a few decades after the Armada battle.

The stockaded settlement of Ville-Marie on the island of Montreal was founded in 1642. On Christmas Day that first year, the little fort housing Maisonneuve and *Messieurs et Dames de la Société de Notre-Dame pour la conversion des Sauvages de la Nouvelle-France* was threatened with imminent destruction by floodwaters of the swollen St. Lawrence.

On 6 January, the day of the Feast of St. Joseph, 1643, Maisonneuve carried to the mountain top a newly fashioned cross and the settlers erected it there in gratitude for their deliverance. On returning to the fort, the tiny garrison continued the celebration "by the firing of the cannons that stood on a platform to defend the settlement."[19]

Very few Canadian cities have had the distinction of receiving their names accompanied by a royal salute. Such was the case for Toronto. It was 24 August 1793 and the site, protected from lake-borne gales by Toronto Island, had for inhabitants a few friendly Indians and a small garrison. It was at this time that Lieutenant-Governor John Graves Simcoe learned of the Duke of York's victory at Famars earlier in the year. To celebrate the victory and to mark the naming of the new station, York, Simcoe soon marshalled his resources. Drawn up on the sandy beach at the edge of the pine forest were twelve- and eighteen-pounders brought earlier from Oswegatchie and Carleton Island, and a detachment of the Queen's Rangers. Offshore lay HM Schooners *Mississaga* and *Onondaga*. All the forces that day participated in the royal salute which simultaneously gave thanks for success against the enemy in Europe and marked the beginning of a great city which would rise out of the wilderness of the New World.[20]

Finally, there is one royal salute that must surely have confounded the queen's enemies. It was 2 June 1953 in the Canadian lines opposite Hill 227, to the northward of Panmunjom in Korea. In the celebration marking the coronation of Queen Elizabeth II, "a bounteous rum issue provided the wherewithal for a toast to Her Majesty" by the 3rd Battalion, the Royal Canadian Regiment. But, not to be outdone by the "footsloggers," the divisional artillery and tanks of Lord Strathcona's Horse (Royal Canadians), supporting the RCRs, fired salutes. Some of these salvoes revealed themselves to be red, white and blue smoke enveloping "two humps known to be occupied by the enemy."[21]

2
The Mess

The word "mess," in the Service context, conjures up different pictures for different people. It is a matter of time and place. In the Canadian Forces, there are separate messes for commissioned officers, warrant officers and sergeants, and junior ranks. There are unit messes, base and station messes, and messes in HMC ships.

Derived originally from the Latin *missum,* the Old French word *mes* had the meaning of a dish, a serving of food or a course of dishes and, eventually, a serving dish holding food for four people. This, in turn, took on the connotation of a group of four who habitually sat together at table and helped themselves from the same dishes — hence a mess.

The usual definition for mess indicates the functional, practical role — the home of all those officers, men and women, who live in; the club for all serving personnel; the centre of social life on a base or station, or in a ship. Indeed, in the two hundred years we have had messes, the continuing theme common to all is that the mess is where officers and men take their food, whether they are bivouacked in the field, comfortably housed in a modern barracks, hanging on to the mess table in a ship at sea, or dining amidst the splendour of plate and crystal, good cheer and sparkling repartee, of the finest mess in the land.

But the mess is more than that. There are characteristics that tend toward the abstract, and are therefore not so readily defined. The seasoned regimental sergeant major knows the value of the friendly, informal atmosphere of the unit mess where, over a period of time, the Service attitudes and professional competence of junior sergeants are slowly but surely built into something approaching the peak of perfection — far better than can be done in the classroom.[1] The same kind of learning process, so essential to a professional fighting force, goes on continuously in every wardroom and every unit officers' mess ashore, where that blend of authority and mutual respect, of friendship and good-humoured sharing of experience, contributes so much to *esprit de corps* and pride in service. This whole concept is something unique to the military.

Since time out of memory, organized fighting forces, unless compelled to live off the land, have been provided by their masters with rations of food and water, essential as they are to survival. It is likely that messes designed for communal eating first came into being in the name of economy of time, expense and effort. The common pot or kettle was the more efficient way to prepare the soldier's stew and the sailor's lobscouse. But, no doubt, companionship had much to do with it, too. As Falconer's dictionary put it back in 1815, "Mess among seamen, implies any company of the officers or crew of a ship, who eat, drink and associate together."[2]

The beginnings of organized messes in the army seem to be eighteenth century in origin. Certainly, there is a marked difference between officers' messing arrangements in the Seven Years' War and those at the close of the Napoleonic Wars. As Montcalm prepared for the defence of Quebec in the spring of 1759, Amherst was gathering his forces at New York, and a glimpse of regimental life may be seen in the daily order book of one of his regiments, the 42nd Royal Highland Regiment, under date of 14 March 1759: "Such of the Gentlemen of the Regiment as intend to mess with Mrs. Calender, the sutler, for next campaign, to give their names to the Adjutant by Monday morning. Divine Service tomorrow as usual."[3]

In other words, in the forthcoming advance up the Hudson and down the Richelieu to Montreal, Amherst's officers could make their own arrangements for cooking their rations, or, for a fee, could sit down to table with other officers in the tent of Mrs. Calender, one of several sutlers who customarily followed on the heels of armies in the field for the purpose of turning a profit.

To indicate the advances made in the concept of messing, it is of interest to note what amounted to an elaborate mess dinner in the field during operations in the year 1812. One of Wellington's young subalterns during the Peninsular War described the tactical situation on the Tagus River in the spring of that year and a "jollification dinner" in which all officers and men of the 34th Regiment of Foot participated:

So we determined to get up a big mess dinner for the whole regiment once for all, to celebrate the battle of Albuera.... We selected a pretty spot outside the town, under some cork-trees, marked out the size of our table on the green sod, and cut a trench all round. Our legs in the trench, we sat on the ground, with the table in front, but without a table-cloth. This was our arrangement.[4]

In garrison, organized mess life received a real impetus when permanent barrack buildings came into vogue. Certainly, at Halifax in 1787, where there were three barrack blocks, the army officers' mess was the centre of the port's social life. The members' rations for a week, valued at three shillings, sixpence, were augmented by means of a levy of two dollars, to purchase extras for the table, though there were complaints from the officers of the 4th Regiment of Foot about the high cost of mutton at sixpence a pound and twenty pence a bottle for sherry and port.[5]

Army officers early in the nineteenth century dined well during passage at sea, though, on occasion, their mess facilities were not as stable as when in garrison ashore. In January 1809 HMS *Fisguard,* frigate, was escorting a troop convoy to reinforce the British army in Spain. Brigadier-General William Dyott recorded an incident in the army officers' mess on board the *Fisguard* in the notorious Bay of Biscay:

In the night another gale of wind came on, and it blew extremely hard the next morning. We were sitting at breakfast in the cabin, when a wave struck the ship, and in consequence of our all clinging to the table hands and feet, the lashings gave way, and coffee, tea, ham, biscuits, generals, aides-de-camp, sailors, etc., were sprawling on the floor, paddling away in different fluids, some with a slice of ham plaistered to his cheek, others with his eye closed by a pat of butter; it was the most ridiculous scene possible.[6]

Naval messes afloat are institutions of great antiquity. Emphasis has been not so much on organization, as upon actions and attitudes distilled over the years into a body of customs that have withstood the tests of time and of social and technological change. Much of what we see in ships' messes today has been dictated by space limitations in ships and by conditions imposed by the long sea passage. Indeed, in a sense, conditions which obtained in Drake's *Golden Hind* prevail in HMC submarines today.

The ship, in terms of the numbers of officers and men embarked and the masses of fighting equipment borne, is a relatively small vehicle. Add to this fuel, stores, the means of propulsion and the ships' capacity to keep the seas for long periods of time, and the problems of living cheek by jowl and at the same time preserving the strictest discipline essential to top fighting efficiency become readily apparent. It is these factors, which down through the centuries of seafaring have produced the customs routines and what may be called "a system of manners," that govern mess life at sea.

In the days of sail a ship-of-the-line had several decks. The seamen had their quarters, their home, on the lowerdeck, the lowest of the gun decks, where the ships heaviest guns were ranged on both sides, each with its port through which it was aimed and fired. To this day, the ratings, or other ranks as they are called now, of the ships' company, are known collectively as "lowerdeck."

A visit to HMS *Victory* at Portsmouth will reveal how these gun decks in action had an unimpeded, clear sweep the length of the ship. It was over the guns that the seaman slung his hammock and, in groups of six or eight, called a mess, sat down at a movable mess table secured between the guns.[7] One man, on a rotating basis, called the "cook of the mess," carried kettles to the galley, drew his mess's cooked rations, and divided them between his messmates. This was called "broadside" messing, a system largely discontinued in the Royal Canadian Navy in the 1950s with the arrival of new construction ships and dining hall cafeteria messing. (However, HMC submarines *Ojibwa* and *Onondaga* still have broadside messing.) Today, the spaces where seamen sleep are still called "messdecks."

The naval officers' mess is called the wardroom, a term in use in the Royal Navy for well over two hundred years. It has a curious derivation. In a sailing ship of war, the great cabin, which was the captain's quarters, was under the quarter-deck. Below that, at the after end of the upperdeck, was what was called in the seventeenth century the ward robe, adjacent to which were the cabins of the ships's officers. This ward robe was originally a store room for items of value taken from captured ships. When empty, ships' officers, off-watch, would congregate there and use it as a mess, and ward robe became wardroom.[8]

In a military force, no matter what the defence policy of a nation may be, the primary objective must be professional military competence, the ability and the readiness to carry out military operations of a very high standard. Such a goal requires leadership, discipline, skill, courage and equipment. But in war, and in peacetime, too, all of these are of little avail without one more ingredient — morale, or *esprit de corps*. Here, the mess has always had an important contribution to make, and that contribution takes several forms, some of which newcomers to the military may be quite unaware.

After the formal classroom and on-the-job training is complete, it is often in the day-to-day contacts in the mess that professional competence is honed to a fine edge. Of necessity, the military is an authoritarian form of social organization where all are subject to the same code of discipline. Yet it is the mess where that delicate balance between formality and informality promotes a healthy spirit amongst its members, seniors and juniors alike, building that sense of mutual respect and trust so necessary in a fighting force. Where men are forced to live in confined quarters, such as the wardroom of a small ship or the mess of an isolated station on land, it is the time-tested philosophy of custom and routine, of civility, good manners and good taste, a basic and lively consideration and respect for others, that encourages the healthy relationships so essential in a first-class fighting unit. Inevitably, the tone and attitudes of the mess are almost electrically reflected in those of the unit as a whole. The great British admiral, Earl St. Vincent, was very much alive to this when he wrote: "Discipline begins in the Wardroom. I dread not the seamen. It is the indiscreet conversations of the officers and their presumptuous discussions of the orders they receive that produce all our ills."[9]

3
Dining in the Mess

The uniquely military institution, the mess, has always had the connotation of the taking of food at table in a congenial atmosphere. One of the difficulties of the novice in understanding this aspect of mess life is the variety of terms used in connection with mess dining. We are not concerned here with the snack-bar facilities provided in some messes, but rather with properly served meals.

Normally, in a unit's or ship's mess, breakfast and luncheon are informal meals. In wartime, generally speaking, the evening meal is of the same category, properly served to mess members who are properly dressed in accordance with the mess rules, but still, informal.[1]

In the navy this evening meal, served without formality, where members may come or go as they see fit, is called supper. In home ports, or large ports elsewhere, normally supper is served in the mess. In large ships, where dinner in the evening is daily routine, an early supper is also served for those who for any reason, including duty, cannot dine. In small ships, supper is the norm and more formal dining is arranged periodically as circumstances afloat permit.[2] The Royal Air Force has used the word "supper" in this sense since its inception and there was a similar tradition in the former Royal Canadian Corps of Signals.[3]

Mess dining, on the other hand, means that there is a degree of formality, or ritual, governed by customs which have proven their worth over the years, together with rules developed by the mess, both of which contribute so much to the sense of satisfaction of good fellowship and good dining.

While different terms are used in different messes ("different ships, different long splices!"), mess dining can be broken down into three categories — dining in, mixed formal dinner (for want of a better term), and the mess dinner. The word "formal" is really redundant in this context because all military dining enjoys a degree of formality. Also, in reading various unit standing orders, many variations of terminology were found for these three types of mess dining. Because messes differ so widely in terms of size, location, amenities and historical background, the wide variety of protocol and custom in mess dining in the Canadian Forces serves to enrich military life.

A dining-in is less formal than attending a mess dinnner, but it is a parade, ensuring the attendance of all members unless there is just cause. In some messes, this kind of dinner is used to welcome new members and to say farewell to those leaving the unit. In the navy, it is called "dining in the mess" and is normal routine in large ships. In the Royal Regiment of Canadian Artillery, there is what is called ordinary guest night, which may be a dining-in once a week for living-in officers only, attired in dinner jackets, or may be a more formal regimental guest night, say once a month, where mess dress is the order of the day.

A mixed formal dinner is a dinner in the mess to which lady guests have been invited. (It is an awkward term, for the dinner by mess definition is formal, but then an impression of the courses being mixed would be undesirable, too.) Procedure for this type of dinner is that of a normal mess dinner except that members escort into the dining room the lady seated next to him according to the seating plan, not his wife or lady guest. Also, the lady guests leave the table when smoking commences and proceed to another room for coffee and liqueurs. As often occurs, protocol does differ, and a member is well advised to know beforehand the customs of the mess. For example, CFP 195 *(Military Knowledge Manual)* states one should seek out and escort the lady to be seated on one's left, while various regimental standing orders say it is the lady on the right. One can readily imagine the foul-up scene!

The high point of mess life is, of course, the mess dinner. One has only to participate in a well conducted mess dinner to appreciate how over a period of two centuries a whole series of customs, usages and rituals have been fashioned into a work of art which is a pleasure to the eye and a challenge to the mind, as well as a delight to the palate. Mess dinners are intended to be happy "family" occasions, not doleful, stuffed-shirt affairs. Rather uniquely, they allow for camaraderie in a setting governed by formal rules of conduct. Juniors and seniors meet in the mess on a footing of social equality, though not professional equality, and in the mess, it being the home of living-in officers, the good manners of ordinary home life, such as respect and deference to one's seniors, are very much alive. The mess dinner affords the opportunity for all members, of whatever rank and responsibility, to meet on a friendly but formal occasion.

Like a dining-in, a mess dinner is a parade; all members are expected to attend. Basically, it is a dinner for the members of the mess alone, although, upon occasion, guests of the mess may be invited. Some messes set aside particular mess dinners as guest nights, to which both guests of the mess as well as guests of individual members may be invited. But whatever term is used to describe the occasion, the mess dinner is the most formal function held there. It is where every member is turned out in his sparkling best, and the mess plate graces the table; where punctuality, ceremonial hospitality and good manners are the order of the evening; where the traditional rituals of military dining foster good fellowship in an atmosphere of what might be called "spirited formality."

The proceedings of mess dinners vary according to unit tradition. This is particularly characteristic of army messes where dining customs have come down from individual regiment or corps practice, while naval and air force messes tend to share a single Service background. However, common to all are four stages of mess dining — assembly, the meal itself, the Loyal Toast and the conclusion.

The usual time for members to assemble in the ante-room or lounge area of the mess is 1930 hours (sailors consider the word hours superfluous when speaking of time and say simply "1930") which allows a half hour for a friendly glass with friends before dinner. It also affords an opportunity to speak to the commanding officer or the senior officer present, and, in some messes, the president of the mess committee known as the PMC. If it is a mixed formal dinner, this is the time for each member to view the seating plan and determine which lady he is to escort to the table.

During the half-hour assembly there are sound signals or calls which inform the members the amount of time left before dinner and the time to proceed into the dining room. The number of calls and the method by which they are sounded differ from mess to mess.

In messes of the Royal Regiment of Canadian Artillery and 1st Canadian Signal Regiment, the half-hour dress (meaning one half hour until dinner), the quarter dress and the officers' mess calls are sounded by one or more trumpeters, and at the first two of these calls, members go on chatting as if the signals had not been heard. In the Queen's Own Rifles of Canada, the officers' mess call is called the "dinner horn."

At a mess dinner of the warrant officers and sergeants at CFB Kingston the three traditional warning calls, including the five-minute call, are sounded by trumpet, and then, when dinner is ready, and in recognition of the number of sailors on base and the contribution made by the ship's company of the former naval communications establishment, HMCS *Gloucester,* a "bo's'n of the day" pipes "hands to dinner."[4]

In naval and air force messes, the senior mess steward simply informs the mess president that dinner is ready to be served and a few quiet words soon has the members heading for the dining room.

The Hastings and Prince Edward Regiment has the unusual custom of the vice-president of the mess committee, "Mr. Vice," assembling all but the head table in the dining room five minutes before dinner, where the members stand behind their chairs to await the arrival of the head table officers and guests who meanwhile have been marshalled by the PMC.[5]

Les Fusiliers Mont-Royal, during the half-hour assembly, have two interesting events — formal reading of the dinner proclamation by the adjutant and the presentation of guests to the guest of honour.

In most messes, smoking is permitted during the assembly in the ante-room or lounge, but traditionally, in air force messes, there is no smoking during the pre-dinner assembly right through until after the Loyal Toast.

In some messes, for example those of the North Saskatchewan Regiment and the Loyal Edmonton Regiment, officers and guests are played into dinner by the commanding officer's piper leading the way. But, if a unit is fortunate enough to have a band in attendance, the old tradition of walking to the tune of "The Roast Beef of Old England" is likely to be observed.[6] This piece of music has been a popular officers' mess call for many years ashore and afloat. A captain of the Royal Navy, writing of service in HMS *Leander*, 50 guns, on the North American station in 1804, referred to the drum beating "The Roast Beef of Old England', the well-known dinner signal of the officers."[7] Interestingly enough, this call is employed to this day in ships of the United States Navy.[8]

On entering the dining room, mess members proceed directly to their places, led by the president who escorts the guest of honour if there is one, although in some messes this honour goes to the commanding officer, or senior officer present. In army and air force messes, members remain standing behind their chairs until grace is said, but in naval wardrooms officers seat themselves as soon as the president has done so, after which grace is said.

If a chaplain is present, he is usually asked to say grace, if not the president does so, or he may ask any member to ask the blessing. Traditionally, grace is the simple "For what we are about to receive, thank God." However, variations are permitted and are heard, but the idea that the navy's grace is the abrupt "Thank God!" is a myth and is generally discouraged when attempted. Yet, these very words — Thank God — comprise the reverently offered grace of the Royal Canadian Hussars, of Montreal.

In the Canadian Forces, the whole matter of what officer is responsible for the conduct of the mess dinner encompasses considerable variety of tradition.

"Mr. President" ("Madam President") may be the PMC (president of the mess committee), the president of the mess, or a president for the day. In each case, he is assisted by "Mr. Vice" ("Madam Vice") (the vice-president) who may be the vice PMC or simply vice-president for the day. Very often, he is the junior member of the mess. In many regimental messes, the PMC certainly arranges the dinner and the mechanics of its smooth running, but it is the commanding officer who presides over the dinner proceedings. In the air force tradition, the president may invite the station commander to lead the way into dinner and escort the senior guest, but retain actual control of the dinner.[9] In naval messes, the picture is quite different owing to the internal organization of a ship of war and its confined spaces. The captain of one of HMC ships has his own quarters and dines alone; he is not a member of the wardroom. In a large ship, the president of the mess may be any officer appointed to that ship. In destroyers and below he is most likely to be the executive officer of the ship. At a naval mess dinner the president is in complete charge and always leads the way into dinner. The captain may attend as an invited guest or as an honorary member. Also, unless it is a large dinner with a seating plan, naval officers take their seats without reference to rank.[10]

The dinner itself consists of several courses with appropriate wines. Conduct throughout the meal is intended to be congenial but formal and most presidents will "nip in the bud" any attempts at horseplay or practical joking until after the conclusion of the dinner. Smoking is not permitted at table until after the Loyal Toast. Indeed, over the centuries dining rules have evolved which have proven to contribute considerably to a sense of well-being and the enjoyment of dining in the mess.

Traditionally, and in fact at the risk of sanctions, a member may not without the permission of the president, whatever his rank; come in late and sit down at the table; leave the table, or return to it after being permitted to leave; read or write; partake of a course before the president; use coarse language or tell off-colour stories; discuss or place bets; discuss political, religious or other potentially highly controversial issues; "talk shop" of other than general Service interest; mention a woman's name unless she is a member of the Service or a well known public figure; speak in a foreign language; or propose a toast on his own initiative[11] — all of which make a mess dinner sound like a heavily circumscribed affair, which it is not. It is just that these rules, which have become customs, help to ensure good dining in an atmosphere of relaxation, moderation, courtesy and stimulating conversation.

Once the meal has been consumed, preparations are made for the Loyal Toast and the other toasts which may follow. All is cleared from the table except the port glasses. It is at this point that a curious custom is practised in the messes of the Royal Regiment of Canadian Artillery which traditionally use runners on the table. On a signal, given as soon as the cutlery and china have been removed, the mess stewards take up position at the ends of the table. There they proceed to twist the runners, the number of turns depending on the length of the cloth. When ready, the stewards at the foot of the table pull the cloths clear of the length of the table with one swift motion.[12] The decanters of port wine (sometimes madeira) are now placed on the mess table in readiness for the Loyal Toast.

The custom of toasting or drinking healths comes down to us from ancient times. Greeks and Romans drank to their gods and libations were poured to honour the ladies. In the course of time, "good health" became an expression of greeting. The word "toast" dates from the closing years of the Tudor period and originally was associated with the custom of drinking to the ladies. A bit of toast was placed in the wine in the belief that it improved the flavour.[13] To this day the toast remains one of the most cherished customs of mess life.

Even though in the course of a mess dinner there may be several toasts, dining in the mess today is the acme of moderation compared to that of our military ancestors. A young subaltern of the 4th Regiment of Foot in garrison at Halifax in 1788 left a record of a mess dinner honouring His Royal Highness Prince William Henry, Captain of HMS *Andromeda:*

> We sat down twenty to a very good dinner . . . . After the royal toasts, and after he had given the Prince of Wales and the Duke of York, we had three times twenty-one, and two bands playing 'Rule Britannia.' We drank twenty-eight-bumper [brim-full] toasts, by which time, as may be well supposed, we were in pretty good order. At nine o'clock a 'feu de joie' was fired by the garrison from the citadel. Those that could walk attended. I was one of the number that got up the hill.[14]

Another glimpse of the toast of an earlier time in Canada may be seen in the journal of a French nobleman, travelling in North America at the time of the French Revolution. In the summer of 1795, he was at Kingston, Upper Canada. There he was invited to a mess dinner of the 60th Regiment of Foot in celebration of the detachment of the regiment forming the garrison being relieved by another detachment of the 60th. Le duc de la Rochefoucauld-Liancourt reported:

> The ingenuity of the English in devising toasts, which are to be honoured with bumpers, is well known . . . . Unwilling to oppose the general will, which becomes more imperious in proportion as heads grow warmer, you resort to slight deceptions in the quantity you drink, in hopes thus to avert the impending catastrophe. But this time none of us, whether French or English, had carried the deception far enough,

and I was concerned to feel, the remainder of the evening, that I had taken too lively a part in the event of the two detachments relieving each other.[15]

As in colonial times, the Loyal Toast in Canadian Forces messes today follows the ritual of passing the port. The table cleared, a decanter of port wine is placed before both Mr. President and Mr. Vice.

At this point customs differ in some messes, but, generally, the PMC removes the stopper from the decanter before him and charges his glass, as does Mr. Vice. In HMC ships, however, the president unstoppers the decanter and passes it; he charges his own glass last. This is also the case in artillery messes.

In some messes, the PMC takes a sip to test the quality of the port, but this is also a relic of our suspicious ancestors who insisted, as guests, on being reassured that the wine proffered had not been poisoned.

One aspect of the passing of the port that is common to all messes, is that the decanter is always passed to the diner's left. But the manner of its passing is another matter. In most air force messes and some units, for example, the Royal Westminster Regiment and les Fusiliers du St. Laurent, the decanter as it is passed is not allowed to touch the table. In naval messes, and in regimental messes such as the Canadian Grenadier Guards, the Royal Canadian Regiment and the Royal Regiment of Canadian Artillery, the matter of decanters touching the table is of no account. In the Queen's Own Rifles of Canada, the custom is to set down the decanter to one's left with a light but distinct thud. On the contrary, in wardrooms, the decanter is slid along the polished table-top from member to member (in fair weather; in heavy weather deliberately dampened linen may be employed), practices dictated no doubt by "the gentle motion of the waves" against the ship.

When the president is satisfied that all glasses have been charged with wine (or it may be water, though the sailor's superstition dies hard that the personage toasted in water will depart this life by drowning), he stoppers the decanter, raps the table for silence and says, "Mr. Vice, the Queen," in English or French. Mr. Vice alone rises and proposes the toast "Gentlemen (or Ladies and Gentlemen), The Queen of Canada," in the other official language. If a band is present, the first six bars of "God Save the Queen" are played immediately upon Mr. Vice proposing the toast, for which, of course, all members stand. All present at table then raise their glasses and reply, "the Queen."

Here, again, unit tradition is very much alive. In artillery messes it is considered improper to add the fervent "God bless her," which is the normal response in other messes, for example, officers of field rank and above in the Queen's Own Rifles of Canada.

The custom of drinking a toast to the health of the sovereign is universal in the Canadian Forces, but, as can be seen, the procedure is not uniform in all units, ships, stations and bases, and in these matters it is incumbent upon hosts to inform and assist their guests at dinner.

While the Loyal Toast is in most messes drunk standing, such is not the case in HMC ships, where the health of Her Majesty the Queen is honoured while seated. The origin of this privilege enjoyed by naval officers has been attributed to several sovereigns. But the story generally accepted is the one about King Charles II returning to England in 1660 after the Cromwellian interregnum, who, replying to the Loyal Toast, rose and struck his head on a low deckhead beam, typical of ships of the time, and declared that, henceforth, wardroom officers should drink the king's health safely seated. Some idea of the antiquity of this custom may be seen in a print published in 1793 showing King George III, who reigned from 1760 to 1820, with a group of officers in the great cabin of a ship-of-the-line, glasses in hand for toasting the royal guest, and seated.[16]

In this connection, the officers of CFB Halifax to this day adhere to the old *Queen's Regulations for the Royal Canadian Navy* (QRCN) which ordered that the health of Her Majesty the Queen shall be honoured while seated in all naval messes whether on shore or afloat, even when "God Save the Queen" is played, on all occasions except when Her Majesty or a member of the royal family is present (when the personage's pleasure as to procedure is previously sought), or when official foreign guests are present.

In addition to the Loyal Toast, depending upon circumstances and tradition, there may be other toasts at a mess dinner, including those proposed to: foreign heads of state when their official representatives are present; the colonel-in-chief; "fallen comrades"; the regiment; "the ladies," and others. In ships of war, one of these is called the Toast of the Day, and there is one for each day of the week. There may be slight differences in wording, but the substance of the daily toast has remained constant for many years:

Monday — Our ships at sea
Tuesday — Our men
Wednesday — Ourselves (as no one else is likely to bother)
Thursday — A bloody war or a sickly season (to ensure quicker promotion)
Friday — A willing foe and sea room

Saturday — Sweethearts and wives (and the usual wag's aside — May they never meet)

Sunday — Absent friends[17]

The date of origin of these daily wardroom toasts is not known. Those for Thursday and Friday are limited pretty well to historic interest today, though in the days of sail they expressed a real hope. A young officer writing about service on the West Indies Station at the close of the eighteenth century during the wars with Napoleon, recorded that "Their toast in a full bumper of grog [rum and water] of an evening was usually 'a bloody war and a sickly season.'"[18] The toast for Saturday night is of even greater vintage. The Chaplain in HMS *Assistance* recorded on 26 June 1675, a Saturday, while cruising in the English Channel; "And towards evening we lie on the deck, and drink healths to the King and our wives, in bowls of punch." On subsequent Saturdays in the Bay of Biscay and off the Portuguese coast, these entries were made: "We end the day and the week with drinking to our wives in punchbowls," and, again, " . . . and punch like [that is, as plentiful as] ditchwater; with which we conclude the day and week in drinking to the King and all that we love; while the wind blows fair."[19]

Speech-making is not generally a feature of mess dinners. Indeed, in most messes, speeches are actively discouraged, and if tolerated, they must be brief. Traditionally, dining in the mess means the taking of food and drink in a congenial atmosphere with a degree of formality in which stimulating, intelligent conversation is a major feature, and not a captive audience for a speaker. However, occasionally, a guest of honour is invited to dine and to deliver an address, the subject of which is known to be of more than passing interest to the members of the mess.

A mess dinner comes to a conclusion when the commanding officer or the president, as the case may be, rises, and leaves the table, escorting the guest of honour if there is one. At this point, members are also free to leave the table.

As mentioned, dinings-in and mixed formal dinners usually conform in most respects with the format which has evolved in each mess for the mess dinner. But in army messes, there is another, the annual regimental dinner, the main feature of which is the reading by the commanding officer of his summary of the year's achievements in the regiment. The annual regimental dinner is a mess dinner, but the usual order of things is altered. A good example is that of les Fusiliers Mont-Royal of Montreal. The following procedural order of the dinner reveals how one regiment of the militia conducts this much anticipated event:[20]

Cocktails in the mess lounge; reading of the dinner proclamation by the adjutant; presentation of the guests to the guest of honour; parade of the head-table guests into the dining room; the Grace; a moment of silence for fallen comrades; the toast to Her Majesty the Queen; the parade of "l'allumeur"; the parade of the main course; the parade of the snuff; the CO's toast to the bandmaster; the CO's toast to the head chef; the introduction of the head-table guests; address by the guest of honour; annual report of the Commanding Officer; the toast to the Regiment; the toast to the guests; the singing of the Regimental Song: "Nous sommes les Fusiliers du Mont-Royal"; the National Anthem.

4
More Mess Customs

It is a characteristic of men and women everywhere that symbolism is used from day to day to convey ideas and feelings that cannot be expressed otherwise except in the time consuming spoken or written word. Thus it is that friendliness is expressed in the simple handshake, reverence or respect in the bowed head. As in civilian life, the observer sees these symbolic acts, however inconspicuous, in the home that is the mess. A member, entering the mess, is a good example.

In many messes, for example le Régiment de Hull, a member pauses very briefly at the door and comes to attention before entering. Sometimes, as in the Queen's Own Rifles of Canada, such symbolism represents what might be called regimental spirit, something akin to the feeling one gets when the toast "To the Regiment" is made — a moment of reflection and respect for those who have gone before. Or take the messes of the Lake Superior Scottish Regiment, of Thunder Bay, or le 62e Régiment d'Artillerie de Campagne, of Shawinigan, where the custom is a simple mark of respect for Her Majesty the Queen. In others, for example the 48th Highlanders of Canada, Toronto, it is a mark of honour for the colours encased in glass in the anteroom, another expression of pride in the unit in which one serves.

A custom similar in feeling and meaning is to be seen in the Queen's Own Cameron Highlanders and the Royal Westminster Regiment, where the colours are uncased and displayed at every mess dinner.

The toasts which follow the Loyal Toast after the meal is over afford an opportunity to honour units within the Commonwealth with which regiments of the Canadian Forces are allied. A reminder of this in the Royal Montreal Regiment is the figure in sterling silver of a mid-eighteenth century boy drummer which always stands before the commanding officer when the regiment dines. The statuette was presented a half century ago by the unit's new ally, the West Yorkshire Regiment (Prince of Wales' Own).

The shared glass of port is a tradition which through the years has contributed on formal occasions so much to the feeling of mutual respect which is so important to the sense of well-being amongst the several elements of a unit. In the Royal Regiment of Canadian Artillery, the Stormont, Dundas and Glengarry Highlanders, the 8th Canadian Hussars (Princess Louise's), and many other units, there is a long tradition of the commanding officer sharing a cup with the bandmaster and the cook in a spirit of goodwill and common purpose.

Typical is the Piper's Toast proposed at mess dinners of the Canadian Scottish Regiment (Princess Mary's) of Victoria by the pipe-major, with the response by the commanding officer. This little sidelight reflects the ancient Scottish relationship between the clan piper and the clan chief. It is symbolic of the prestige of the pipe-major within the regiment. In the Candian Scottish, he pipes himself around the table and comes to a halt facing the commanding officer. The latter rises and each takes up a quaich or quaigh (from the Gaelic *cuach* — a kind of shallow drinking cup usually made of wood, sometimes of silver). Each holds up his quaich while the pipe-major recites the mottoes of the famed 16th Battalion of the First World War Canadian Expeditionary Force, and the other battalions which are perpetuated by the Canadian Scottish. This done, they both drain the quaich at one draught, turn it upside down and kiss the bottom of the quaich to show that the contents have been entirely consumed.[1]

In the Royal New Brunswick Regiment, they have what they call "The Passing of the Quaich," right after the toast to Her Majesty. The commanding officer invites the bandmaster and the pipe-major to the table and passes the quaich first to the pipe-major who proposes the toast to the regiment in Gaelic. He takes a draught and returns the quaich to the commanding officer who responds. Then the quaich is passed, being replenished from time to time, to the bandmaster, the senior guest and each member of the mess in turn. The last officer sees to it that the quaich is properly drained and turns it upside down to prove it.[2]

On occasion, the Scottish quaich plays a part at mess dinners of air command bases. A lone piper, in this event, leads the members into the dining room, marching round the perimeter until all the diners have found their places. Later, he may play during the passing of the port in preparation for the Loyal Toast. Then comes the Piper's Toast, a bit of ceremony very much like that of the Cameron Highlanders of Ottawa and many other Scottish regiments.

The piper, leaving his pipes in the ante-room, enters the dining area, marches round the perimeter, halts and faces the base commander and salutes. The base commander rises to greet the piper while a tray bearing two silver quaichs is brought forward. As the president raps his gavel for silence, the piper raises his quaich and gives the ancient Gaelic toast:

Slàinte mhath (pronounced Sl*awn*-cha Vah') meaning "Good Health to You."

To which the Commander replies:

Slàinte (pronounced Sl*awn*-cha) meaning "Good Health."

Having drained the scotch whiskey from their quaichs in one draught, they are returned to the tray and the piper salutes the base commander, turns smartly about and marches briskly out of the room.[3]

Typical of the rich variety of mess customs observed with enthusiasm in the militia regiments are those of the Loyal Edmonton Regiment. Dating back to when the regiment's forbear, the 49th Battalion, took its pipe band to France in the First World War, the honorary colonel of the regiment is to this day piped to dinner in the mess. And all new officers who have joined since the last mess dinner are presented to the honorary colonel at the mess table and with him drink a toast to the regiment.

In the messes of armoured regiments, there are often reminders of their cavalry origin. When the PMC of the British Columbia Dragoons demands silence at the table in preparation for the Loyal Toast, it is not the gavel, but the riding crop, with which he raps the table-top. The riding crop used was originally owned by an officer of the regiment killed on active service in Kashmir in 1950.

The Royal Canadian Hussars, Montreal, are also very proud of their cavalry background. It is a tradition at dinner that after the Loyal Toast the commanding officer declares a ten-minute interval to "water the horse." The "last parade" of the Hussar's regimental dinner is a memorable event called "The Ride" and is presided over by a senior officer who served in pre-Second World War days when the regiment was horsed. At the orders "prepare to mount" and "mount," all members place their index fingers on the table. At "walk march," the fingers are raised and brought sharply down in rhythmic slow time. Through "trot," "canter," "gallop" and "charge" one can imagine the rising crescendo (and hilarity) as the finger tips are drummed as rapidly as possible, followed by the reverse process and the welcome order to "make much of your horses."[4]

On a more sombre note is the traditional toast to fallen comrades, usually observed in silence but in some messes accompanied by the plaintive, yet poignant, music of the lament played by a lone piper.

In the 48th Highlanders of Canada this is a very moving scene. When the toast, "fallen comrades," is proposed, the members remain seated and the piper plays the lament, "Flowers of the Forest," after which the members drink the toast in silence with the commanding officer drinking from a silver chalice. The last lines of the old ballad convey the sorrow after the battle long ago just as they do today:

> The Flowers of the Forest that fought aye the foremost,
> The prime of our land lie cauld in the clay.
>
> We'll hae nae mair liltin' at the ewe milkin',
> Women and bairns are heartless and wae;
> Sighin' and moanin' on ilka green loanin',
> The Flowers of the Forest are a' wede away.[5]

Perhaps the most colourful customs in mess life are those traditionally observed in Scottish regiments. One such custom is the proposing of a toast with "highland honours."

The Calgary Highlanders wear a special shoulder badge bearing an oak leaf and acorn awarded for the famous counter-attack by the regiment, as the 10th Battalion, CEF, in the Battle of St. Julien near Ypres in 1915, during the first German assault using gas. It was in a stand of oak trees known as Kitchener's Wood, hence the design of the badge. Ever since, the toast to the regiment has been to "The Glorious Memory of the Twenty-second of April," with full highland honours.[6]

In the Queen's Own Cameron Highlanders, Winnipeg, the giving of highland honours is almost exclusively reserved for the "dining out" of the commanding officer on relinquishing the command of the regiment.

When the 48th Highlanders of Canada, Toronto, dine in the mess, each company of the regiment is honoured in the course of the dinner by the band playing each company's march and by a toast with highland honours.

To those unacquainted with the toast proposed with highland honours the ritual gives a glimpse of the lively night scene long ago in the clan chief's great hall by torch-light. Today, highland honours in the mess of the Toronto Scottish Regiment is described thus:

> ... all members stand with the left foot on the chair, right foot on the table, face the portrait of the colonel-in-chief (Her Majesty Queen Elizabeth the Queen Mother) and, after the Piper's tune, drink the toast.[7]

Another tradition of Scottish dining is the "Piping of the Haggis." A revered dish of great antiquity, the haggis consists of the heart, lungs and liver of a sheep or calf, chopped up with suet, onions and oatmeal, seasoned and boiled in a sheep's stomach. The parade of the haggis, which after the ceremony is served as a side-dish with the main course, is carried out in different ways in different messes, usually immediately after the grace.

Two junior subalterns leave the table and meet the piper in the ante-room. The haggis is carried on a board having two handles on each end designed to rest on the young officers' shoulders. Led by the piper, the haggis bearers are followed by the officer designated to make the address, the whole party being piped around the entire mess, eventually coming to the centre of the mess table where the steaming haggis is brought to rest. It is at this point that Robert Burns' time-honoured address, "To a Haggis" is recited:

> Fair fa' your honest, sonsie face,
> Great chieftain o' the puddin race!
>
> Auld Scotland wants nae skinking ware
> That jaups in luggies;
> But, if ye wish her gratefu' pray'r,
> Gie her a Haggis![8]

There follows the ceremonial slicing of the stomach-bag using the Scottish officer's dagger, the dirk.

The West Nova Scotia Regiment enjoys a tradition of more than twenty years in the "Parade of the Stag's Head." It seems that, originally, this parade was carried out the day after a buck was shot when the unmounted head was presented to the first lady mayor of Kentville. Ever since, when dining in the mess, an antlered deer's head mounted on a tray of wood is brought to the mess table in symbolic memory of earlier regiments absorbed, and in gratitude for the abundance of food produced in Nova Scotia.

Immediately preceding the main course, the stag's head, surrounded with food, is paraded to the music of "Floral Dance" on the shoulders of four subalterns led by the adjutant. This officer presents the stag's head to the commanding officer with a brief address featuring a dubious use of the language of heraldry:

Sir: Nova Scotia being the recognized province of plenty, I present to you a stag's head, emblematically denoting meat which is the main food of our province [The Land], flanked by lobsters which are rampant in the sea around us [The Lunenburg Regiment (1870)], and surrounded by dormant apples, denoting the sweeter dishes [The Annapolis Regiment (1869)]; all of which makes us truly thankful for our rich heritage.

To which the commanding officer replies: "Which we are honoured to defend. On with the feast."[9]

An interesting custom in several messes is the ancient one of passing the snuff, particularly in Scottish regiments. Traditionally the snuff is contained in a silver snuff box or mull recessed in the skull between the horns of a handsomely mounted ram's head, known in the Stormont Dundas and Glengarry Highlanders as "His Lordship."

In the Toronto Scottish Regiment, the toasts completed, the PMC stands and calls: Mr. Snuff. The subaltern delegated retires to the ante-room where he picks up the regimental snuff mull, and re-enters the dining room. The piper pipes him to the mess table where he offers snuff to the commanding officer, then to all members and guests. He then returns to the commanding officer who rises and offers snuff to Mr. Snuff. Retrieving the ram's head, the subaltern is piped out to the ante-room.[10]

Service in Normandy during the Second World War brought new customs to several Canadian units. One such practice that has matured into a highly cherished tradition is the proposing of particular toasts in calvados, the Norman drink distilled from the apples for which that district of France is so well known. In le Régiment de Maisonneuve, the toast to the regiment is always in calvados, as it is in le Régiment de la Chaudière.

In another Montreal regiment, there is a curious yet strongly held belief that calvados makes *un trou* (a hole) in the stomach, and that somehow this assists the second part of the meal to be more easily consumed. This is why it is that part way through the main course the commanding officer traditionally rises and proposes the long anticipated toast "Trou Normand" and the calvados is downed in one draught, just as the 17th Duke of York's Royal Canadian Hussars were wont to do some thirty odd years ago on the battlefields of Normandy.[11]

Over the years, colourful traditions have grown up which reflect the culture of the region from which the unit has sprung. This is particularly so amongst French-speaking regiments. An example of this is the wearing of the many-hued sash and tuque of the *habitant* over mess dress when dining in the mess of les Fusiliers Mont-Royal.[12]

Similarly, to be present at a mess dinner of le Régiment du Saguenay is to see observances which have come down from the native Indians of the Lac Saint-Jean country, and from the early French settlers in the valley of the Saguenay.

Immediately after the toast to the Queen, there commences the colourful ritual of the peace pipe's *"la touche de l'amitié"* or the "puff of friendship."

It all begins when all members, their right hands over their mouths, make the wild, five-second Indian cry. The PMC at once breaks into the ancient Indian folk-song "Ani Couni, Ani Couna," members joining enthusiastically in the chorus.

Then commences the ritual of the peace pipe, when two previously designated officers rise and, with arms crossed at shoulder level, proceed to the fire cauldron. Standing face to face they don feathered bonnets and raise their right hands above their heads in the traditional Indian greeting of peace. Going to their knees the two simulate digging a hole and bury the "war hatchet" or tomahawk beneath the bearskin rug.

Then seated on the bearskins with legs crossed, the two chiefs, facing each other across the fiery cauldron, take up the pipe of peace, fill it with tobacco and light it with a twig of cedar. Each then takes a "puff of friendship."

The two chiefs rise, and, in time with the song, still being lustily sung, pass the pipe from guest to guest. The puffing completed, the chiefs return to the cauldron, empty the pipe and ceremoniously place their bonnets on the bearskins.

The second custom much enjoyed by the mess members is *la lampée de caribou* which might be called "The Swig of Caribou." Caribou is a cup of welcome of long tradition in the province of Quebec. It is a fiery drink of fortified wine. As the members voice "La Marche du Régiment du Saguenay," two officers approach the jug of caribou and put on their woollen tuques. The jug is carried around the mess table enabling each guest to have his swig of caribou. Then all together they drink to the health of the regiment and utter the long "ahh" of satisfaction reminiscent of the very expressive belch of the nomad of the desert after feasting on mutton.[13]

Another set of customs with a regional quality about them are observed with zest in Cape Breton Island, specifically at Canadian Forces Station Sydney. Indeed, there is something reminiscent of Champlain's *L'Ordre du Bon Temps* in the founding in 1956 of the unofficial, but very real, Royal Cape Breton Air Force. Not that Sydney, Nova Scotia, is isolated as is many a radar station, but it is considered by the station's people to be off the beaten track of military traffic, hence the establishment of the very successful RCBAF some twenty years ago, a concept which has enhanced mess life markedly.

At dinner, mess dress includes the colourful bow tie fashioned in the Cape Breton tartan. The Loyal Toast is followed by another in special rum with all due solemnity, and with one foot on the table highland fashion: "Chimo — the RCBAF!" — all in keeping with the spirited, if impolite, motto of the mess, *Nil Illegitimus Carborundum.*

In lieu of the usual farewell mug to a departing member, is the presentation of a sword for the defence, in time of crisis, of the homeland which, naturally, is Cape Breton. It is said that no visiting officers are allowed into associate membership unless they demonstrate the ability to write decent reports about the station, and the rank of honorary marshal of the RCBAF is bestowed only on those with fifteen years continuous duty at CFS Sydney![14]

A tradition widely observed in air force messes is a singular antipathy towards speeches in the mess. But there is an exception, and that is when a member is about to be re-appointed out of the squadron or base and he is asked "to say a few words." Before he is allowed to utter a word, he is suffered to endure a rendering by the mess of the following rollicking ditty, "The Chug-a-Lug-Song." When the line, "So drink chug-a-lug" is reached the speaker is required to drink the contents of his specially prepared glass in a single draught and turn the glass upside down over his head to prove "mission completed."

> Here's to . . . ,
> He's true blue,
> He's a drunkard,
> Through and through,
> He's a drunkard,
> So they say,
> Tried to go to Heaven,
> But he went the Other Way,
> So drink chug-a-lug,
> Drink chug-a-lug etc.[15]

Dining in the mess is a formal occasion, but the high jinks, fun and games which often follow the concluding of the dinner are anything but formal. The arrangements for entertainment are often left to the younger, high-spirited members of the mess, and they seldom fail to come up with activities of a lively kind. The game described here has been chosen because it illustrates the boisterous nature of these affairs, and also because it has enjoyed a long popularity in all branches of the Service. It is called "Greasing the Gun."

The long mess table is tilted by supports placed under the legs of one end to form a polished, inclined plane. Chesterfield cushions are spread out on the floor at the lower end of the table. The "volunteer" is placed face down on a blanket on the table top. The gun's crew on either side grasp the blanket edge, and, in accordance with the rhythmic orders of the "NCO" — "one — two — fire!," slide the victim back and forth to gain momentum. On the order "fire," they release their grasp and the victim is propelled at a considerable rate of knots off into mid-air and the inevitable crash to follow.

But the point is, that, before being launched, the "projectile" has a match and match-book in hand, and if he fails to ignite the match while in flight, a misfire is declared, and the fun commences all over again.

The base officers' mess at CFB Petawawa is located on an eminence with a fine view of the Ottawa River and the Laurentians. Just outside the entrance is a venerable red oak tree with great spreading boughs. It is known as the "drinking tree" or "subaltern's tree."

It has often been said that on certain evening occasions, subalterns stationed at Petawawa climb the subaltern's tree and seated out on the spreading boughs, champagne in hand, render wondrous songs on the night air, and such goings-on are duly recorded in the drinking tree log-book.

As the mess, formerly the gunner's mess, is an old temporary building, and has been slated for demolition, fears have been held that the subaltern's tree might also become a victim of the bulldozer. But, ever resourceful, the young officers have assured their beloved tree a considerable degree of life expectancy.

There on the trunk is a highly polished brass plate designating the spot as an official bench mark of the Dominion of Canada, and therefore sacrosanct: elevation, 507.3 feet; latitude 45° 55′12″ north; longitude 77° 17′23″ west.[16]

5
Words and Expressions

Customs and traditions serve many purposes, one of which is that they span the years of Service life from one generation to another. One aspect of this is language, words and expressions used from day to day in the course of a Serviceman's duty, in both peace and war. Language in the Service is a part of custom and tradition which bridges the years forming a living continuity between the Serviceman and Servicewoman of today and those who have gone before.

Able Seaman
The rank, or rating as it was once called, of able seaman, or AB, is the equivalent of the private in the army and air force. It was fully established in the Commonwealth Navy of Cromwell in the seventeenth century.[1] As the words imply, the able seaman is fully trained for upper deck duties. In the days of sail, the saying was "able to hand, reef and steer," that is, fully capable of going aloft to take in sail and to take charge of the helm.[2]

Adjutant's Tea
Adjutant's tea is sherry served in the field before breakfast, for example in the Grey and Simcoe Foresters.

Admiral
The rank of admiral signifies the commander-in-chief of a nation's navy; a senior naval officer in command of a fleet or squadron, or of a command or station ashore. Before unification of the forces, admirals with such appointments were known as flag officers. The word admiral is derived from the Arabic *emir* or *ameer* meaning "chief." It made its way westward from that

cradle of navigators, the Mediterranean Sea, from the medieval latin *amiralus*, through the Old French *amirail* and the Spanish *almirante*. In Britain, the term admiral developed in a rather complex way from medieval times, but became firm as the commander-in-chief at sea in the seventeenth century. In a large fleet at sea in the days of sail, the main squadron in the centre with the Admiral of the Fleet was preceded by a squadron in the van or lead and bearing the second-in-command, the vice-admiral of the fleet, hence the rank of vice-admiral. The rear of the fleet was covered by a third squadron or rear-guard, bearing the rear admiral of the fleet, hence the rank today of rear-admiral.[3]

A curious use of the term in our own maritime heritage is to be seen in a Royal Proclamation dated 26 June 1708 concerning the "fishing admirals." Each year, fishing fleets would arrive in Newfoundland waters, base themselves in numerous coves and havens and land their catches there for drying, before returning to Europe in the fall, their holds full of dried fish. Good order was maintained in these outports by appointing the captain of the first ship to arrive "season admiral of the said harbour or creek," the second ship, vice-admiral, and so on. The admiral's decision about foreshore rights and disputes which might arise was binding.[4]

Artillery

Guns used by the army; the arm or branch of the land forces that uses guns. Of early French origin, the word is derived from *artiller,* to equip or arm. Originally, artillery encompassed a wide variety of war equipment, including all missile-type weapons. In 1539 the "Guylde of Artyllary of longbowes, Crossbowes and handegonnes" marched from Aldgate, City of London, to Westminster, where it was reviewed by King Henry VIII.[5]

Awkward Squad

This term of good-natured derision is still occasionally heard. It refers to recruits who have difficulties of co-ordination and therefore are slow to come up to the standards of their drill instructors. This is a phenomenon of long standing. General Amherst, on the march up the Hudson River in 1759 bound for Montreal, required the awkward men to be exercised by themselves twice a day, and infantrymen who fired before the word of command were punished with extra drill with the "acquart men" in the evening.[6] Similarly, at the raising of His Majesty's Newfoundland Regiment of Foot, 1780-1783, early provision was made to exercise the awkward men.[7]

Barn

A barn is a hangar.

Battalion

The origin of this word is obscure. It dates from at least the sixteenth century in the old French form, *battaillon,* and is believed to have a common root with the word battle.[8] The battalion, traditionally, is a unit of infantry composed of several companies and forms part of the larger brigade or regiment. In the organizational sense, the structure of the battalion has had many changes through the centuries to meet the needs of changing roles and tactics, and of advances in the technology and doctrine of war. Today in the Canadian Forces the term battalion has two applications: an infantry regiment, which may consist of one, two, or more battalions, manned and equipped as fighting units; the administrative unit for support troops, called service battalions.

Bird

Naval slang for a sailor with a long record of disciplinary misdemeanours. It has the same origin as "jail-bird," one who has been confined in prison which often was called "the cage." In earlier times such felons were often sentenced to serve in the Royal Navy.

Bivouac

An encampment without tents or huts. It is thought to be derived from the German *Beiwacht,* having a connotation of watch or guard.

Blue Bark

An example of Service jargon which has become official language in regulations. A blue bark is a passenger travelling via Service aircraft for compassionate reasons to attend the funeral of a member of his or her family. The term came into use in the early 1960s and is particularly associated with service in Europe. The origin of the term is not known but is thought to stem from "embarkation" and travel priority categories.

Boatswain

The term boatswain (bo's'n) is the oldest title in the sea service. It is derived from the Old English *batswegen* or *batsuen* (boat's swain or husband). In Saxon times the boatswain was in command. In medieval England, he was the officer who made the ship go, having charge of the masts, yards and sails, and was second only to the master. Nathaniel Boteler in his *Dialogues,* in the reign of King Charles I, showed the wide responsibilities of the boatswain in the early seventeenth century. He had charge of all ropes, anchors, sails, flags, colours, and care of the long-boat. He called up the watches to their duty, kept the sailors "in peace, and in order one with another," and he saw to it that all offenders were punctually punished (boatswain's mates had to wield the cat-o'-nine tails), "either at the Capstan, or by being put in the bilboes, or with ducking at the main yard-arm."[9] It is readily seen that through the centuries the boatswain has had the duties not only of command, but those associated with the coxswain and the late master-at-arms. But through it all the boatswain has remained to this day the seaman specialist, particularly in terms of equipment related to seamanship. In HMC ships today, the boatswain, usually a master or chief warrant officer, looks after small arms, anchors and cables, hawsers and fenders, paints, life rafts and demolitions, as well as parade and small arms training.[10]

Boatswain's Mate
In harbour, the boatswain's mate is a member of the gangway staff under the officer of the day. He pipes all orders and generally assists the quarter-master. At sea, he keeps his watch within hail of the officer of the watch.

Boondocks (Boonies)
Area not considered part of the runway or taxiway, or a relatively isolated base or station.

Brigadier-General
The rank between colonel and major-general. A definition of the time of Wellington, it has stood the test of time, if not terminology, rather well: "Brigadier, a military officer, whose rank is next above that of a colonel, appointed to command a corps, consisting of several battalions or regiments, called a brigade."[11] The term has its origin in the Italian *brigata* meaning company, related to *brigare* (brawl) and *briga* (strife). For a time in the Canadian army the rank was simply brigadier. The term brigadier-general was reinstituted in 1968.[12]

Buffer
Slang term for the chief boatswain's mate, usually a petty officer, dating from the eighteenth century. Its derivation is obscure. While the boatswain is responsible today for all the upperdeck seamanship equipment, the chief boatswain's mate, or buffer, is the "foreman" of the hands who keep the internal spaces of the ship in good repair. In destroyers and lesser ships, the boatswain and the buffer are likely to be one and the same person.

Camming-up and Camming-down
The fitting up and taking down of camouflage netting as used, for example, to hide the positions of guns and vehicles.

Captain

In the Service today, the term captain has several meanings. In terms of rank, the naval captain is equivalent to colonel, while the army and airforce captain is the rank between lieutenant and major. In terms of office, there is the captain of a ship, and the captain of an aircraft. Captain is derived from the Latin *caput* meaning head. With the head being the directing or controlling portion of the anatomy, it is not difficult to see how the Romans came to use *capitaneus* to denote the director or leader of troops. There is a very long tradition of the captain as the officer commanding a company-size unit of from one hundred to two hundred men. Even in the navy the term captain is of military origin. The seamanship and navigation essential to making a passage at sea were in earlier times the province of the boatswain and the master, the latter term being still very evident in the merchant service. The captain came on board with his soldiers to do the fighting, while the master, the seaman, conveyed the troops to the right place to engage the enemy at sea or on a foreign shore. With the advent of "great guns" in ships in the sixteenth century, the master became the captain who not only directed the ship, but led his fighting seamen.[13]

Chit

Shortened form of chitty, an Anglo-Indian word from *chitthi,* meaning a written note, or a voucher tendered in lieu of cash for refreshments in the mess.

Colonel

A rank which today denotes a senior staff officer, not yet a general officer, but no longer the senior officer in a regiment — with one exception. The Canadian Airborne Regiment, consisting of three commandos capable of operating independently, is commanded by a colonel.[14] The term dates from the late sixteenth century and early seventeenth century when the process of merging the normal army formation, the companies under their captains, into regiments under their colonels, was well advanced. The origin of the word itself is unknown. Sometimes it was spelled "coronel" as in the French of the period, which suggests "crown." This, itself, raises several conjectures including insignia, also the authority for the colonel's commission. In the Italian *colonnello,* there is a relationship with *colonna,* meaning a column.

Colour Sergeant

The title given to warrant officers in regiments of foot guards; the title given to selected non-commissioned officers having the honour and distinction of attending (escorting) the queen's and regimental colours of foot guards and certain other infantry regiments.[15] It was the Duke of Wellington who initiated the idea of the colour sergeant "for the encouragement of good men,"[16] and it was established as a rank in the British army in 1813, the general order making it clear that "the duty of attending the Colours in the field shall be at all times performed by these Sergeants."[17] In the days when the colours were carried into battle at the centre front of the regiment, they were prime targets for the enemy, and casualties among ensigns and colour sergeants in the defence of the colours were high. So, while it was considered a great honour to be given the custody of the colours, it took men of high courage to accept that honour. Today, colour sergeant is not an official rank, as it was prior to 1919 in the Canadian Militia.[18] It is a traditional title in the foot guards and an office or appointment of honour on specific occasions as in the "trooping of the colour."

Commander

The rank of commander evolved from the split command situation in the early warship where the captain commanded the soldier fighting men and the master navigated the ship by commanding the mariners. After the arrival of great guns in ships of war in the time of Henry VIII, sailors both worked the ship and fought the ship. As ships developed in tonnage and gun-power, the captain in command of a ship-of-the-line had under him a master as his chief navigator, but in lesser ships the two offices were combined in one officer called "master and commander."

In the mid-eighteenth century the "master and" part was no longer needed when an officer was placed on complement to relieve the commander of his navigating duties, but it was not until 1794 that the rank of commander came into official use in the Royal Navy.[19]

In 1875 the lieutenant of eight years seniority was given the well known "half-stripe" of the lieutenant commander, and this title was officially recognized in 1914.[20]

Commando

A body of troops, highly trained for specialized tasks or missions. In the Second World War, British commandos were amphibious shock-troops often employed on raids or operations with limited objectives. It is a Portuguese term derived from *commandar* (command), and from the late Latin *commandare*. Commando was used by the Boers and became a familiar term during the South African War at the beginning of the twentieth century. The word is used today in the Canadian Forces to denote the three components of the Canadian Airborne Regiment — the two parachute commandos and the mechanized commando.

Commodore

Unlike the Royal Navy, commodore is a permanent rank in the Canadian Forces, between captain and rear-admiral. At sea the commodore traditionally is in command of a detached squadron. Today the appointment of senior officer afloat is that of a commodore. The term is from the Dutch *Commandeur* introduced by them in 1652. King William III of Orange brought the title to the Royal Navy in 1688.[21]

There is an old saying connected with the commodore. Well into this century, it was the custom to fire a gun at sunset, when in harbour, and lower the colours. On hearing the evening gun fired, one would hear, "the commodore has fallen down the main hatch," meaning his day's work is done and so is mine.[22]

Company

The dictionary meaning of this word is given as "a body of persons combined for common object," and this definition applies to the use of the term today: a sub-division of an infantry battalion, or of a naval reserve division for parade purposes, or simply the ship's company or ship's crew. It is also used to denote a detached unit of support services. There is a curious commercial origin to the term company. Towards the end of the medieval feudal period, mercenary bands of professional soldiers appeared in Europe, whose captains would accept contracts to fight for or against anyone. Money was invested in these bands, which soon were called companies, to share in the profits obtained from plunder and ransom.[23]

Corporal

The master corporal of today is the corporal of earlier times, a leader of men. This attribute is reflected in the derivation of the word — the Italian *capo* (head), *di squadra* (of the squad), sometimes written *capo de escadra*, referring to squad, or squadron, or to the earlier fighting formation, the square. The French called this man *caporal* and, in English, he became corporal. Sir James Turner, soldier, in his *Pallas Armata* (1683) made some rather pithy remarks in describing the function of the corporal of old:

A caporal . . . hath an absolute command of his squadron, neither may any in it disobey him; if any do, the caporal may beat him with his sword, and commit him to prison . . . and he is bound to teach them how they are to behave themselves when centinels, . . . to teach all that belong to his squadron their postures, and to handle their arms. So you see this caporal of ours hath work enough to do, for all the pay or wages he gets.[24]

Coxswain

The coxswain (cox'n) today is the senior non-commissioned seaman in the ship, usually a chief warrant officer. He is the connecting link between the ship's officers and the lower deck other than that provided by the divisional system. He sees that daily routines on board are carried out, and attends the captain's and the executive officer's tables when requestmen and defaulters are being seen, formerly the duty of the ship's master at arms. In action, or in confined waters, he takes over the ship's helm. A second meaning for coxswain is the seaman in charge of a ship's boat when away from the ship — coxswain of the boat. The name coxswain is a very old one at sea. It is derived from the medieval Latin *cussus,* the Old French *coq* and the Old English *coc,* all meaning "cock" as in "cockboat," that is a small boat. In recent years, the coxswain has lost ground in professional status as a seaman. As a specialist seaman, command of the ship once devolved on him if say, in action, all the executive branch (seamen) officers had been incapacitated. This is no longer so.[25]

Crabfat

Aircrew. (Used in good-natured derogation by fishheads.) Early in the twentieth century, crabfat meant the relatively new paint colour (battleship grey) used on the hulls and superstructures of warships. The modern usage may have originated between the two world wars when the RAF, in their blue-grey uniforms, provided the aircrews for Royal Navy aircraft carriers.

Dhobey

Sailor's term for washed clothes. It is derived from the Hindu word *dhob* meaning washing.

Dragoon

Today, a dragoon is a member of an armoured regiment. Before the days of self-propelled vehicles, a dragoon was a mounted infantryman. The word is thought to derive from "dragon," a form of cavalry pistol of the early seventeenth century, mounted on a swivel in a sling, later replaced by the carbine. One early writer quaintly described dragoons as " . . . a sort of Mungrels betwixt the Two [that is foot (infantry) and horse (cavalry)], who are bound to fight either on Foot or Horseback . . . "[26]

Engineer

Today there are many forms of engineers in the Service — aeronautical, marine, flight, and others — but the longest established is the military engineer. His appearance, historically, long pre-dates the civil engineer. Throughout the ages, the military engineer had charge of the "engines of war." This is why the engineer and the artilleryman can trace their ancestry back to a common source, guns being engines of war. The engineer has been described as one who designs and constructs military works. An engine is a mechanical contrivance. Ingenious means clever at contriving. All of these words are derived from the Latin *ingenium,* meaning cleverness.

Ensigns

Ensigns are colours that are worn chiefly by ships for purposes of national identification. They are normally flown at the ensign staff at the stern. In battle, one or more ensigns may be hoisted in a variety of positions for distinguishing friendly from enemy ships — at the peak of the gaff, at the yardarm, or at the masthead. These are called battle ensigns.[27] A ship may wear a masthead ensign when dressed for a celebration. The ensign worn by HMC ships is identical to the national flag and should not be confused with the Canadian Forces ensign which is not worn at sea.

The ancient rank of ensign is still used by certain regiments of the Canadian Forces in lieu of second lieutenant. It was his duty to carry the colours into battle.[28]

Fishheads

Surface ship sailors. (Used derogatively by submariners and maritime airmen.)

Flak

Anti-aircraft fire, from the German *fliegerabwehrkanone*; also used in the sense of verbal objection to policy decisions, etc.

Flight

A subdivision of an air squadron, a group of say three or four aircraft under a single command — hence the source of the former air force ranks of flight lieutenant and flight sergeant. In the early fifteenth century the term was used in much the same sense, as in "a flight of goshawkes" and "a flight of douves." The word is derived from the Old Saxon *fluht,* meaning the action or manner of moving through the air.

Flip
Flight in a Service aircraft.

Fly-Away Kit
An air cargo consignment of one or more large metal containers (Paul Bunyan's), containing all the essentials for a given number of men for a particular mission to a particular geographical region, all prepared and packed from a permanently held check list.

Flying a Desk
A pilot suffering through a non-flying tour of duty.

Formation
Derived from the Latin *formatio*, the term formation was used in Roman times to describe the disposition of troops going into battle. In the Canadian Forces today the word has two connotations: one, in a sense, static; the other, one of movement. The first is an ordered arrangement of troops and/or vehicles (used in the broadest sense of the term) under a single command, such as an air division, a brigade group, or a naval task force, organized for a specific purpose. The formation having the connotation of movement is as in the traditional air force sense of formation flying where two or more aircraft are led and manoeuvered as a unit. This latter meaning for formation is also seen in the drilling of troops, in tanks advancing, say, in echelon, and in a squadron of destroyers making, say, a torpedo attack.

Fusilier
There are six fusilier regiments in the militia today. Down through the centuries, the fusiliers performed the role of light infantry, with a special capability of protecting artillery and the encamped battalion. They were armed with a light musket called a fusil fitted with a sling so that it could be carried on the fusilier's back, leaving his hands free for other defensive duties.

The word is derived from the French *fusil* and the Italian *focile*, both of which have their origin in the Latin *focus* meaning hearth or fire. The soldier called a fusilier appeared in the seventeenth century and coincided with the introduction of the flintlock musket or fusil which gradually superseded the earlier matchlock.[29] This lighter, shorter musket carried by the fusilier had an important technical advantage. The spark from striking the flint was kept close to the pan containing the powder, whilst with the matchlock, a sputtering fuse was used to ignite the musket charge, an ever present danger when protecting the artillery train and its attendant powder tubs. The first fusilier regiment in the British army was raised in 1685, the Royal Fusiliers (City of London Regiment).[30]

General

Together with admiral, the highest rank in the Canadian Forces. The term was used in the English language of the Middle Ages, having come from the Old French and, originally, from the Latin *generalis*, with its root *genus* meaning kind of things or species. The question of why a major-general is junior to a lieutenant-general may be answered by looking at the seniority and precedence of general officers in the Parliamentary Army of the Civil War period in Britain in the seventeenth century. This army was commanded by a captain-general, the horse (or cavalry) by a lieutenant-general, and the infantry by a sergeant major general. When the term sergeant was dropped from the title of the most junior of these general officers, it muddled up the accepted sequence of precedence.[31] The term captain-general is not used in the Canadian Forces, with one exception. Her Majesty the Queen bears the honorary appointment of captain-general of the Royal Regiment of Canadian Artillery.

General Officers

The collective term for officers of the ranks of: general and admiral; lieutenant-general and vice-admiral; major-general and rear-admiral; brigadier-general and commodore.

Goofing Stations

A piped announcement used in HMC ships to give off-watch members of the crew ample notice of an unusual spectacle to be seen from the upper deck. The term originated in the icebreaker arctic patrol ship, HMCS *Labrador*, during her first voyage when she became the first naval ship, indeed the first big ship of any description, to navigate the North-west Passage (1954). The pipe "hands to goofing stations" was made so that the enthusiastic would not miss the sight of polar bears, walruses and huge icebergs close at hand.[32] The term was used earlier, in HMS *Kenya* on passage in the Indian Ocean, 1943.[33]

Grenadier

Through the centuries, there have been several types of foot-soldiers. One of these is the grenadier, represented in the Service today by the Canadian Grenadier Guards. The grenadier came into being in the seventeenth century, initially in France. They were the men picked from each company of the regiment as having the height and strength to hurl a hand grenade, usually shown badge-wise as a sphere spouting flame, with great accuracy and effect.

Thus the grenadiers became the élite of the infantry and to this day jealously guard their ancient title. Like the fusilier, the grenadier slung his musket over his back to free his hands as he led the attack hurling his grenades, which word, incidentally, comes from the ancient French *pome grenate*, or pomegranate. The relationship between the pomegranate, that large fruit containing an abundance of seeds, and the grenade, is abundantly clear in Durer's famous painting of the Emperor Maximilian (1519), even to the orifice-like appendage from which the flame is traditionally shown being emitted. Similarly, the heraldic device representing the city of Grenada in Spain is the pomegranate.

Grey Funnel Line
Her Majesty's Canadian ships.

Grunt
A soldier.

Guidon
A swallow-tailed pennon or flag. It is to armoured regiments what the regimental colour is to infantry regiments. The present system of guidons and colours came into being in the British army in the mid-eighteenth century and guidons were the special mark of dragoons. The term, guidon, is derived from the ancient French *guydhomme*, the leader of horse.[34] Eventually, the word shifted from the idea of the rank of the officer who bore the guidon into battle to the colour itself.

Hangar Queen
An aircraft having the status of AOG (aircraft on ground) in a hangar from which parts are taken to keep other aircraft operational. Such transfer of parts and equipment is of a temporary nature and not to be confused with "cannibalization" or permanent removal.

Heads
Naval term for toilets. It originated from the location of the seamen's latrines in the days of sail — out over the open bows at the ship's head with no protection from head seas other than a canvas dodger or screen. The heads were sometimes used for other purposes, which explains an amusing incident in HMS *Thetis*, frigate, on the Pacific station in 1853. A sheet of flame was seen forward and a heavy explosion shook the ship. The *Thetis* was quickly put before the wind but it was soon evident there was no fire. It turned out that

"... the gunner's boy, instead of throwing the powder [sweepings from the magazine] overboard, had tilted it down the head-shoot" and a sailor's burning pipe ashes had ignited the powder![35]

HMCS

The four block letters, HMCS, standing alone, bring memories to many, of the silk cap "tallies" of naval ratings during the Second World War. There was no ship's name on the ribbons, just the four letters in gold, so as not to broadcast to enemy ears the identity of ships in harbour. But there was no mistaking the meaning of the letters; the wearer was a member of the ship's company of one of His Majesty's Canadian ships in commission. These letters represent a centuries-old tradition.

Originally, the sovereign was personally responsible for the defence of the kingdom, and the ships intended for that service, as distinct from ships owned by merchants, were called the King's ships, later His Majesty's ships. From time to time in the seventeenth century, the word "Majesty's" was, in the written form, abbreviated, but the letter abbreviation did not come into fashion until the late eighteenth century. Early examples were references to HMS *Phoenix* (1789), HMS *Alfred* (1795) and HMS *Diadem* (1795).[36]

The first ship in the Royal Canadian Navy was a light cruiser, and at her commissioning on 4 August 1910 (four years to the day before she would be at war) she was called HMCS (for His Majesty's Canadian ship) *Rainbow*. The custom continues to this day.

Hoochie

A soldier's shelter made from natural materials in the field, for example, a lean-to made of evergreen boughs. Also used in a figurative sense for billet or accommodation.

Hussar

Today, a hussar is a member of an armoured regiment. The term dates from the fifteenth century and originated in Hungary. Hussars through the centuries were light cavalry.

Infantry

Soldiers who fight on foot. From the Italian *infanteria* and *infante* meaning youth, or foot soldier, as opposed to the more mature cavalryman of earlier times.

The oldest infantry regiment in the Canadian Forces is the Canadian

Grenadier Guards, of Montreal, established 17 November 1859 and styled the "First Battalion Volunteer Militia Rifles of Canada."

Jock or Jet Jock
A pilot, or more specifically, a jet pilot.

Junior Officers
The collective term for officers of the ranks of: captain and lieutenant(N) (for Navy); lieutenant and sub-lieutenant; second lieutenant and acting sub-lieutenant.

Killick
Slang term for leading seaman, the sailor equivalent to corporal. Killick dates from the seventeenth century, its derivation unknown. It means a heavy stone used in small craft as an anchor. Such a stone, usually encased in strong pieces of tree branches to facilitate securing with a rope, is the earliest form of anchor. The leading seaman received the name killick because his badge of rank on the left sleeve of his jumper was the single anchor. The rank of leading seaman was established in the Royal Navy in 1853.

Kye
Hot cocoa. Prepared by the duty cook, kye has traditionally been available when the hands are called in HMC ships, also in training establishments ashore before "pipe down" at night. Kye is also traditionally available during the night watches at sea. Certainly, during the Second World War, this was much appreciated in small ships in heavy weather. Back in 1881-2, during troubles in Ireland, the Royal Fusiliers were guarding Pembroke Dockyard, Milford Haven, Wales. The "queen's cocoa" was issued to all night sentries, a personal gift of Queen Victoria.[37] In 1941, the last class of boy seamen in the Royal Canadian Navy were given a hot cup of kye each morning, having been turned out at 0530 by the duty PTI (physical training instructor).[38] There was once a custom in the army called "gunfires," or "gunfire tea." The custom still survives but the term seems to have disappeared. It consisted of hot tea or cocoa served from the cookhouse immediately after reveillé and "before PT — to hold one until breakfast." The term "gunfire" came from the practice of firing a gun at reveille.[39]

In HMC ships today, the traditional kye has all but disappeared, largely because of improved facilities in the messes where, throughout the night watches, it has become routine for hot coffee and food to be available.

Interestingly enough, the traditional naval kye or hot chocolate is still very much a live custom for the cadets of the Royal Military College, Kingston.

Liberty Boat
Ship's boat which carries the liberty men, that is, men permitted to go ashore — on liberty, that is, on short shore leave.

Lids-Off
This is a term peculiar to the Royal Military College, Kingston. A lids-off is very much like a "stand-down," an unplanned period of relaxation from normal duties, with this difference — while a stand-down usually applies to everyone except the duty watch, a lids-off is awarded to only a portion of the main body, say a squadron, a group, or a team, for a job particularly well done.

Lieutenant
A commissioned officer immediately below the rank of captain in the army and air force, and immediately below the rank of lieutenant-commander in the navy. A word of ancient French origin, lieutenant originally meant one who acts for, or in lieu of, a superior officer. The land and air forces pronounce this rank "leftenant," while seamen say "letenant." The rank of sub lieutenant, between midshipman and lieutenant, was introduced in the Royal Navy in 1861.

Lieutenant-Colonel
The rank between colonel and major in the land and air forces. He is the commanding officer of an armoured or artillery regiment, or of an infantry, signals or service battalion. By the time of the civil war in Britain in the seventeenth century, the process of establishing regiments by amalgamating the independent companies was well advanced, and in Cromwell's New Model Army fighting against King Charles, the second company of a regiment was commanded by the second-in-command of the regiment, the lieutenant-colonel.[40] Such regimental ranks and company commands, within the regiment held by the colonel, the lieutenant-colonel and the major, are commemorated today in the Canadian Forces by the "differencing" of the company colours carried by regiments of foot guards.

Major
The rank in the land and air forces between lieutenant-colonel and captain. In

the period bridging the close of the sixteenth and the beginning of the seventeenth centuries, when the independent companies were being collected into regiments for more effective command in the field, the colonel commanded the regiment, but he also commanded the first company in the regiment. Similarly, the second-in-command of the regiment, in addition to his regimental staff duties, commanded the second company of the regiment. He was called the sergeant major, that is, "greater sergeant," and in due course, the commission rank of sergeant major was shortened to major.[41] Later, when the rank of lieutenant-colonel was introduced, he was second-in-command of the regiment and also personally in command of the second company. The major, once called the sergeant major, now commanded the third company.

Master Seaman
A new naval rank is the master seaman, created to conform with the concept of the single rank system of the unified force. The master seaman is between the leading seaman (or killick) and the petty officer second class, just as the master corporal is midway between the corporal and the sergeant.[42]

Matelot
A sailor, from the French. Pronounced mat'lo.

Militia
Reserve regiments today are officially part of the reserve force as opposed to the term regular force. But the term militia continues to be used in the reserve regiments and, indeed, their geographical groupings are called "militia areas." The word itself is derived from the Latin *militare*, and *miles, militis* meaning soldier. Traditionally, militia has the connotation of a citizen army, a constitutional force raised under the sanction of government for the defence of the realm in time of emergency such as threatened invasion.[43] This idea can be traced back to the ancient Saxon *fyrd*, which was a compulsory levy of all the able men in the country. In England the term used in Elizabethan times was "trained bands."[44] In the London of 1660 there were six regiments of trained bands.[45] Traditionally, the militia has been raised locally, in the cities, towns and counties. In the old French colony of New France in the valley of the St. Lawrence, the militia, made up of all the able-bodied men, contributed to the defence of the colony.[46] It was militia regiments in British North America which were called out for service in the Fenian Raids and, after Confederation, in putting down the North-west Rebellion of 1885. A series of Militia Acts in the latter half of the nineteenth century prepared the way for

the reserve regiments which until the unification of the forces were collectively known as the militia.

Milk Run
Routine mission.

Mule
A tractor for towing aircraft and supporting equipment on an air station or aircraft carrier.

Muster by the Open List
A surprise muster of ship's company where every man reports who he is, his rank, and his duties on board. This was to counteract the practice of some pursers of having non-existent people on the ship's books. Today, a muster by the open list is sometimes used by a senior officer on taking up a new appointment to meet and size up the people of his command.

Orderly Officer
Duty officer of junior officer rank in the army and air force who, during a twenty-four hour period of duty on a base, station or in the field, is responsible for the smooth running of routine proceedings and the maintenance of good order and Service discipline. His duties are comparable to those of the officer of the day on a ship of war in harbour.

In an earlier time, there was little disciplinary action which could be taken by a commanding officer against erring subalterns other than by the ponderous court martial. Extra duty, such as service as orderly officer, had a salutary effect on the offender.

Other Ranks
A collective term of all those not of commissioned rank.

Paul Bunyan
A large box-like container for crating air cargo.

Petty Officer
Today, the naval rank of petty officer second class is equivalent to that of sergeant in the army and air force; petty officer first class to warrant officer; chief petty officer second class to master warrant officer and chief petty officer first class to chief warrant officer. The rating of petty officer was known in the Royal Navy in the eighteenth century. The captain chose his seaman petty

officers from the best able seamen. The master-at-arms (that is, instructor in small arms, later to take on police duties), the armourer, the sail-maker, and the ship's cook, were all early petty officers, literally small or minor or inferior officers, taken from the French *petit*, including pronunciation. The rank of chief petty officer dates from 1853.[47]

Pigeon
An airman.

Pioneers
A proportion of a force equipped with spades and other tools which precede and prepare the way for the main force. In Canadian infantry regiments today, pioneers are to be seen on ceremonial occasions, heading the parade smartly turned out in white leather aprons and gauntlets with shining broad axes. But pioneers have not always enjoyed such exalted prestige. One early writer stated that pioneers in camp were summoned to their labour by the "pioneers' call" — "round heads and cuckolds, come dig!" — and a private soldier could be demoted to pioneer.[48] Sometimes, pioneers were employed in large numbers. Major-General James Wolfe, on board HMS *Richmond*, frigate, in the St. Lawrence in 1759, ordered three hundred pioneers to parade ashore with tools under the direction of an engineer.[49]

Piquet or Picquet
Of ancient French origin, the word picquet originally meant a pointed stake used in a palisade, and piquet, a small pointed stake used to tether a horse. The present military term thus carries the same connotation of security as did the original meaning of the words.

Also, during and after the civil war in Britain, the pike of the infantryman was gradually replaced by the musket. By the end of the seventeenth century, pikemen formed only a small body whose duty it was to protect the colours, and here the relationship can be seen between the terms pikeman and picquet or picket.[50] To this day, the orderly officer of a guards regiment is called the picquet officer.

Pongo
A soldier.

Poopy Suit
Rubber ditching or anti-exposure suit.

Private

The Concise Oxford English Dictionary defines private as an "ordinary soldier without rank, one below non-commissioned officers." In eighteenth century rolls, he was listed under the heading of "private men." Shakespeare, in the sixteenth century, used the term "private soldier" in his play, *Henry IV* (part 2, act 3, scene 2). Some authors relate the word to the close of the medieval period when a soldier, no longer bound to his feudal master, might make a private contract for military service.[51] Other researchers associate the word with British seventeenth century usage. Elite regiments at the time of Charles II recruited "private gentlemen" into the ranks. Also, before the Restoration, in Cromwell's army, there is evidence of dissatisfaction with the designation "common soldier," which originally intended no disparagement, but rather had the same sense as the navy's age-old rating of "ordinary seaman."[52]

Prop-blast

An airborne term referring to a party in celebration of qualifying as parachutists. In the technical sense, prop-blast means the buffeting a parachutist experiences from the slip-stream of the aircraft.

Pukka

A word of Hindu origin having in its military sense a connotation of genuineness, of being solidly built. A "pukka-sapper" is a certificate awarded by members of the military engineering branch to a non-engineer who has made some significant contribution with or to military engineers.

Pusser

This is a distortion of purser, the supply officer in HM ships in earlier times. Because the purser was not paid in the same way as the other officers of the ship, he was permitted to operate what amounted to a concession for the sale of personal gear to the seamen, for example, clothing — purser's or pusser's slops. In time the term described government or regular issue — such as pusser's rum or pusser's dirk (seaman's knife). Pusser, today, also has the connotation of that which is regular, or proper, as opposed, say, to "tiddley" items acquired ashore.

Quartermaster

Quartermaster has two distinct meanings in the Service today, one used on the land, the other in ships. Historically, the quartermaster in the army was responsible for providing billets for troops on the march, or when on garrison duty before the day of barracks, and for laying out a camp during operations in the field. Today, he is responsible for unit equipment, food — receipt, accounting, care, custody, control, and maintenance — and proper distribution of all material on charge to the unit,[53] much like the air force's supply officer.

The naval quartermaster is a petty officer, leading seaman, or able seaman who, at sea, is the helmsman who steers the ship, receiving his orders from the bridge. In harbour, he keeps watch under the orders of the officer of the day, is a member of the gangway staff, pipes routine orders and generally assists the officer of the day in seeing that harbour routines are properly carried out.

Rank and File
A collective term for all below the rank of sergeant.

Rattle
"To be in the rattle" is the sailor's expression for being on the list of defaulters to be paraded before the ship's executive officer for a hearing regarding an alleged offence, that is, being on charge.

Recce
Reconnaissance or reconnoitre.

Regiment
The regiment is a permanent recruiting and training unit of the army with a permanent depot or home station, and is divided according to its function into companies, squadrons and batteries. The meaning of the word, even today, is a complex one. Sometimes it has the "total family" meaning of the infantry, including the depot, as well as the battalions, the operational units of the regiment. In armour, the regiment itself is the operational unit, while in the artillery there are regiments within the regiment. In a signal regiment the squadrons, which make up the regiment, are capable of independent, detached service. Before the seventeenth century, the military unit was the company. But, as the management of land forces advanced in the tactical sense, the need soon arose to collect these independent companies into groups under the rule (or regimen or regime or regiment) of a single officer who was called the colonel.[54] (Several regiments of the militia in Canada came into being in the late nineteenth century in the same way, the combining of independent companies.) Hence the word regiment, from the Latin *regimentum*, meaning rule.

Rig of the Day
The uniform clothing to be worn by a sailor as laid down by pipe or by routine order. The pipe "hands to clean!" does not mean cleaning; it means that the ship's company is to dress in the rig of the day as specified.[55]

Rodents
A name worn with pride by the cadets of Royal Roads Military College, Victoria, British Columbia.

Sapper
The basic rank of a member of the Royal Canadian Engineers, or a collective term for the military engineer branch. Sapper is derived from the French *saper*, to undermine, which points up the original role of the sappers — demolition. In the days of fixed fortifications and defensive positions, sappers and miners were employed in tunnelling right under the enemy's walls which were then breached by the use of explosives. The advancing of trenches for the purpose of reaching enemy positions was known as sapping, and the men as sappers. (New Westminster was originally called Sapperton because of the work of the Royal Engineers in the early days of British Columbia.) "Sappers are soldiers belonging to the artificers or engineers, whose business it is to work at the saps — a gallery sunk underground . . . , these serve in sieges to carry on the approaches under cover . . . "[56]

Scran
Slang for ship's food. A scran bag or scran locker is a repository for stowing personal gear left sculling about the mess decks, which is recoverable only by paying a fine. Scran, of unknown derivation, dates from the eighteenth century. The scran bag was originally a bag in which discarded bread and sea biscuits were collected. Because ships' companies have always lived in such confined spaces, passage-ways have had to be kept clear and the blockage of pumps by clothing, et cetera, avoided. Much importance was, and is, attached to keeping mess decks cleared up. Within living memory, belongings committed to the scran bag could only be redeemed at the price of a piece of soap[57], but today it is a nominal cash fine which goes to the ship's fund.

Scuttle-butt
Ship's rumour, or gossip. In the days of sailing ships of war, scuttle-butt was literally a scuttled butt or breached cask, " . . . a cask having a square piece sawn out of its bilge, and lashed upon deck. It is used to contain the fresh water for daily use, whence it is taken out with a leaden can."[58] Just as the women of

European villages met daily at the village fountain to draw water and exchange gossip, so did sailors meet at the scuttle-butt. The same occurs to this day round the office water fountain or the coffee vending machine.

Senior Officers
The collective term for officers of the ranks of colonel and captain(N) (for navy); lieutenant-colonel and commander; major and lieutenant-commander.

Sergeant
Non-commissioned officer above master corporal. This title has come down from the English of the Middle Ages, from the Old French *sergent* and the Latin *servire*, to serve, *serviens*, servant or military servant, and *serviens eques*, serving knight.[59] Long centuries after the weapon was obsolete, the special mark of the sergeant of infantry was his carrying of the halberd. This pike-like weapon on a long wooden shaft was effective against cavalry. The head consisted of a spear-head to seek out chinks in the knight's armour, a hook to pull him out of the saddle, and an axe blade.[60]

Sheriff
In air force slang, the orderly officer.

Shine Parade
One hour in barrack routine, usually just after the evening meal, devoted to cleaning, pressing clothing and polishing personal equipment.[61]

Sick Bay
Space or quarters in a ship for treating the sick and hurt. The first of such quarters, called "sick birth" or "sick berth," were ordered to be fitted out in every line-of-battle ship of the Mediterranean fleet of the Royal Navy by Earl St. Vincent in 1798. They were not to be in the dark, smelly bowels of the ship, but just under the forecastle deck on the starboard side. The forecastle bulkhead or wall at this time was square, but when rounded bows were introduced shortly after Trafalgar, the rounded timbers of the bulkhead suggested the curve of a bay to seamen, and sick berth in the sailor's jargon became sick bay.[62]

Silent Hours
This is the period of the night watches in HMC ships between "pipe down," when those not on watch turn in for the night, and the calling of the hands in

the morning. It is customary during the silent hours to avoid disturbing the watch below by performing the routine duties of working the ship as quietly as possible. Even the marking of the hour by striking the ship's bell (when this was carried out in HMC ships) was largely suspended during the silent hours. The term silent hours is used similarly in Canadian Forces bases to denote that period between the close of one working day and the beginning of the next.

Skylarking
Seaman's term for frolicsome, mischievous behaviour, tricks and practical jokes. In the days of sail, skylarking included racing and chasing up the ratlines and shrouds of the rigging and sliding down the royal-stays and back-stays for amusement — hence skylarking. This sometimes led to serious accidents. Moresby reports that in HMS *America*, 44 guns, in 1844 off Cape Horn, he and two other "youngsters" "... were mastheaded, — one at each masthead, I at the mizen — for skylarking about the rigging."[63]

Slops
Dating from the fifteenth century, slops are ready-made clothing worn by seamen and usually procurable from naval stores either afloat or ashore. Pursers (supply officers) made handsome profits by the sale of slop clothes to sailors in HM ships of the early seventeenth century when such were ordered "to avoyde nastie beastlyness by continual wearing of one suite of clothes, and therebie boddilie and unwholesome ill smells in every ship."[64]

Soldier
Member of an army; the word soldier has been in common use in English since the fourteenth century. It has its origin in the idea that a soldier is, and almost always has been, a hired fighting man. This is to be seen in the medieval English *souder* and Old French *soudier* for soldier and *soude* meaning pay, as well as the medieval Latin terms *solidarius* and *solidus*, the coin with which the soldier was paid.

Sprog
Air force slang for student pilot, but, in the navy, recruit or novice sailor. While the word's origin is obscure, its use in the Service is related to another use of sprog, meaning an infant.

Squad Boss
In air force slang, the squadron commander.

Squadron
This term has a wide application. It denotes a grouping or organization of air-craft, armoured vehicles or ships. Airmen, signalmen, military engineers and cadets are members of squadrons for administrative and operational purposes, and in some cases for parade drill. Squadron is derived from the Italian *scadra* or *squadra*, which in turn came from the Latin *quadra*, meaning square. The early regiments of horse in the British army were divided into squadrons, as were Canadian cavalry regiments in their day.

Stand Down
A stand down is a period during which normal work routines are suspended. It is very similar in meaning to the sailor's "make and mend" or "makers." Like the French *descente de la garde*, stand down has the connotation of going off duty, or marching off guard, that is, standing down after a period of standing to, say, on the ramparts of old, expecting an attack. There is also the technical meaning of standing down or immobilizing a piece of equipment, for example, grounding an aircraft for purposes of refit or repair.

Standard
A square flag which is the colour of certain regiments and of air squadrons. In the Middle Ages, the standard flown by armies of the time was a large flag made to stand before the tent of the army's commander as opposed to being carried. Considered superior to the guidon, the standard, by the mid-eighteenth century in the British army, was the mark of a regiment of dragoon guards. The only regiment in the Canadian Forces today which is distin-guished by its standard is the Governor-General's Horse Guards, of Toronto.
   The flying squadron standard is a rectangular flag of light blue silk eligible for presentation when an air squadron has attained twenty-five years of service. Perhaps the best known standard is the queen's personal Canadian flag, which is an adaptation of the Royal Standard and is flown when Her Majesty is resident in Canada or is borne in a ship or aircraft of the Canadian Forces.

Stick
A group of parachutists who jump from one exit of an aircraft during a single pass.

Sticks and Bricks
Construction engineers.

The 2nd Battalion, Princess Patricia's Canadian Light Infantry, in combat dress, parading the colours on the anniversary of the Battle of Kapyong, Korea (1951), CFB Winnipeg, April, 1972. (Note the United States presidential citation, awarded to the unit for gallantry, secured to the regimental colour.)

Subaltern
A commissioned officer of the combat arms of the army below the rank of captain. The word is derived from the Latin *sub* (under) and *alternus* (alternate).

Subordinate Officers
The term for officers of the rank of officer cadet.

Tanker
A member of an armoured regiment equipped with tanks, as opposed to reconnaissance vehicles.

Thumperheads
Field engineer junior ranks.

Troop
Historically, this word was in use in the sense of a troop of horse, that is, part of a squadron of cavalry, as early as the sixteenth century. Indeed, a troop of horse at this time could be a formidable force. King Charles II, describing his escape to France after the Battle of Worcester, 1651, encountered a troop of Cromwell's horse amounting to "twice twelve score."[65] Its origin is obscure, but it is generally believed that troop came from the French *troupe* or *trope*, and from the Latin *troppus* (a flock). Troop today denotes a part of a squadron of armoured vehicles, and is also used colloquially in the collective sense, "the troops," meaning other ranks.

Voltigeur
The voltigeur is a member of a light infantry unit specially chosen for his agility and rapid movement. This class of soldier was first raised by Napoleon in 1804 and has the distinction and privilege of leading the attack. The voltigeurs were literally "springers and leapers," usually men of small but wiry physique, capable of taking full advantage of surprise and shock tactics in the field. The term is still extant in the Canadian Forces in a regiment based in Quebec City, Les Voltigeurs de Québec.[66]

Wake
When friends and fellow pilots gather in the mess following the death of a fellow officer. Sometimes provision is made previously by the deceased to pay for the spirits consumed.

Wardroom

Naval officers' mess. The precise origin of this word is not known. It has been said that wardroom evolved from ward robe, a store room for stowing valuables taken from captured prizes. It was located beneath the captain's cabin which was right aft under the quarter-deck. When empty, the ward robe, being adjacent to the cabins of the ship's officers, was used as a mess.[67] This was in ships-of-the-line. In frigates and lesser ships officers messed in the gun room. The midshipmen, who normally served in the larger ships of the fleet, slept and messed down in the bowels of the ship, in the "cockpit" or midshipmen's berth.[68]

Almost certainly, the word wardroom or ward room came into use in the eighteenth century.[69] An early use of it in print is to be found in a report from off the Portuguese coast in April 1758, the year of Louisbourg. When a ship-of-the-line of ninety guns was lost by fire, the first word received by the ship's lieutenants not on watch was when "the word was passed into the ward room, by the centry, that the fore part of our ship, the *Prince George*, was on fire."[70]

Warrant Officer

Today, these words are used to designate the three senior non-commissioned officer ranks in the Service: chief warrant officer, which has replaced the former warrant officer class one of the army and air force and corresponds with the chief petty officer first class in HMC ships; master warrant officer, the former warrant officer class two, and the equivalent of the chief petty officer second class; and the warrant officer, which encompasses the quartermaster sergeant, the staff sergeant and flight sergeant of the former Services, and is the opposite number of the petty officer first class in HMC ships.[71]

The word warrant can be traced to medieval times and the ancient French *warant*, itself a variant of *guarant* or *garant*. There are similar roots in the early German *warent* and *wahren*. Even today, the word has many meanings but, in the military context, it contains the idea of an authority granted by one person to another to do something which he has not otherwise a right to do, not unlike a commission.

Indeed, a chief warrant officer today receives a warrant, a document, bearing the signature and seal of the minister of national defence, which reads in part:

By virtue of the Authority to me, by His Excellency the Governor-General in Council in this behalf given, I do hereby Constitute and Appoint you the said ... to be ...

from the . . . and to continue in the said Office during the pleasure of the Honourable the Minister of National Defence.

The melding of the warrant ranks (and their equivalents) in the three former Services began in 1949 when the rank structures and pay scales, but not rank titles, were made uniform. It was at this time that the naval warrant officer of old (who wore a thin ring), and the commissioned warrant officer (who wore a thick ring, the same as a sublieutenant), both of whom lived in the wardroom, began to disappear. Indeed, it was this standardization in the rank structure which pointed up the vastly different origins of these senior non-commissioned officers, who over the centuries were given positions of authority between the men and the commissioned officers.

Historically, the warrant officer of the army and the air force evolved from the experienced soldier with leadership capability specially selected for the job by the colonel of the regiment,[72] much as the captain of a ship of war selected his petty officers from his ablest able seamen.

But the old naval warrant officer was a very different person from a petty officer. This special breed of warrant officer had his origin not in the warrant or document giving authority to act, but in the warrant or document by which material or stores were requisitioned. This concept dates back to the beginning of the Royal Navy under Henry VIII in the sixteenth century.

When the sovereign required a ship for naval service, she was requisitioned from her merchant owner by warrant which in Tudor times meant that the ship arrived in the king's yard complete with stores and the ship's standing or warrant officers. It would be unthinkable in those days for a ship to be taken into service without her master, boat-swain, carpenter and cook, and, later, the gunner. They were part of the ship — standing officers, acquired by warrant. They went with the ship, and even stayed with her when in ordinary, that is, in reserve. They were the officers who made the ship go. When it came time for the fighting, the king would put his soldiers and their officers on board, the commissioned officers bearing the sovereign's commission. When the operation was over, they went ashore again, but not the warrant officers.[73]

White Knuckle Airlines
Service air transportation (usually non-scheduled flights).

Wing
A wing is an organization of two or more air squadrons — hence the origin of the former air force rank of wing commander. The term is also used in a parade square sense, wing drill being similar to battalion drill.

Zip Driver
A CF-104 Starfighter pilot.

Zipperheads
Junior ranks of an armoured regiment.

6
Mourning Observances

Down through the centuries of human history, there have been many customs related to death and mourning, partly owing to religious belief and partly because of the prevalence of superstition. There is little doubt that much of the concern for the departed was, and still is, related to the sheer mystery of life and death. A few of the customs connected with grief and mourning are still to be seen in both civilian and military life today, and one of these is the use of black fabric as a symbol of mourning.

The sombreness of black has long been linked with subdued sound as, for example, in the use of black shrouds to muffle the drums of the funeral procession, or the muffling of oars when the bier is being moved by barge.

An example of the muffling of drums more than two centuries ago is to be seen in an order relating to the death of Princess Elizabeth in England in 1759: "The Baize to cover the drums and the Crapes for the Officers' Sashes will be delivered out of the Great Wardrobe in Scotland Yard."[1]

Today, the drum is muffled by encasing it in a piece of black fabric having a draw-string, thus damping the sound. Muffled oars, in the funeral context, are seldom seen now, but when this kind of ceremonial procession is carried out, as in the case of some famous seaman, black canvas or matting is wrapped round the loom of the oars. This muffles the creaking sound of oars against thole-pins or rowlocks in precisely the same way as a sailor's jersey did when cutting out a ship from under an enemy shore battery, or, nowadays, when rowing guard in harbour on a dark night.

Though the wearing of the black crepe armband has largely disappeared from civilian life, this old custom of indicating grief and bereavement, or simply as a mark of respect, is still very much alive in the military. By regulation, a mourning band is worn on the left arm when court mourning or Service mourning is directed. It may also be worn in the event of personal bereavement.[2] This custom goes back a long way.

In 1767, King George III decreed, upon the death of the Duke of York and Albany, "Officers of the Army should not wear any other Mourning on the present melancholy occasion than a black Crape round their Left Arms, with their Uniforms."[3]

A typical reaction of a ship's company losing their highly respected captain occurred in HMS *Berwick*, 74 guns, near the close of the eighteenth century: "...they divided their black silk handkerchiefs, and wore one part round their hats and the other round their arms...; and they walked through the cabin in ranks and bowed to the coffin while passing, and most of them in tears..."[4]

Late in 1805, after Trafalgar, a seaman of HMS *Victory* wrote: "There is three hundred of us Pickt out to go to Lord Nelson [*sic*] Funeral. We are to wear blue Jackets white Trowsers and black scarf round our arms and hats...."[5]

Customs relating to death and mourning remind us of the variety of symbolism practised and understood by our ancestors. One such theme appealed to the superstitious, the idea that at certain times, particularly during periods of grief, men's hearts become defenceless against evil. In many ancient churches, special doors were left open so that when the Host was brought in the front door, the devil was encouraged to scuttle out the back. Some scholars see this idea in the firing of the three volleys over the grave — to frighten the ever-encroaching devils away.[6] Fortescue has traced this custom of prayers said over the departed and the three volleys fired in the name of the Holy Trinity back to the companies of German mercenaries of the sixteenth century.[7] Today, of course, the three volleys are simply a farewell salute to one's comrade-in-arms.

Some idea of the antiquity of firing over the grave may be gathered from an account of the burial of Sir Peter Carewe in 1575 in the days of the first Elizabeth:

... the drummes strake upe, and theirwith all the soldyers dyschardged ther peeces 4 or fyve tymes together, wherewith the Churche was soe full of smoke that one coulde scarse discirne another. Lastlye, a nomber of chambers, wch were in the church yearde, and all the greate ordynaunces in the towne, and yn the shippes in the ryver, and at the keye, were also dischardged.[8]

Regrettably, this ancient military rite recently fell victim to the levelling effect of the unification of the Forces (1968), inasmuch as the Royal Canadian

Air Force had dropped this bit of ceremonial back in 1960.[9] However, at time of writing, the decision has been taken to reinstate the use of funeral firing parties.

Another recurring theme of mourning is slovenliness, a feeling of not caring, brought about by a sense of distress and "a sinking of the heart," perhaps best conveyed in the French *je suis désolé*. Today, when some nationally recognized figure dies, the national flag atop the Peace Tower on Parliament Hill is half-masted as a mark of respect and national mourning. This custom comes from the sea practice of half-masting the ensign. But, as every sailor knows, to have a halyard not hoisted close-up is a mark of sloppy seamanship,[10] a sin almost as reprehensible as leaving loose rope-ends trailing over the side. The custom of half-masting the colours is said to date from the sixteenth century.[11]

There is an interesting reference to half-masting the flag in the mid-eighteenth century. In November 1759, HMS *Royal William* brought the body of Wolfe from Quebec to Portsmouth and, upon anchoring, two guns were fired to signal the removal of his remains. "At nine the body was landed and put into a hearse, attended by a mourning coach, and proceeded through the garrison. The colours on the forts struck half flag-staff, the bells muffled, rung in solemn concert with the march, minute guns were fired. . . ."[12]

This particular example of mourning custom related to slovenly seamanship is not unlike the one practised in the days of sail. In harbour, with all sail off the ship, it was normal practice, indeed mandatory, that all the yards must be properly squared off, the yards being the spars suspended from the masts and on which the sails are set. They must be at right angles to the masts and at right angles to the fore-and-aft line of the ship. No self-respecting seaman would have it otherwise. Yet the mark of a ship in mourning was to "scandalize" her yards, that is, yards topped to starboard and to port, said to be "set aslant" or yards "a-cock-bill," in the most unseamanlike fashion.[13]

This same theme of neglect, albeit a studied neglect, may be seen in the idea of things being in reverse to what they should be. To visit Langemarck in Belgium is to see, in a setting of the traditional cypress and crimson roses, a massive, brooding figure in stone, a steel-helmeted Canadian soldier of the Great War, his head bowed in sorrow, his hands resting "on arms reversed" — the St. Julien Memorial. Or take the funeral of General Sir Arthur Currie, commander of the Canadian corps in the Great War, who died in Montreal in 1933. In the cortège were two cavalry detachments, three university contingents and four infantry regiments, "all with arms reversed." "Immediately behind the gun-carriage is the general's charger, with boots reversed in the stirrups, and the empty sword-scabbard hanging from an empty saddle."[14]

Consider the last respects paid in 1929 to Sir William Otter, veteran of the Queen's Own Rifles of Canada at Ridgeway (1866), commander of the Battleford Column in the North-west Rebellion (1885), and acclaimed Canada's first native-born general. The casket was borne on a gun carriage, "the led riderless horse with the jackboots reversed in the stirrups . . . ; the firing party with arms reversed; the detachments from every unit in the city; and, over all, the slow measured tread to the "Dead March from Saul" played with muffled drums."[15]

Such scenes had changed little from a ceremony conducted on the western prairie nearly a century ago. The officer commanding the Midland Battalion in the North-west campaign, a Lieutenant-Colonel Archer Williams, succumbed on board the steamer *Northwest*, and the funeral service was held at Battleford, truly an impressive sight:

> The plain board coffin, wrapped in the folds of the old flag under whose shadow he had fought so honorably and well was lifted on a gun carriage, behind which a soldier led his riderless horse. His own fine regiment, now going home without a leader, followed as chief mourners, with arms reversed, and the cortège numbered fully fifteen hundred armed men. Brass bands were there with muffled drums, and the wild lonely upland echoed the wail of the "Dead March in Saul," as slowly and sadly we conducted the gallant dead to the once beleaguered fort. . . . [16]

Fortescue states that the drill of "resting on arms reversed" dates from the funeral of the Duke of Marlborough who died in 1722.[17] However, the idea of neglect of arms as a mourning observance comes down from a much earlier time, as the following account confirms. Sir Philip Sidney died at Arnhem in 1586, just two years before the famous fight with the Spanish Armada. His body was embalmed and preparations were made for moving the remains to England:

> . . . it was conveyed to the water's edge, followed by twelve hundred of the English soldiers, walking three abreast and trailing their swords and muskets in the dust. . . . As they marched, solemn music was performed. Rounds of small shot were thrice fired by all the men present, and from the great ordnance on the walls, two volleys were discharged as the corpse was taken from the shore.

Later, in London, in the state funeral,

> A hundred and twenty unarmed citizens were in attendance, and about 300 citizens trained for war, all holding their weapons reversed . . . , the body was interred under the Lady Chapel [in old St. Paul's] . . . , and a double volley of shot from the churchyard informed the world outside that Sir Philip Sidney had been buried.[18]

To this day, at regimental dinners of le 12e Régiment Blindé du Canada, at Trois Rivières, a special table is always set in front of the head table, and the place settings of crystal, china and cutlery are laid in reverse. In this way, the regiment honours its dead.[19]

When a sailor, soldier or airman dies, the coffin, during the funeral service, is covered or draped with the national flag or the Canadian Forces ensign, in token that he died in his country's service. This very old custom is particularly appropriate for a burial at sea. In the absence of a casket, the deceased is sewn into a canvas hammock with weights at his feet to facilitate rapid sinking. The draped ensign helps to obscure the form of the corpse, for the flag is held fast to the ship's rail when the body is reverently slipped from beneath the ensign over the side, "plunging with a splash to its last resting place 'full many a fathom deep.'"[20]

Finally, in military customs related to funerals, there is the recurring theme of the Light after the Darkness, choose life, not death. Remember the past, but march with spirit and faith into the future, for tomorrow is a new day. This ancient theme is seen in the traditional opening words of the funeral service: "I am the resurrection and the life . . . . "

This idea is seen also in the movements of the funeral escort and the accompanying band music. In the approach to the graveyard all is governed by the solemnity and measured pace of the traditional funeral march, "The Slow March from Saul."[21] But once the burial service is over, the escort is clear of the graveyard, and the shrouds have been removed from the drums, the funeral party, at a sharp word of command, breaks into the quick-march and the band strikes up a regimental march, or in the case of the navy, the stirring notes of "Heart of Oak," beginning "Come, cheer up, my lads . . . ."[22]

This dramatic switch from the slow to the quick is of ancient origin. In 1675, a boatswain of HMS *Assistance* was buried ashore "like a souldyer." The well known diarist, the Reverend Henry Teonge, recorded on this occasion: "and as soone as wee were out of the church yard the trumpetts sounded merry levitts [musical strain or call to rouse soldiers in the morning] all the way."[23]

First post and last post were, until recent years, the last two trumpet or bugle calls to be heard in a military camp or barracks at the close of the day. They had to do with the posting of guards or sentries, the setting of the watch for the night. Today, last post is heard almost exclusively in the funeral service and in Remembrance Day observances from coast to coast. It is not difficult to see the symbolism involved. One does not soon forget the thoughtful impression made on the mind by the pause near the end of last post, followed by the great welling up of that final high E and its eventual drifting away on the night air. In the funeral service, last post is followed by reveille, which is

One of HMC ships preparing to leave harbour for a burial at sea, October, 1966. (Note the rifles of the sentries are in the reverse position and the ship's ensign is at half-staff.)

consistent with the ageless theme of the new day; life must go on; there is duty to be done.

Today, in the Canadian Forces, there is a regulation which has a bearing on uniform dress early in the month of November. It reads in part: "The Remembrance Day Poppy... shall be worn... on the left side of the headdress..."[24] Although associated with the tragedy of war by generations of Europeans, the wearing of the poppy in Canada dates from the years closely following the Armistice of 1918.

There is much conjecture about how this scarlet emblem came originally to be associated with the remembrance of war dead. Certainly in the Low Countries of Europe, which have known the clash of arms for countless centuries, the poppy grows in great profusion in the grain fields, and is considered a weed.

However, there is no doubt about how the red poppy became for Canadians, indeed for the whole allied cause, the symbol for sacrifice, for remembrance, and for the prayerful hope that man would somehow, someday, eliminate the horror that is war. It was fifteen lines of verse written in a dug-out in the trenches not far from battle-torn Ypres in Belgium, in 1915. "In Flanders Fields" was the quiet, thoughtful outpouring of the heart of a courageous, compassionate medical officer of the Canadian Expeditionary Force, Lieutenant Colonel John McCrae, of Guelph, Ontario. These are the words, so familiar to so many for nearly sixty years:

> In Flanders fields the poppies blow
> Between the crosses, row on row,
> That mark our place; and in the sky
> The larks, still bravely singing, fly
> Scarce heard amid the guns below.
>
> We are the Dead. Short days ago
> We lived, felt dawn, saw sunset glow,
> Loved, and were loved, and now we lie
> In Flanders fields.
>
> Take up our quarrel with the foe;
> To you from failing hands we throw
> The torch; be yours to hold it high.
> If ye break faith with us who die
> We shall not sleep, though poppies grow
> In Flanders fields.
>
> John McCrae[25]

7
Some Service Customs

Banyan

An example of the custom that continues to evolve or change over the years is the banyan, a special kind of party peculiar to the navy. In spite of the changing nature of the banyan party, there are three constants: it is always a fun occasion, it is held outdoors, and the emphasis is on good food, good drink and good fellowship — something along the lines of the old-fashioned picnic.

Banyan in the navy originally meant a meatless, and therefore an unpopular, day. As a sea term, it dates from the seventeenth century. Mondays, Wednesdays and Fridays were banyan days designed to conserve the supply of kegs of "salt-horse," that is, salted-down beef, during sea passages which often took many months. The staple on banyan days was a kind of porridge made from dried peas.

The term is derived from the Banians, a caste of Hindus in India, who abstained from the use of meat on religious grounds, a reverence for life.

While this practice continued well into the nineteenth century, flag officers were not above changing the rules when the operational situation warranted. Vice-Admiral Sir Alan Gardner, writing to the Admiralty from his flagship HMS *Queen* in 1794, informed their Lordships:

> ... when the British fleet was in sight of the Enemy ... I ordered the Company of His Majesty's Ship the *Queen* to be supplied with an allowance of Pork for their dinner, it being a Banyan day; and finding them exceedingly fatigued after the actions of the 29 May and 1st June, I directed them to be served with half an allowance of wine more than their daily portion. ...

He closed with the request that the ship's purser be compensated for this extra expense![1]

Banyan days gradually changed from meagre or lean days to much more pleasant ones. For one thing, especially in private ships or detached squadrons on lengthy voyages, fishing from the ship's side was encouraged, and this diversion from ship's routine was much enjoyed. Also, seamen became adept at stowing away palatable foodstuffs of the more tasty kind acquired during "runs" ashore or by barter from bumboat proprietors in harbour. These "goodies" would be brought out in the various messes to tide over otherwise drab meals.

Also, captains came to understand that picnics ashore, particularly on an isolated beach far from civilization where desertion would likely not be attempted, were good for ship's morale. Perhaps one such occasion was in 1850 when HMS *Thetis*, a beautiful sailing frigate of 38 guns was on passage from Valparaiso to her station at Esquimalt. Moresby tells of a picnic ashore on the coast of Chile when, "after a glorious supper of fish, grog, songs and bonfire, we started at a late hour to return [to the ship], and found we had mislaid the boatswain!"[2]

The idea of parties ashore in rather isolated locations continued, particularly in training squadrons, well into the 1950s. After a week of strenuous training exercises, watch and watch about, day and night, frigates such as HMC ships *Beacon Hill* and *Antigonish* would send all but the watch ashore in Bedwell Harbour or near Port Hardy in British Columbia waters, for a banyan of beer and hamburgers. In such places there were no distractions and sailors under training were not likely to get into any mischief!

In 1971 when Her Majesty the Queen was in British Columbia waters in HM Yacht *Britannia*, the royal family, on passage from Powell River to Comox, put ashore in Stag Bay for a quiet picnic. This allowed one of the escorts, the destroyer HMCS *Qu'Appelle*, a bit of relaxation. "After a full day of activities, which included a fishing derby, crab hunting and oyster picking, all hands enjoyed a quarterdeck "banyan" of steaks and broiled oysters."[3]

While sailors will always look forward to getting ashore, the banyan, owing to social and technological advances, is also changing. Today, most ships of the fleet are miniature aircraft carriers, providing uncluttered flight decks for helicopters. And the men of the fleet in the 1970's are a much better educated and more sophisticated lot than their predecessors. As a result, and in spite of the attractions of big-city ports, banyans today are often held right on board ship, even in harbour, and splendid occasions they are.

Indeed, so popular is the modern banyan that even submariners with their restricted upper deck are not to be denied. Providing the sea is quiet to avoid someone being washed overboard from the narrow casing, a half oil drum can barbecue the most tasty steaks to be washed down with a cool beer beneath a sunny sky.

Finally, there is a more recent new twist to the banyan as evidenced by the experience of the ship's company of the twenty-two thousand ton ship, HMCS *Preserver*. Traditionally, the banyan has always been a self-starter, the initiative coming from within the ship. In 1974, when the *Preserver* landed many tons of supplies as a gift from Canada to the impoverished people of an isolated parish in Haiti, the Haitians responded by joining the *Preserver's* company in one tremendous banyan on a nearby island, a party which featured calypso music and folk dancing as well as the ship's band, a very colourful scene under gasoline generated lighting rigged by the ship's electricians.[4]

The Boatswain's Call

One of the oldest customs of the fleet today is the use of the boatswain's call, "making a pipe" to pass an order. The instrument itself, which is essentially a whistle suspended on a chain round the neck of the boatswain's mate or the quartermaster and made up of parts called the gun, buoy, keel and shackle, has changed little in five hundred years service in the Royal Navy.

"To pipe" means to sound the boatswain's call and follow up with the spoken order, usually over the ship's broadcast, such as "hands to stations for leaving harbour" or "special sea dutymen to muster." On the other hand, some pipes are orders in themselves requiring no spoken word, such as "hands to supper" or "pipe down." The boatswain's call epitomizes the smooth, orderly fashion in which the routines of the twenty-four-hour day on board a warship at sea are conducted.

Some idea of the timeless practicality of the pipe may be gained from the definition given in Falconer's Dictionary of 1815:

> Call, a sort of whistle, or pipe, of silver or brass, used by the boatswain and his mates to summon the sailors to their duty, and direct them in the different employments of the ship. It is sounded to various strains, adapted to the different exercises, as hoisting, heaving, lowering, veering away, belaying, letting-go a tackle, &c., and the piping of it is as attentively observed by sailors, as the beat of the drum to march, retreat, rally, charge, &c., is obeyed by soldiers.[5]

One can imagine the impression on the mind of a sixteen-year old midshipman joining his first ship and hearing for the first time the sound of the pipe as it floated out over the water. The ship was HMS *Blonde*, frigate; the place, the anchorage at Spithead, England, in 1793. "After a severe pull we got alongside as the boatswain and his mates were piping to dinner."[6]

The captain of HMCS *Preserver* being piped aboard for the first time at the commissioning of the ship at Saint John, New Brunswick, July, 1970.

"Piping the side" is a form of salute honouring certain personages as they board or disembark from one of HMC ships. If that person boards from a boat he is piped twice, once as the boat approaches the ship and again as the person mounts the accommodation ladder. If the arrival is over the brow or gangway, he is piped once. Here again, this ancient call is associated with the giving of orders.

In the days of sail, captains often had occasion to visit other ships in company, perhaps for a council of war, or to repair on board the flagship, "booted and spurred," that is, with sword and medals, to "collect a bottle" for some misdemeanour such as needlessly crossing his admiral's bow, or simply to dine with a brother captain. Perhaps it was because of heavy weather, or typical eighteenth century portliness from over-indulgence in port wine and multi-course dinners, that certain personages such as flag officers and captains were lowered into their barges, or hoisted on board, in a contrivance not unlike a boatswain's chair suspended from a whip at the yardarm. This spared them the exertion of climbing the accommodation ladder. Piping the side today sounds very much like the notes of yesteryear which meant "hoist away," "handsomely" and "avast hoisting."

In recent years some changes have been introduced regarding piping the side. Over the centuries the ceremony has been considered a purely nautical one in that the honour was accorded exclusively to the sovereign; a member of the royal family in naval uniform; flag officers; captains of HM ships and foreign naval officers.[7] "No Military Officer, Consular Officer or other civilian is entitled to this form of salute."[8] Today's regulations reflect the single Service nature of the Canadian Forces, for this honour is now accorded to "General officers of the Canadian Armed Forces when in uniform."[9]

Another change that has come about is reflected in the statement: "The side is never piped in a shore establishment."[10] The fact is that today this custom, carried out with spirited dignity and precision, is a much cherished tradition in the naval divisions, HMC ships *Donnacona* (Montreal), *Star* (Hamilton) and *York* (Toronto).

Traditionally, the side is piped when a corpse is brought on board, taken ashore or committed to the deep.

The term, "pipe down," has been used for several centuries in the navy and is one of those expressions that has been accepted in civilian life. It has meant variously: a holiday from all work that is not essential; an admonition to keep quiet after "lights out"; or, simply, an order to dismiss the hands from the deck when a particular duty has been carried out on board ship. The antiquity of this pipe, so popular today, is to be seen in the era of Trafalgar in the case of the new commanding officer of HMS *Diamond*. "The hands were turned up and his commission read." Turning to the first lieutenant of the ship after the ceremony, the captain ordered: "That's all, pipe down if you please, sir."[11]

A long tradition related to the boatswain's call which is little known outside the navy is that whistling is forbidden in HMC ships so that it will not be confused with the pipe.

With the possible exception of the seaman's knife, the boatswain's call, in whatever form, is probably the oldest, and certainly the most distinctive, item of personal nautical equipment. How old is not known. A form of pipe or whistle was used in the galleys of ancient Greece and Rome to control the stroke of the oars manned by slaves. In the course of time the call or pipe evolved in that cradle of western civilization, the Mediterranean, into the practical whistle of command, but also into a form of symbolism, the whistle as a badge of office, and also as a highly regarded badge of honour.[12]

In the time of Henry VIII, an ornate whistle of gold on a golden chain was the badge of office of the Lord High Admiral of England. Something of the aura surrounding this golden call may be seen in the action of Sir Edward Howard in the sea fight with the Chevalier Prégant de Bidoux off Brest in 1513. When Howard, the Lord High Admiral, was surrounded and cut off on board the French flagship, his last thought before being felled was to hurl his precious badge of office into the sea.

> None else, he cried, shall wear, and mocking say
> This was his badge, token of England's might,
> High Admiral of England.[13]

The boatswain's call's long heritage in control and command at sea was well known to Shakespeare. In the first scene of his drama, *The Tempest*, he has the master calling to the boatswain:

> .... speak to the mariners: fall to't yarely [nimbly],
> or we run ourselves a-ground: bestir, bestir. [exit]

and the boatswain shouts to the crew:

> Heigh, my hearts! cheerly, cheerly, my hearts! yare,
> yare! Take in the topsail. Tend to th' master's whistle.

The same kind of control and command, this time in battle action, is to be seen in an eyewitness account of Drake in the *Golden Hind* in the Pacific off South America in 1579.

About nine o'clock at night, the English ship crossed the course of San Juan's vessel and, immediately, came alongside...they blew a whistle on the English ship and the trumpet responded. Then a volley of what seemed to be about sixty arquebuses was shot, followed by many arrows, which struck the side of the ship, and chain-balls shot from a heavy piece of ordnance carried away the mizen and sent it into the sea with its sail and lateen yard.[14]

The Changing of the Guard

A very popular feature during the summer months in the nation's capital is the colourful ceremony known as "the changing of the guard." Though the guard duty itself is carried out at Government House (sometimes called Rideau Hall), which is the residence of the Governor-General and the home of Her Majesty the Queen when residing in Ottawa, the elaborate pageantry and military precision of the changing of the guard occurs daily on the lawns of Parliament Hill.

Some one hundred and twenty-five officers, non-commissioned officers and guardsmen participate in this centuries-old ceremony. Essentially it is the relief of the old guard by the new. Attired in their traditional bearskin headdress and scarlet tunics, the guardsmen present a stirring scene as, attended by a band, they parade their queen's colour (when Her Majesty or the Governor-General is in residence) and their regimental colour.

Commencing in 1959, the public duties detachment of the Regiment of Canadian Guards performed this duty every summer for eleven years. Today, two militia regiments share the responsibility — the Governor-General's Foot Guards of Ottawa, and the Canadian Grenadier Guards of Montreal.

A point of interest is that the new detachment arriving for guard duty is called "the duties." Once it has passed an exacting inspection by the adjutant who sees it is properly turned out and fit to perform guard duty, only then is the detachment called the "new guard" and the officer commanding takes over his command.[15]

Following the inspection, the colours, with their armed escort, are marched through the ranks. Then the old guard pays its compliments to the new by presenting arms, and the compliment is returned. This is followed by the ancient Ceremony of the Key in which the commander of the old guard turns over the key of the guardroom to the commander of the new guard. The two guards then change positions, march past the adjutant and leave Parliament Hill, the new guard to take up its duty, the old to leave its cares behind.

To most observers, the changing of the guard means "spit and polish," colour, precise movements and the spirited music of the band. It is refreshing to see another view, the good-humoured grousing but solid sense of duty traditionally inherent in the make-up of the guardsman. A veteran Cold-streamer put it this way:

> We did lots of ceremonials in the Guards — troopin' the colour, guardin' the Tower of London, and what not. Stood on parade four and five hours at a time — with a 14-day detention if you fainted. The trick is to keep your weight off your heels. That's why Guards' boots bulge in front — lots of room to wiggle your toes without anybody knowin'![16]

The Commission

"Commission, in a military sense, is the authority by which every officer acts in his post."[17] This eighteenth century definition assesses the meaning of a parchment or linen-backed paper scroll which a man or woman receives on becoming a commissioned officer. The queen's commission is a delegation of authority to exercise command, on behalf of Her Majesty, over one's subordinates. In Canada, the commission scroll is signed by the Governor-General as the queen's representative, and by the minister of national defence.

Over the centuries, the sovereign's commission has, from time to time, been changed in wording, but for the most part the format and message conveyed have remained constant. The officer commissioned is named, his duties and obligations are outlined in general terms, and there is an expression of trust and confidence in him. In the Canadian Forces, an officer may be given only two commissions, one when he is first commissioned, usually in a junior rank, and a second if he should reach the rank of brigadier general or commodore. An officer holds his commission at the pleasure of the sovereign.

The commission scroll bears the coat of arms of Canada. The signature of the Governor-General is in the centre, over which is the impression of the Governor-General's privy seal. The signature of the minister of national defence is at the base of the scroll which reads:

> Elizabeth the Second, by the Grace of God of The United Kingdom, Canada and Her other Realms and Territories Queen, Head of the Commonwealth, Defender of the Faith.
>
> TO
>
> (Name in Full)
>
> HEREBY appointed an Officer
> In Her Majesty's Canadian Armed Forces
>
> With Seniority of the   day of   19
>
> We reposing especial Trust and Confidence in your Loyalty, Courage and

Integrity, do by these Presents Constitute and Appoint you to be an Officer in our Canadian Armed Forces. You are therefore carefully and diligently to discharge your Duty as such in the rank of   Or in such other Rank as We may from time to time hereafter be pleased to promote or appoint you to, and you are in such manner and on such occasions as may be prescribed by Us to exercise and well discipline both the inferior Officers and men serving under you and use your best endeavour to keep them in good Order and Discipline. And We do hereby Command them to Obey you as their superior Officer, and you to observe and follow such Orders and Directions as from time to time you shall receive from Us, or any your Superior Officer according to Law, in pursuance of the Trust hereby reposed in you.

IN WITNESS Whereof Our Governor-General of Canada hath hereunto set his hand and Seal at Our Government House in the

City of Ottawa this   day of

in the Year of Our Lord One Thousand Nine Hundred and

and in the

Year of Our Reign.

BY COMMAND OF
HIS EXCELLENCY THE GOVERNOR-GENERAL

MINISTER OF NATIONAL DEFENCE

The wording of this modern Canadian commission may be compared with that of a lieutenant's commission in 1809 in the Honourable Artillery Company of London:

...you are, therefore, to take into your charge and care the said Company, and duly to exercise the inferior officers and soldiers of the same in arms; And also to use your best care and endeavour to keep them in good Order and Discipline, commanding them respectively to obey you as their Lieutenant. And you are also to obey your Superior Officers (according to the Discipline of War) in pursuance of the Trust reposed in you.[18]

A later commission of the same unit, dated 1879, looks more like the modern format. Beginning with "Victoria, by the Grace of God, of the United Kingdom of Great Britain and Ireland, Queen, Defender of the Faith, &c," it uses the ancient formal language of the sovereign addressing a subject: "To Our Trusty and Well-beloved, Greeting."[19]

Indeed, there is little change from this Victorian commission to a Canadian army commission of 1940, except that emphasis is placed on the trust and confidence the sovereign has in the newly appointed officer. Signed at the upper left by the Governor-General, the Earl of Athlone, the commission reads in part, after the formal greeting:

> We, reposing especial Trust and Confidence in your Loyalty, Courage and good Conduct, do by these Presents Constitute and Appoint you to be an Officer... to exercise and well discipline in Arms, both the inferior Officers, and Men serving under you and use your best endeavours to keep them in good Order and Discipline... according to the Rules and Discipline of War, in pursuance of the Trust hereby reposed in you.[20]

A post-war commission in the Canadian army signed by Viscount Alexander of Tunis in 1949 was identical to the wartime version except for changes such as the sovereign no longer being Emperor of India and the deletion of the words "Dominion of" in reference to the nation.[21]

A commission in the Royal Canadian Air Force signed by the Earl of Athlone in 1945[22] and one signed in 1950 by Viscount Alexander of Tunis[23] were in almost all respects identical to those of the Canadian army, including the minor changes in wording. Indeed, the scroll used in 1959, in the new reign, revealed few changes from that used by the air force during the Second World War.

The introduction of a common commission after the unification of the Services in 1968 has removed a historic, but rather curious, aspect of the naval officer's commission. While the former army and air force scrolls emphasized, by repetition, the trust and confidence in the newly commissioned officer, the navy, while mentioning these qualities, ended up with the dire threat: "you will answer the contrary at your Peril."

The anomaly may be explained by going back to an earlier time when there were marked differences between the actual control of the British army and the Royal Navy. The sovereign delegated his authority directly to the subalterns in the army, but exerted no direct control over the navy. The royal authority was delegated to, and jealously exercised by, the Lords Commissioners of the Admiralty, even to the wording of commissions, hence the threat was an admiralty threat.[24]

Two other differences in naval commissions, though minor ones, were that they bore the personal arms of the sovereign, and the newly appointed officer was invariably addressed as "Mister." But the major difference was in the language used.

A commission in the Royal Canadian Naval Volunteer Reserve (the RCNVR — who during the Second World War formed by far the great majority of the officers and ratings manning the fleet), signed by the Earl of Athlone in 1945, read in part:

> By the Governor-General and Commander in Chief of the Dominion of Canada . . . . By virtue of all powers me hereunto enabling, I do hereby constitute and appoint you a Sub Lieutenant in the Royal Canadian Naval Volunteer Reserve, Charging and Commanding you in that rank . . . to observe and execute the General Printed Instructions for the Government of His Majesty's Naval Service . . . And likewise Charging and Commanding all Officers and Men subordinate to you . . . to behave themselves with all due Respect and Obedience to you their Superior Officer.[25]

Oddly enough, the traditional admiralty threat is not in the RCNVR wartime commission, but it was in that of the permanent force navy of the post-war period. This document is an interesting one, because, besides bearing the personal arms of the sovereign, it shows the queen as granting the commission. It also contains the admiralty threat of old. Moreover, "good conduct" of the army and air force becomes "integrity" in the navy and the admonishment about subordinates behaving themselves is forgotten.

A commission in the Royal Canadian Navy signed by Governor-General Georges P. Vanier in 1960 reads:

> Elizabeth the Second, by the Grace of God of the United Kingdom, Canada and Her other Realms and Territories, Queen, Head of the Commonwealth, Defender of the Faith.
>
> To Mr . . . . hereby appointed Lieutenant Commander in Her Majesty's Canadian Fleet.
>
> We reposing special Trust and Confidence in your Loyalty, Courage and Integrity, do by these Presents Constitute and Appoint you a Lieutenant Commander, Royal Canadian Navy, Willing and Requiring you from time to time to repair on board and to take upon you the Charge and Command of Lieutenant Commander in any ship or Establishment to which you may hereafter at any time be duly appointed, or the charge and Command of any other Rank to which you may be promoted or appointed, strictly Charging and Commanding all the Officers and company of the said Ship or Establishment subordinate to you to conduct themselves jointly and severally in their respective employments with all due Respect and Obedience unto you, and you likewise to observe and execute the Queen's Regulations and Orders for the Royal Canadian Navy and such Orders and Instructions as you shall from time to time receive from Naval Headquarters or from your Superior Officers. Hereof nor you nor any of you may fail as you will

answer the contrary at your Peril. And for so doing so this shall be Your Commission.[26]

It has been a custom in all three services for many many years to celebrate a promotion, in which, of course, the promoted one pays for the refreshments consumed in his honour by his friends and fellow members of the mess. It is generally known as "wetting the stripe."[27]

A similar celebration called "wetting the commission" has been observed a long time, too. Describing an incident which occurred three years before Trafalgar, in 1802, the first lieutenant of HMS *Volage* recounts being on shore and encountering eight "jolly midshipmen" from his ship seated around a table holding a gallon-bowl of strong punch. "Number one" was invited to partake of the punch in honour of one of the "mids" who had just learned of his promotion to lieutenant. The officer wryly noted that the bowl's contents were soon gone despite the taste of parchment and the fact that most of the ink was gone from the scroll.[28]

Crossing the Line
One of the oldest customs of seafaring men, as well as the most boisterous, is the centuries-old, farcical ceremony of crossing the line, meaning the equator. Dating at least from the early seventeenth century, this elaborate occasion for horseplay and skylarking illustrates the sailor's enthusiasm and ingenuity in making the best of an otherwise boring situation. The seemingly endless days of the listless rolling of the windship and the flapping of her canvas, while drifting through the light airs of the doldrums, provided the opportunity for initiating people variously called greenhands, tadpoles or novices, into the "Mystic Rites of the Freedom of the Seas, according to the Ancient Customs of King Neptune and his Watery Realm."

As one would expect, the ceremony has had many variations through the years in dress, props, and procedure, depending on the imagination and talents of King Neptune and his motley retinue.

On the great day, as HMC ship approaches the imaginary line (the ship having been placed out of routine except for the watch, and officers and men alike having taken up every vantage point to watch the hilarious spectacle), a hail is heard from somewhere forward demanding to know "what ship?" An equally great voice replies from the bridge and soon learns that King Neptune is about to board the intruder.

Said to enter by the hawsepipe, a strange company is soon seen on the fo'c'sle making its way aft, led by King Neptune, bearded and bewigged with rope-yarn, oakum and sea-weed, bearing in solemn majesty his crown and trident. In his wake trips the heavily rouged, amply endowed, but suspiciously muscular, Queen Amphitrite, to the tune of a fiddle or recorder and the inevitable ribald remarks of the ship's company. Then come the barber, with his huge wooden straight-edge razor and sundry swabs, the doctor, with his large galley syringe, mallet and mystical physic, and, bringing up the rear, the bears, sometimes called constables, with their persuaders.

Having demanded the presence of all the greenhands in the ship's company irrespective of rank, King Neptune lectures them on the impending ordeal to be suffered before being admitted to His Oceanic Majesty's realm as shell-backs (i.e. proper, full-blown, deep-water sailors), and warning them of dire results should they ever in the future neglect to see that all future tadpoles receive similar treatment.

There follows the time-honoured ceremony of seating the blindfolded tadpole on a tilting plank over a canvas pool specially rigged for the occasion. Each time the candidate opens his mouth to answer a question, he receives the barber's swab of soap lather and eventually is shaved with the outsize razor, with little regard for nose and ears. The physician then profers his special brand of treatment, including an enormous pill concocted by the co-operative sick bay "tiffy" and the galley crew. Finally, the candidate is tumbled into the pool, there to be ducked thrice by Neptune's willing henchmen, the bears. Of course, through all this, the victim struggles valiantly, resulting in an uproar much to the liking of the jubilant company assembled.

After the presentation of flowery-worded, often artistically executed, certificates to the new shellbacks, King Neptune and his entourage disappear over the side.

While the making of a shellback is traditionally tied to crossing the equator, there are numerous instances over the years, as well as today, where crossing the line has been adapted to crossing the Tropics of Cancer and Capricorn, the Polar Circles, and even the passing of famous headlands such as at the Strait of Gilbraltar or Cape Horn.[29] Such customs go back into early Canadian history.

In *Jesuit Relations*, that magnificent documentary of life in New France, for the years 1647-48, is a description of what happened on board ships bound for Quebec on reaching that part of the St. Lawrence River opposite the "Mountains of Notre Dame," when the ship's crew amused themselves "by baptising the new passengers, unless, by means of a present, they turn aside the flood of that baptism, which is made to pour in abundance over their heads."[30]

Two centuries later the same custom was being practised in the emigrant ships on reaching the Grand Banks of Newfoundland. On 3 May 1855

Neptune, King of the Sea, boarded the ship *Ocean Queen* to receive the newcomers on board "this being their first visit to the Banks of Newfoundland going to Quebec in America."[31]

Soldiers, too, on passage to distant stations, have enjoyed crossing the line. Lieutenant-Colonel William Dyott, in his journal, tells of taking his regiment to Barbados and the ceremony involving his troops as they crossed the Tropic of Cancer in January, 1796. He writes:

> Then comes on the barber's work, who after daubing the face and head of the fast-bound stranger with the vilest of all possible compositions, of tar, grease, etc. etc., proceeds to shave him with a piece of old iron, which not only takes away the sweet-scented fine oily lather, but scrapes the face (carrying some particles of skin with it) to that degree to cause howlings most hideous.[32]

Nor are modern soldiers averse to participating in the good-natured festivities of crossing some imaginary line at sea. In April, 1951, the Royal Canadian Regiment, bound for Korea, crossed the 180th meridian of longitude in the Pacific and duly marked the occasion with "certificates of the Order of the Golden Dragon" signed by no less a dignitary than Davy Jones himself.[33]

At one time, crossing the line was an ordeal of considerable hazard. In January, 1782, a regiment of Light Dragoons was in a convoy of the Royal Navy out of Portsmouth, headed for the East Indies. On crossing the equator, eighty-one people paid tribute, leaving one seaman and two boy seamen as the only greenhands. They were "accordingly ducked three times from ye Lee Main Yard Arm."[34]

A good description of this rough and ready method of entertainment on board ship is in a journal kept nearly a century earlier in 1702, in the *Arabia* of 16 guns.

> This day likewise we crossed the equinoctial line, into the Southern part of the World . . . The manner of ducking is this; there is a block made fast to the main yardarm, through which is reeved a long rope, one end whereof comes down on the Quarter Deck, the other to the water, at which end is made fast a stick about a foot and a half long thwartways, on which the person sits across holding fast with his hands the rope as it goes up having a running knot about him; when being ready he is hoisted up close to the yardarm, by the people on the Quarter Deck, and at once let run. His own weight from that height plunges him under the water, as low as the ship's keel; then they run him up again as fast as they can and so serve him three times, then he is free and may drink with the others that paid.[35]

Sailors over the centuries have enjoyed the high jinks of crossing the line, but ever since the advent of the long-range aircraft, there's been a new twist to the ancient ceremony where all the hilarity is at the expense of the novice. High above the clouds, over the equator, the Arctic Circle, or even the Pole, the same tradition prevails, albeit with new factors introduced, such as cramped space and speeds measured in the hundreds of knots.

But the people of air transport command (now group), ingenious as they are, have made adequate adjustments. King Neptune is now the captain of the aircraft and he has only a few henchmen, just enough to attend to the blind-folding of the unfortunate tadpole, who now on bended knee listens to a litany of transgressions, all the while his left hand suspended in a hastily concocted preparation (warm vegetable soup and shaving cream are quite standard ingredients); there follows a thick beverage of mushroom soup and ginger ale, and on removal of the blindfold, the cold water treatment![36]

However, to compensate in part for these indignities, the now fully fledged member of the "Winged Order of Neptunus Rex" is given a handsome, signed certificate, much like the sailor's, so that he will never again be suffered to endure such an ordeal.

It is of interest to note that the elaborate certificate, though it is not embellished with beautiful mermaids as is the sailor's, does make rude remarks about those interlopers "Davey Jones and all his admirals of the fleet and their minions," and also reminds the veteran of the polar skies who boasts about the rigours and dangers of the Canadian Arctic, that this certified journey, "unlike that of the admirable Admiral Byrd, was conducted at so and so feet in air conditioned comfort" and that the only ice encountered by our adventurer "was in a glass container" — a far cry from being ducked at "ye Lee Main Yard Arm"!

Embarkation

There is an old saying in Service life that with responsibility goes privilege. This idea is seen today in the custom whereby seniors board a transport aircraft last and disembark first, to spend the least possible time confined in the aircraft, subject as it is, when on the ground, to the heat of summer and the cold of winter. This custom is centuries old and comes from the sea. Indeed, the word embark is derived from the old poetic term "bark" or "barque," meaning any ship or boat.

If a destroyer, for example, is lying at trots, as opposed to a jetty, or is anchored in a roadstead, passage to and from the shore or other ships is made in the ship's boats. All ranks may go in the same boat, but juniors in rank embark first and disembark last.

In the days of the "wooden walls," when this custom began, there was very real discomfort and a likelihood of getting soaked by the brine when the ship's launch, with a bit of a sea running, was being fended off by the boat's crew at the foot of the accommodation ladder. For the boat was much livelier than the ship; it rose and fell more rapidly. It was to avoid, as much as possible, having seniors exposed to the inconveniences of an open boat in a seaway that this bit of protocol developed centuries ago, yet it is still practised today in spite of the relative luxury of the Boeing 707 transport.

Feu-de-joie

A feu-de-joie is a salute fired on occasions of rejoicing, just as the expression suggests — a bonfire, a fire of joy. The firing of muskets replaced the bonfires of ancient France and developed into the present ceremonial salute. A British admiral described the feu-de-joie a century ago as "a salute fired by musketry on occasions of public rejoicing, so that it should pass from man to man rapidly and steadily, down one rank and up the other, giving one long continuous sound."[37]

The feu-de-joie, or "running fire," down through the centuries has been an expression of joy and celebration for a great variety of occasions. Sometimes it was on the grand scale. A recruit in the 56th (Essex) Regiment of Foot in 1799 described how Abercromby's victory in Holland was celebrated by troops at Barham Downs awaiting passage to the battle zone: ". . . we were nearly 20,000 strong . . . being formed in one extensive line, the firing of the feu de joie produced a fine effect . . . certainly the finest sight I had ever witnessed."[38]

As is often the case, a military custom may have its counterpart in civilian life. Admiral John Moresby tells how he experienced, as a youth in Somerset in the early nineteenth century, the excitement at the time of the apple harvest and the crushing of the fruit in the cider-presses:

> . . . as night closed in, the custom, descending from heathen times, of wassailing the apple trees was faithfully observed. Every old gun, blunderbuss, or pistol that the village could produce was brought out, and masters and men, women and children, all trooped to the principal orchard. . . . Then, with shouting and cheering, and a general feu de joie over the trees, all joined in the chorus: 'Old apple-tree, I wassail thee,' etc. etc.[39]

It is rare for a feu-de-joie to be fired at sea, but such was the case in HMS *Basilisk* off the coast of New Guinea in 1873. Moresby, as captain of the

Men of the 1st Battalion, Queen's Own Rifles of Canada, firing a feu-de-joie, Work Point Barracks, Victoria, June, 1967.

Basilisk, describes the occasion when the possession of some islands was proclaimed. "The Jack was then run up and saluted amid three hearty cheers . . . . A feu de joie was then fired, and I said: 'Lads, in honour of what old *Basilisk* has done, we will splice the main brace tonight [that is, serve out an extra ration of rum to all hands].' "[40]

Meanwhile, on the other side of the world, the queen's forces were celebrating quite different occasions. Barely a month after its organization, the forerunner of the Queen's Own Rifles of Canada on 24 May 1860 fired a feu-de-joie for Queen Victoria. The order read in part:

> . . . the Active Militia Forces of No. 5 Military District of Upper Canada . . . will parade in brigades on Thursday, the 24th inst. in the field on the west of the Parliament Buildings, Toronto, at a quarter before noon, for the purpose of firing a 'feu-de-joie' in honour of Her Majesty's Birthday.[41]

Twenty-five years later, on the old queen's birthday, another feu-de-joie was fired, this time in an operational situation at Battleford on the North Saskatchewan River during the North-west Rebellion. Two columns of Canadian militia celebrated the Twenty-fourth of May with a divisional parade and a full feu-de-joie was fired, including artillery. "This show of strength so impressed the Indians that they came flocking in to surrender . . . . "[42]

In modern times the feu-de-joie has been fired in Canada on numerous occasions. On 6 May 1935 the Calgary Highlanders joined with other units in a grand parade to Victoria Park, Calgary, where a feu-de-joie was fired as part of the celebration marking the Silver Jubilee of the reign of King George V.[43]

On 12 May 1937 the temporarily-styled Royal Regiment of Toronto Grenadiers joined with its sister regiments, the Queen's Own Rifles of Canada and the 48th Highlanders of Canada, at Queen's Park, Toronto, to celebrate the coronation of His Majesty King George VI.[44]

Another memorable occasion was on 23 June 1959 on the Plains of Abraham, Quebec, when the three regular battalions of the Royal 22e Régiment were presented with new colours by their colonel-in-chief, Her Majesty Queen Elizabeth II. After Her Majesty addressed her regiment in French, the ceremony, which opened with "God Save the Queen," ended with the regiment firing a feu-de-joie and the singing of "O Canada."[45]

Just as it had done more than a century before, the Queen's Own Rifles of Canada celebrated its 110th birthday in 1970 with the firing of a feu-de-joie.[46]

A very unusual occasion was the honouring of the late Colonel R.S. McLaughlin, honorary colonel of the Ontario Regiment for forty-seven years, on the attainment of his one hundredth birthday. At a special parade of his regiment in September, 1971 a feu-de-joie was fired in the colonel's honour.[47]

The Fly-past

It was after the Second World War that the ceremonial fly-past came into its own as a traditional form of salute on occasions of national importance. Over Ottawa, as well as other centres, such occasions are Battle of Britain Sunday, Canadian Forces Day, and Dominion Day. Aircraft fly in formation over a prescribed flight-path and an honoured personage in a conspicuous location formally takes the salute. In several respects it is not unlike the ceremonial attending the march-past of troops and vehicles and the sail-past of the fleet.

Though this form of salute is largely a post-1945 practice, the first large-scale, ceremonial fly-past of the Royal Air Forces actually took place in 1935 at Duxford, England, when some two-hundred aircraft of the RAF passed overhead in review in celebration of the Silver Jubilee of King George V.[48]

Of course, long before 1935, small-scale fly-pasts honouring commanding officers of stations and other dignitaries were fairly common. They probably had their origin in the Royal Flying Corps and Royal Naval Air Service when squadrons returning from missions during the Great War flew past their stations at low altitude before landing.

Today, in addition to fly-pasts of nation-wide significance, the ceremony is performed locally on the occasion of a change of command or to participate in some civic observance.

Freedom of the City

One of the most prized honours of a marching unit is the conferring upon the unit of the privilege and distinction of the freedom of the city — the honour for all time of marching through the city with drums beating, colours flying, and bayonets fixed. Several regiments have been so honoured in Canada in recognition of their honorable record and to demonstrate the affection and esteem with which they are held by the citizens. Nor is the granting of the freedom of the city exclusively a regimental affair. In the port city of Vancouver, the naval reserve division, HMCS *Discovery*, takes pride in being the first and only unit to be so honoured (1973). Similarly, the city of Trenton conferred the privilege on Royal Canadian Air Force Station Trenton in September, 1967.

Usually, the freedom of the city is granted to a unit which has enjoyed a long and happy relationship with a city. An example is the Royal Regiment of Canada which, in 1962, on the occasion of the one hundredth anniversary of the founding of the regiment, was so honoured by the city of Toronto, the first in the city's history. At the same time the regiment was reminded of its obligation "to hold itself, as a regiment, as the first official protectors of the city."[49] But sometimes the honour is granted to mark a people's gratitude for a heroic service, as in the case of Princess Patricia's Canadian Light Infantry. In its jubilee year, 1964, the freedom of the city of Ypres in Belgium was conferred on the Patricias for their exploits a half century before.[50]

The conferment of the freedom of the city means, in the physical sense, the granting of the privilege to march through the city with "drums beating, colours flying and bayonets fixed." Of course, everyone is familiar with the colour and pageantry of the military parade, which immediately raises the question, what is so important about the granting of this privilege? As is the case with so many of our traditions, this custom goes back more than three centuries in British military history.

There has ever been amongst British peoples a deeply seated antipathy towards a large standing army; large regular forces as garrisons in British cities have seldom been welcomed by the populace. This goes back to Tudor times, before and since, when the city of London jealously guarded its ancient rights and depended on its own trained bands to keep the peace and defend the city. Throughout our history, both in Britain and the Commonwealth, there is a strong tradition against the war-like appearance of large bodies of troops in the streets disturbing the civil repose and posing a threat, real or imagined, of infringement of ancient civic rights.

Even the time-honoured method of recruiting "by beat of drum" was highly suspect in the citizen's mind because of past incidents not unlike those associated with the press gangs of the Royal Navy. Thus it became customary to request the permission of the chief magistrate, the lord mayor, before any such foray was undertaken.

Sometimes the sequence of words — drums, colours, bayonets — differs, reflecting different times and different conditions. For example, when the custom of conferring the freedom of the city first took hold after the Restoration of King Charles II in 1660,[51] the bayonet was not yet in use. Today, the naval division has no colour. And it is only in relatively recent times that bands have come into use as opposed to the fife and drum of an earlier age. This would seem to favour the recognition of historical development in today's usage — first, the ancient drum; next, the colours; and lastly, the bayonet.[52]

The ceremony of granting the freedom of the city hearkens back to an even earlier time when cities had walls and gates were barred to friend and foe alike — to the foe for obvious reasons, to the friend until the city authorities were assured of the troops best behaviour and the purpose of the presence of the regiment seeking entry. Today's ceremony reflects the ritual which had to take place in the days when troops on the march had no barracks and required being billeted in the town for the night. The following was written more than two centuries ago:

> As soon as the Town-Major . . . has notice from the Sentinels that the Regiment is in view, he should take a Serjeant and a file of men, and go to the outermost Barrier, and order one of the draw-bridges to be drawn up after him, till he has examined the original orders or route of the Regiment, lest the enemy, by having notice of the march of the Regiment, should, under that pretence, endeavour to surprise the town.[53]

These same procedures of long ago are to be seen today whenever a unit of the Canadian Forces is honoured by a city. The 2nd Battalion, the Royal Canadian Regiment, is a good example. As the battalion marched into the city of Fredericton in June, 1973, the chief of police stood his ground in the middle of the road, just like the city marshal of yesteryear, stopped the regiment and enquired of the commanding officer as to the purpose of the presence of the regiment on the march in the city. As the troops waited beyond the barrier of old, the commanding officer was escorted to the mayor who called a formal session of the city council, whereupon a resolution granting the freedom of the city was voted upon and approved. There followed an inspection and review of the battalion by the city's chief magistrate, and an exchange of scroll and gifts — all for the purpose of demonstrating the mutual esteem and respect of the citizens and the regiment.[54]

The wording used in the scroll normally presented to a unit at the time of the granting of the privilege of marching through the city with "drums beating, colours flying and bayonets fixed" is colourful and varied. The following is the text of the illuminated scroll presented to the Hastings and Prince Edward Regiment by the City of Belleville in 1964.[55]

FREEDOM OF THE CITY OF BELLEVILLE

TO

THE HASTINGS AND PRINCE EDWARD REGIMENT

THIS DAY AND HENCEFORTH MAY IT BE KNOWN THAT, on this occasion of the Presentation of Colours and in honour of the history and tradition of The Hastings and Prince Edward Regiment and its predecessor units, that the Corporation of the City of Belleville in the realm of Canada of her Gracious

Majesty, Queen Elizabeth, the Second, by virtue of the authority of a resolution passed unanimously by the Council of the said Corporation on the sixth day of January, One Thousand, Nine Hundred and Sixty-Four, HEREBY PROCLAIMS AND GRANTS TO THE HASTINGS AND PRINCE EDWARD REGIMENT

The Freedom of the said City of Belleville and all rights and privileges pertaining thereto, as long as the waters of Quinte Bay embrace the shores of the said city, to enter therein and march throughout its streets, thoroughfares and highways, without hindrance or trespass on any and all occasions with Colours and Battle Honours flying, bayonets fixed and bands playing,

This Freedom is granted and confirmed in grateful acknowledgement and recognition of services rendered and duty bravely performed since the formation of the Regiment's parent units, the First Regiment of Prince Edward Militia in the year, One Thousand, Eight Hundred, and the First Regiment of Hastings Militia in the year One Thousand, Eight Hundred and Four and continuing throughout a distinguished record of service in the wars of 1812, the Rebellion of 1837, the Fenian Raid of 1865, the North-West Expedition of 1885; the war in South Africa in 1898, the First World War of 1914 to 1918; the unit formally became the Hastings and Prince Edward Regiment in 1920, and this grant is particularly to perpetuate its feats of bravery, devotion and glory from 1939 to 1945 from North Africa to Sicily, to Italy and to the European Theatre, to witness the capitulation of its enemies and thereafter, in causes dear to the hearts of the said City and all its citizens.

In particular and without limiting the foregoing, This Freedom is granted and to be recognized as a memorial to all ranks from said Regiment and its predecessors contributing to its distinguished history, who have given their lives on the altar of freedom in the performance of their duty and earned for their comrades and all who came after them the honours now recognized and being secured to them in perpetuity by their fellow citizens hereby recorded.

SIGNED AND SEALED on behalf of the CORPORATION OF THE CITY OF BELLEVILLE on this *seventeenth* day of May, in the Year of Our Lord, One Thousand, Nine Hundred and Sixty-Four.

J.R. Ellis
Mayor

SEAL

A.S. Stalker
Clerk

Levee

The levee has a long tradition in the Canadian Forces as one of the activities associated with New Year's Day. Officers of the various units and headquarters receive and greet in their messes visiting officers and other guests in the convivial spirit of the first day of the new year. Hospitality is dispensed in a variety of forms, from the special flaming punch of the Royal Canadian Hussars of Montreal, a concoction bequeathed to the regiment by the old 1st Motor Machine Gun Brigade and which takes a month to prepare, to the famed Athole Brose, that brew of oatmeal, honey and whisky, of the Seaforth Highlanders of Canada, Vancouver.

In line with this tradition, the chief of the defence staff, beginning on 1 January 1975 hosts a levee each New Year's Day in the new National Defence Headquarters at 101 Colonel By Drive, Ottawa.

The levee has an unusual origin. The word itself meant, originally, the action of rising, specifically from one's bed, coming from the French *lever* (to rise). As early as the seventeenth century, a levee was a reception of visitors on rising from bed, a morning reception by a king or person of distinction. In the eighteenth century, in Britain, it was an assembly in the early afternoon by the sovereign at which men only were received.

While the levee is still largely a male preserve, women, unescorted, do attend on New Year's Day. Prince Edward Island and Newfoundland in 1975 are the only two provinces where women are not welcome at the lieutenant-governor's levee.[56]

Make and Mend

A make and mend is a half day (afternoon) when normal work and routines are suspended. The expression is often abbreviated to "makers." Originally, in the days before naval ratings had a standard uniform issued, once a week, usually on Thursdays, the pipe, "hands to make and mend clothes" would be sounded so that seamen could make and mend the clothing which in those days had been purchased from the purser's slop chest. It was an afternoon to catch up on the wear and tear to which sailor's clothing was subjected in the days of sail.

With the advent of issued uniform clothing in the mid-nineteenth century in the Royal Navy, the make and mend gradually took on a recreational purpose including organized sports, both ashore and afloat. This was the case in the Royal Canadian Navy and, traditionally, this was on Wednesday afternoons.

However, even before the First World War, the idea of the make and mend as a time when a seaman afloat had some time to himself was gaining ground. "At one p.m. on Thursday, instead of clearing up decks as usual, preparatory to both watches, falling in, the pipe goes, 'hands make and mend clothes,' which means that the afternoon is for the men to do as they like."[57]

One author, an able seaman, gives a graphic description of what the make and mend meant to the sailor afloat in the 1920s:

... the majority of the ship's company may be relieved of routine duties between noon and seven bells. These are golden hours indeed, when, in summer weather the bluejackets may be seen stretched out on the forecastle enjoying sweeter sleep than any civilian knows.[58]

In the period of the Second World War, in HMC ships, a makers was still a half-day on which ratings not on watch were to muster and repair and wash their clothing, and scrub their hammocks.[59]

Today, with unification and the five-day working week, there is a trend in HMC ships to return to harbour early on Fridays, with a make and mend, meaning leave for all but the watch on Friday afternoons. As a result, the make and mend appears in daily routine orders published in advance so that the ship's company may make their plans for week-end leave. Because the intention to grant a make and mend is known in advance, the pipe, "hands to make and mend clothes," is not heard so often today.[60] At sea, the same result is often achieved simply by piping the order, "pipe down."[61]

An ancient nautical custom, it is of interest to note that the make and mend has an army background, too. An historian writing about the Royal Canadian Regiment in training on Salisbury Plain, England, in 1940, wrote: "On return to barracks... there was the customary 'make and mend' day free from duties; one fifth of the Regiment went on leave and others began to practise for the Brigade sports three days hence."[62]

Indeed, it is rather intriguing that while the navy has lost the original meaning of the term and today uses the term make and mend less and less, in the Royal Canadian Regiment and Princess Patricia's Canadian Light Infantry it is used widely, not only to denote a period of time when normal work and routines are suspended, but to signify, say on a field exercise, time to be devoted to maintenance of personal kit, clothing, weapons, vehicles et cetera, not unlike the old make and mend of the days of sail.

Manning and Cheering Ship

"Manning and cheering ship" is a very old custom. More than a mark of respect, it is an expression of esteem and affection by the whole ship's company for a particular person or another ship's company. This drill or ship's evolution, invariably carried out with spirit and enthusiasm, is to be seen when Her Majesty the Queen or her representative, His Excellency the Governor-General, visit, or make their departure from, units of the fleet; when HMC ships enter harbour after an engagement or victory at sea; and when one of HMC ships sails to her new homeport or to pay off. Sometimes a departing flag officer or other senior officer is so honoured.

The ship's company of HMCS *Gatineau* cheering ship as Her Majesty the Queen in the royal yacht *Britannia* leaves Canadian waters, July, 1959. (Note the historic arrangement of flags in *Britannia*: the Union Jack at the jack-staff; the admiralty flag at the fore; the royal standard at the main; the Canadian ensign at the mizzen; and the white ensign at the ensign-staff.)

In the days of sail, manning and cheering ship made a remarkable sight as each ship of the squadron vied with each other in smartness and speed to man the yards and rigging clear up to mastheads. Today, the ship's company line the rails of the upper deck, and, led from the bridge, give three mighty cheers.

Manning the Side

In the expression, "to man the side," there are two different meanings. One is the example where two warships meet on more or less parallel, reciprocal courses. One would expect to hear the alert sounded by bugle or bo's'n's call in each ship and the hands fallen in on the sides facing each other.[63] This practice has come down from the days of the heavily-gunned windship where, with most of the ship's company on deck or aloft, the guns could not be run out, indicating peaceful intentions.[64]

The other meaning of manning the side is the very old custom of receiving senior officers at the head of the accommodation ladder or the brow with a side party in attendance. Such side party would consist of four or five ratings, once called side boys, all in a line, headed by a chief or petty officer with his bo's'n's call ready to pipe the dignitary aboard.

There is an interesting account of the practice of this custom in Canadian waters more than two centuries ago. It will be remembered that in the summer of 1759 Wolfe spent several weeks assessing the problem of taking Quebec. One day during one of his tours of inspection he encountered a young midshipman recently arrived from New England who had not yet acquired a uniform. Ashley Bowen's journal gives an account of the lively exchange between the general and the midshipman in which the latter proved his identity by detailing how Wolfe was received on board HMS *Pembroke*, fifty guns, Captain John Simcoe RN,* earlier at Halifax. Young Bowen explained how only four hands were ordered to man the side until it was discovered that the visitor was none other than the commanding general, James Wolfe, when the orders took on a note of some urgency. In quick succession, the sergeant of marines, the boatswain and the master-at-arms arrived at the double, and a proper ruff was beat.[65]

---

*HMS *Pembroke*, 50, in Halifax and in the St. Lawrence in 1759, is of special interest as a result of subsequent events in Canadian history. The captain of the *Pembroke*, Captain John Simcoe, died on the passage to Quebec; he was the father of Upper Canada's first Lieutenant Governor, Colonel John Graves Simcoe. Moreover, the master (navigator) in the *Pembroke* was none other than the future famous explorer, James Cook.

Marriage

Social and economic change has had a significant effect on the serviceman and attitudes regarding marriage, and thus on customs related to marriage. In the past, two things militated against early marriage — low pay, and the belief that undivided attention was essential to the young man's success in the learning phase of the military profession.

Ten years before meeting his destiny at Quebec, a young major of infantry, James Wolfe, pointed up a third factor when he issued this order: "Any soldier that presumes to marry clandestinely, . . . that shall not consult his officer before his marriage, that the woman's character may be inquired into, every such offender will be punished with rigour."[66]

This concern for the welfare of the young serviceman still persisted when the Royal Canadian Air Force first spread its wings in 1924. "Permission to marry may be granted by the applicant's commanding officer. Such permission will not be given unless . . . the commanding officer is satisfied that the applicant is financially able to marry and that the woman is a desirable character."[67]

Even as late as 1965 it seemed necessary to admonish young officers to tread softly in this matter of marriage. "If you are married you are bound to have more interests outside your army life, and then your work and learning suffer . . . . You must not expect to have special treatment if you do marry before the official age [23 years]; it would be unfair to the other officers."[68]

But in spite of all the dire warnings, young men and the ladies of their choice found ways to begin their married lives and many were the joyous scenes when the young sailor went over the brow with long, white tapes securing the black silk about his neck, the symbol of his wedding day. That custom, of course, went out with the square-rig of bell bottoms and jumper. However, one custom of this kind does survive, though it is only occasionally seen today — the hoisting of a garland.

When a member of a ship's company is married in the port where the ship is lying, a garland of evergreens is hoisted for the day between the masts of a two-masted ship, or on the forestay of the more likely single-masted ship.

A marriage custom which is very much alive today is the time-honoured arch of swords. In a Service wedding involving a commissioned officer, officer colleagues in uniform acting as ushers make the arch of swords for the bride and groom at the foot of the chancel steps at the end of the ceremony. Or, more often, the weather being fine, the ceremonial arch is made outside the church door, the officer-ushers having made a rapid exit through a side door, leaving the bridesmaids to go down the aisle unescorted.[69]

Two service personnel exchange marriage vows, Nova Scotia, 1957.

A lively marriage custom combining dignity and mirth is the one observed in the Second Regiment, Royal Canadian Horse Artillery at CFB Petawawa. Whenever a member of the regiment marries, he and his bride are joyfully assisted to a special seat mounted on the limber of a 25 pound gun. In this fashion, under tow by a 3/4-ton truck and escorted by a party from the regiment, the happy couple leave the church to begin their honeymoon.[70]

New Year's Day

As in our society generally, New Year's Eve and New Year's Day are times of merry-making and good fellowship throughout the Canadian Forces. In addition to the traditional levees (see page 94), activities, more of an "in-house" kind, are varied and colourful.

Formal balls on New Year's Eve are very popular in units from coast to coast, a typical example being that of the Saskatchewan Dragoons of Moose Jaw, where balls take place simultaneously in the warrant officers/sergeants mess and the officers mess.

New Year's Day in the messes epitomizes the camaraderie and goodwill between all ranks. In most units of the Canadian Forces the officers as a group call on the warrant officers and sergeants in their mess and then, in turn, the NCO's are entertained in the officers' mess.

This custom in its various forms is of long standing. On the western front in 1915, the 3rd Battalion, Canadian Expeditionary Force (called the Toronto Regiment, a forbear of today's Royal Regiment of Canada) had spent Christmas Day in the sodden trenches facing the German army. But by New Year's Day, 1916, the battalion was out of the line in reserve. There, spread out company by company in huts and barns, the troops fashioned trestle tables, decorated them with holly, and sat down to dinners of remarkable ingenuity served by the sergeants and officers in a memorable atmosphere of battle-tried comradeship and good-will.[71]

On New Year's Day, 1944, the Queen's Own Rifles of Canada were stationed at Bournemouth, facing the English Channel. But duties in wartime served only to heighten the sense of good fellowship when the regiment's commanding officer and his officers strode up to the door of the sergeant's mess and were invited in, in the time-honoured tradition, by the regimental sergeant-major, to have a glass together.[72]

The traditional exchange of visits on New Year's Day between the officers and sergeants has, in the case of the 7th Toronto Regiment, Royal Canadian Artillery, an additional happy development. The commanding officer and the regimental sergeant-major join forces and personally cook and serve breakfast to the lot.

A similar occasion is to be seen in HMCS *Star* where the captain hosts a luncheon for all the officers of the Hamilton Naval Division.

In HMC ships in harbour there is a long tradition of sixteen bells being rung on the ship's bell at midnight on December 31, rather than the eight bells which normally would mark the end of the watch. On this occasion the bell is struck not by the quartermaster or the boatswain, but usually by the youngest seaman in the ship, this to the accompaniment of sundry whistles and sirens of other ships nearby.

In HMCS *York*, the Toronto naval division, there is a very lively scene in the chiefs' and petty officers' mess which not only marks New Year's Day but which recalls a three-hundred-year old custom which has only recently disappeared from the fleet. A highly polished, brass-bound rum barrel is appropriately broached at the sound of the time-honoured pipe, "up spirits," and the irreverent but low-key aside, "stand fast the Holy Ghost!"

A new tradition has been building for some years in HMC ships when in their home port for New Year's Day. More and more of the families of the members of the ship's company come down to the harbour at Esquimalt or Halifax to go on board and sit down to dinner in the congenial atmosphere of the mess decks of a ship of war. Where sailors must live in such confined quarters, it is indeed a joyous experience for them to hear the children's voices close at hand while they and their wives enjoy the good fellowship of the occasion.

The old French Canadian custom of gift-giving on New Year's Day is a highly cherished tradition in le Régiment de Hull where at a breakfast party in the armoury each officer and his wife receives a beautiful and tastefully chosen gift, often in silver, from the officers' mess of the regiment.

Reference to the year-end festivities in the Canadian Forces would not be complete without a word about that time of celebration so dear to the Scots — Hogmanay, the ancient expression for the last day of the year. The word itself is thought to have come from an old Norman word *hoguinané*, having the same meaning. To be present at the reciprocal visits between the messes of the Queen's Own Cameron Highlanders of Winnipeg, where the pipes seem to come into play with a renewed spirit and there is joyful camaraderie on every hand, is to see a reflection of the meaning of Hogmanay in the Scottish regiments throughout the land.

The Oath of Allegiance
When a person joins the Canadian Forces, he or she is required to swear an oath of allegiance, or make a solemn affirmation, in these words:

I, (full name), do swear (or solemnly affirm) that I will be faithful and bear true allegiance to Her Majesty, Queen Elizabeth the Second, Her heirs and successors according to law. So help me God. (The entreaty at the end is omitted in the case of the solemn affirmation.)

Such a statement, made under oath, is a form of contract, a solemn promise, between the recruit and the sovereign, who as the queen of Canada embodies the state, the sovereign power. This oath of allegiance, or solemn affirmation, is based on a practice thousands of years old.

In the legions of ancient Rome, the soldier took a military oath called the *sacramentum*. It was a set formula of words voiced under conditions of great solemnity and expressing a commitment so deep that a soldier would seldom dare break it, not so much from fear of sanctions, as from the impossibility of expunging the stain from his personal honour. He promised implicit obedience to his commanders, that he would not desert the Service, "nor at anytime refuse to expose himself to the utmost Perils, for the Safety and Welfare of the State."[73]

This Roman army ceremony was re-enacted at the beginning of each year. It was an impressive spectacle. One soldier would be selected for his strong voice. He would repeat the formulated words after the tribune, whereupon the whole legion, as one man, would shout their consent to abide by the oath, sometimes drawing their short, heavy swords and thrusting them in the air to emphasize their declaration.[74]

Through the centuries, the conditions under which the oath of allegiance was administered, or whether it was administered at all, to recruits, have formed the background of many stories, fact and fiction. Much has been written about the "king's shilling," the acceptance of which at one time constituted an agreement by a man to enlist. Many were the tales of over-zealous recruiting sergeants inveigling a fellow citizen, too long languishing in the tavern, into accepting the king's shilling, the victim waking up next morning wondering how he was to escape being apprehended as a vagabond, or how to muster twenty shillings "smart money" to buy his way out of his "bad bargain." Or, it could go the other way, and that is why a useless soldier or sailor was known as a "king's hard bargain." Or, perhaps, the reluctant recruit never even saw a king's shilling, for in times of great national stress, the dreaded press gang produced "the bodies" if they could not be procured any other way.

However, it is of interest to note that Britons nearly three centuries ago had some protection against arbitrary induction into the forces. Since 1694, the attestation of a recruit was required to be before a civil authority to guard against a citizen "being entrapped, without understanding the nature of it, into a contract, which, even though not a contract for life, is one of a very serious nature."[75]

Although the words of the oath of allegiance have changed over the years, there is a timeless quality in the expression of the relationship binding the sovereign and the subject. For example, there is something almost medieval in the phrasing of the soldier's oath in the days of Queen Anne nearly three centuries ago:

> I swear to be true to our Sovereign Queen Anne, and to serve Her honestly and faithfully, in the Defence of Her Person, Crown and Dignity, against all Her enemies and Opposers whatsoever; and to observe and obey Her Majesty's Orders, and the Orders of the Generals and Officers set over me by Her Majesty. So help me God.[76]

During the Napoleonic Wars, the oath and the certificate of the magistrate or justice of the peace before whom the recruit was attested were printed forms. The oath taken by a soldier in 1799 was reinforced by this quaintly worded document:

> I, (name) do make Oath, that I am by Trade a   and to the best of my Knowledge and Belief, was born in the Parish of   in the County of   and that I have no rupture, nor ever was troubled with Fits, and am no ways disabled by Lameness or otherwise, but have the perfect Use of my Limbs, that I am not an Apprentice; and that I do not belong to the Militia, or to any other Regiment, or to His Majesty's Navy, or Marines.[77]

Promenading

The custom of promenading, as practised in the Canadian Forces today, is said to be one of considerable antiquity, yet, in the military sense, reference to it is difficult to find in print until the twentieth century. Promenading is associated with infantry regiments, particularly guards regiments, and is also practised in some armoured regiments. The word is taken from the French, meaning a walk taken at a leisurely pace for exercise or amusement, to and fro for display, or as part of a ceremony. The term dates from the sixteenth century and, in the eighteenth century, represented a fashionable practice of the European civilian scene.

Indeed, a rather colourful scene was painted in the words of a young officer of the 4th Regiment of Foot nearly two centuries ago, in 1787, recently arrived at Halifax for garrison duty. "There is a square in town called the Grand

Parade, where the troops in garrison parade every evening during the summer; and where all the belles and beaux of the place promenade, and the bands remain to play as long as they walk."[78]

Promenading has been defined as "a custom of long standing in the British Brigade of Guards by which officers on guard meeting, move to and fro in a leisurely, informal style in pairs prior to being called on parade for the changing ceremony. The officers march 25 to 30 paces in one direction, turn about and repeat the process."[79]

Promenading, in relation to the assembly of a battalion, is carried out in some regiments in lieu of the practice where the officers are fairly casually marched on to the parade by the battalions' second-in-command, where they stand in line facing the troops awaiting the order for the officers to fall in or to take post.

In the "Standing Orders of the Royal Canadian Regiment" (1935), it is clear that promenading was practised but the word was not used: ". . . as each Company is formed up . . . Officers will walk to and fro not more than three abreast, well clear of the battallion."

The air force seems to have adopted something approaching promenading, though perhaps in not so informal a fashion. "The officers are to march onto the parade ground and proceed to march in quick time, in pairs, up and down along the directing flank of the squadron in rear of the trumpeter . . . and the drummer."[80]

In spite of the uncertainty of the origin of military promenading, the custom is still very much alive in the Canadian Forces today. In the century-old Drill Hall in Ottawa, at the commanding officer's parade of the Governor-General's Foot Guards, the officers walk informally, in pairs, traditionally with hands clasped behind their backs, behind the saluting dais, prior to taking over their respective commands.

Reveille

It is the rare individual who really enjoys getting up in the morning, particularly when he is being coerced into getting out of bed by some insistent, jarring noise, be it the harsh notes of a bugle, or the "cheerful entreaties" of a sergeant or a ship's quartermaster, or the raucous demands of the simple alarm clock wisely set in a dish-pan. Yet the rising is inevitable and that's what reveille is all about, particularly the dictionary meaning for *se réveiller*, to revive. Like so many things military, the word comes from the French imperative *réveillez*, meaning wake up, originally from the Latin *vigilare*, watch.

However, in spite of the nasty ideas associated with reveille, including that line from an old song — "Some day I'm going to murder the bugler!,"[81] the word reveille, probably more than any other, brings to mind one scene after another at such a rate and in such a variety of time and place, that when all put together conjures up in the mind's eye a most rich and colourful tapestry depicting the military heritage of the Canadian people:

The bright, chill air of an April morning in 1793 and the Queen's Rangers building new quarters at Queenston where the gallant Brock was to fall two decades later in the defence of Canada. "The Bugles sound at 5 every Morning & Coll. Simcoe goes out with the troops & returns to breakfast at nine."[82]

The 2nd Battalion, The Royal Canadian Regiment, at sea off Korea on 5 May 1951. ". . . reveille blew at 0430 hours and debarkation at Pusan began."[83]

Major-General Smith-Dorrien's flying column striking out against Boer guerilla forces in the cold and fog of an African night in 1900. "Reveille sounded at 1:00 a.m. on November 6 and at three o'clock the columns moved off . . . " including the Royal Canadian Dragoons, two guns of "D" Battery, Royal Canadian Artillery, and a pom-pom, which was the advance guard.[84]

The early morning assault of the 3rd Canadian Division over the Normandy beaches. "Reveille on D-Day, 6 June, 1944, was at 0315 hrs. The water in the Channel was rough: the spirits of the men boisterously high."[85]

The 10th Royal Grenadiers from Toronto on the march with wagon train north from Qu'Appelle to bring Riel's rebels to battle, camped on the prairie for the night. Next morning, 11 April 1885, reveille sounded at 4 a.m. and the long march continued.[86]

The makeshift camp of the Calgary Highlanders on the Sarcee Indian Reserve at the outbreak of war in 1939. "Each morning Boy Bugler Bennie Lee would arouse the drowsy recruits — bankers, salesmen, clerks, cowboys, farmers, lawyers and men from all grades of civilian life. In their motley garb ranging from mufti to kilts and home-made glengarries, the troops grabbed pails and raced for the water pumps. The day's training had begun."[87]

The shrill notes of the bo's'n's call in a Second World War destroyer and the timeless language of the sea. "Wakey, wakey, wak-e-ey! Rise and shine! Lash up and stow [your hammock]!"[88]

It was April, 1885, when the men of the 92nd Regiment (Winnipeg Light Infantry) were at Calgary to march to the relief of Edmonton, bent on the capture of Big Bear and his forces after the massacre at Frog Lake. ". . . the strident notes of the bugle band sounded reveille at half past four, and breaking camp early we marched twenty-five miles our first day."[89]

Camp Borden in the days of the old Canadian Air Force of 1922, before the RCAF was established; an office-hut adjacent to the parade square, the living quarters of an RCMP constable (station security) and the assistant postmaster. The latter was a sergeant of the CAF and it was his duty to play reveille early every morning. This he slyly did by poking his bugle out the open window of the hut "for there was nobody else around!"[90]

In September, 1974, in exercise "Potlatch" off the mouth of the Nahwitti River, Vancouver Island, men of One Combat Group bedded down for the night in the cold austerity of the anchor cable space in HMCS *Provider*, took it in stride when a petty officer announced an unusually early reveille for the troops, 0300, "because that's when we drop anchor," and the cable deck is no place to be when that massive chain cable starts rattling out through the hawse.[91]

Although the early morning call or beat of the drum was known in Elizabethan times, probably the earliest instance of reveille in printed English was *Lawes and Ordnances of Warre* by the Earl of Northumberland (1640): "No victualler shall entertain any Souldiers in his house, tent or hutt, after the warning-piece at night, or before the beating of the Ravalee in the morning." A similar warning is to be found in the Articles of War (1673).[92]

In the eighteenth century, reveille was defined as "the beat of a drum, about break of day, to advertise the army that it is day-light, and that the sentinels forbear challenging."[93] Another purpose for reveille, other than for waking people up and marking the cessation of night duties, was as a signal to open the gate to let the horse-guard, consisting of a corporal and half a dozen troopers, do a quick reconnaissance beyond the walls of the town.[94]

Today in the Canadian Forces, people know what reveille means but its use in the sense of a fixed drill or loud, awakening sound has all but disappeared. It is seldom spelled out in routine orders. Indeed, the way people start the working day in the forces reflects a less regimented, "do-it-by-numbers" way of life. The majority of personnel today, whose duty is performed on bases, stations and even in barracks, live on the economy, that is, in their own accommodation in the town or elsewhere. They are expected to get themselves up, transported and in their place of duty on time, and this is their own responsibility.

In barracks today the troops do not normally live in dormitories, but are accommodated two to four in a room, or even in individual rooms. In some barrack situations, the troops are on their own so far as getting up is concerned, while in others a duty NCO goes around knocking on doors to awaken people. At Collège Militaire Royal de Saint-Jean, a duty cadet in each block has the same responsibility.

What it really amounts to, today, is that reveille is far from a standardized routine in the Canadian Forces. There is much variety and flexibility to allow for differences in accommodation and circumstances, for example, duty at a command headquarters, as opposed to arctic training up by the Coppermine River.

It is evident that in regard to the management of daily routine there is a marked difference between what might be called the training scene and the operational environment, a distinct diminution of the outward signs of disciplinary control. For example, at CFB Chilliwack, where people are under training, daily routines are regulated audibly by recorded trumpet calls and band music, electronically controlled from the guardhouse. Similarly, at the Royal Military College, Kingston, reveille is by recorded bugle call, reinforced by the voices of duty cadets, and even by the bo's'n's call in the quarters known as the stone frigate.

On the other hand, when troops are out in the field on a scheme or exercise, rousing people is done by the man to be relieved, by a shake or voice call, or if the tactical situation permits, people may be awakened by the piercing sound of a "deuce and a half horn," the air horn of a 2½ ton truck. But, generally, the further one moves from the training establishment to the routine of the fixed base or station, with factors of shift work (as it is called) and of military duty occupying only a fraction of the weekly span, there is less and less of the outward signs of the traditional military life and more and more of what is called "civilianization" of the Service.

Yet, to visit a line regiment in garrison, is to hear the reveille of old sounding in the crisp morning air. For example, in Princess Patricia's Canadian Light Infantry, to this day, a bugler of the regiment's Corps of Drums steps smartly out on the parade square and sounds reveille in the time-honoured way.

One area where there has been little change is in "rousing the hands" in HMC ships where the factor of having to live in relatively cramped quarters still obtains as it has since the days of Nelson and before. Here the "cheery" twittering of the bo's'n's call penetrates every mess deck by way of the ship's broadcast, "wakey, wakey, rise and shine," followed by a variety of rhymes of doubtful literary merit intended to convince the drowsy matelot that the view from the upper deck is "wondrous fine!"

The Rifle Tradition
When the three former Services were merged into a single unified force by Act

The newly presented colours of the three commandos of the Canadian Airborne Regiment lowered in salute, CFB Edmonton, 1973.

A veteran artillery piece and modern guns of the 30th Field Regiment, Royal Canadian Artillery (the Bytown Gunners), fire a national salute on Canada Day, 1 July 1975, Parliament Hill, Ottawa.

The guidon of the Royal Canadian Dragoons and escort in armoured personnel carriers, while centurion tanks of the regiment fire a feu-de-joie commemorating the regiment's part in the Battle of Liliefontein, South Africa, in 1900 at Lahr, Germany, November, 1975.

The Honourable Pauline M. McGibbon, lieutenant governor of Ontario, and her guard of honour composed entirely of women of the Canadian Forces, CFB Trenton, 1975.

Howitzers of the 30th Field Regiment, Royal Canadian Artillery (the Bytown Gunners), firing a salute in tribute to Canada's war dead, Remembrance Day, Confederation Square, Ottawa, 1975.

The Right Honourable Jules Léger, Governor-General, taking the salute of a guard mounted by the Royal 22e Régiment, Parliament Hill, Ottawa, January, 1974.

A destroyer alongside at Halifax illuminated for the festive season, Christmas, 1971.

The colour of the Royal Canadian Air Force and the newly-presented standard of 439 Squadron being marched past, Baden, Germany, 1973.

The ceremony of changing the guard by the Public Duties Detachment, composed of guardsmen of the Governor-General's Foot Guards of Ottawa and the Canadian Grenadier Guards of Montreal, Parliament Hill, Ottawa, August, 1975. In the foreground is the centennial flame fountain displaying the armorial bearings of the provinces.

The ship's company of HMCS *Quebec*, cruiser, mustered on the fo'c's'le as the ship crosses the equator to the accompaniment of the ancient crossing the line ceremony, 1954.

Crossing Canada's Arctic Circle — a frigid King Neptune and court — HMCS *Proctecteur*, 1973.

King Neptune and Queen Amphitrite about to preside over the crossing the line ceremony in HMCS *Cape Scott* at the equator on the South Pacific on passage to Easter Island, 5 December 1964.

The flypast of Canadian Forces CF-104 Starfighter aircraft on the occasion of presentation of squadron standards by His Royal Highness the Prince Philip, Duke of Edinburgh, in Baden, Germany, May, 1973.

Mayor Charlotte Whitton of Ottawa inspecting the 2nd Battalion, Regiment of Canadian Guards, on the occasion of the regiment receiving the freedom of the city of Ottawa, 1964.

A soldier of the 8th Canadian Hussars (Princess Louise's), leading the regimental mascot, Princess Louise II, 1973.

A quarter guard mounted at the regimental headquarters, the Citadel, Quebec, by the Royal 22e Régiment with the regimental mascot, Batisse, in attendance, June, 1958.

of Parliament in 1968, followed by a programme a year later of kitting up all ranks in a common dark green uniform, the new garb seemed familiar and most appropriate to several units of the Canadian Forces — the rifle regiments. Eight years later, in 1976, when the minister of national defence authorized all rifle regiments to wear their traditional black web belts and sword slings with the Canadian Forces green uniform on ceremonial occasions, it was like coming home, a return to what has become known as the rifle tradition. Units such as the Regina Rifle Regiment, the Royal Winnipeg Rifles, the Queen's Own Rifles of Canada, the Brockville Rifles, the Hastings and Prince Edward Regiment, and other units with forbears of the rifle tradition, all take great pride in being a part of this nearly two centuries old distinctive form of infantry.

It all started back in 1797 in the British army when a special battalion of riflemen was added to the 60th Regiment of Foot (later to become the King's Royal Rifle Corps). Three years later much the same thing happened in the 95th Regiment (later the Rifle Brigade). Unlike the other line regiments who wore red, "the rifles" right from the start were clothed in green like the game-keepers of the forest on whom to some extent the role of the rifles was modelled.[95]

Both in uniform and drill, the rifles tactically represented a fighting man who blended into his environment and, therefore, was less readily seen, and a skirmisher lightly equipped, quick and flexible in movement. He was ideal for the campaigns in the forests of North America. Indeed, the 60th Regiment was raised for that purpose and gave a good account of itself in the Seven Years War and the American Revolution. A century later, the Royal Rifles were at the gates of Fort Garry, near where the Red and the Assiniboine rivers join in today's Winnipeg, to quell Louis Riel's rebellion.[96]

Rifle regiments traditionally, in addition to a green uniform, used black leather (later black web) equipment, black head-dress, and black buttons. There were no fifes and drums, just bugles used mostly for passing orders. They carried no colours and their battle honours were inscribed on their badge, traditionally a maltese cross.

Unlike other infantrymen, who were equipped with the bayonet triangular in cross section, the rifles had a special weapon called a sword, and to this day a rifleman's bayonet is called a sword. It came about this way. Originally, riflemen were equipped with a shorter and lighter rifle than ordinary infantry units to increase their mobility. A longer bayonet was provided to make up for the length of reach lost by the shorter rifle. This bayonet was fitted with a hand grip to use alone for close quarter fighting. For this reason it was called a sword.[97]

On the march, the rifle was carried "at the trail" to be ready for instant action, and the march itself was conducted at a pace faster than the normal cadence of the infantry. Drill movements were quick and quiet with a minimum of orders. Though strictly disciplined, quick, quiet flexibility and resourcefulness were the mark of the rifleman in the field. Emphasis was placed on the individual in developing alertness, stealth and speed of movement. High standards of marksmanship and ability to move away from fixed tactics and drills were hallmarks of the rifle regiment. These traditions are very much alive and proudly preserved by the rifles today.

Rounds
Rounds are routine duties of inspection designed to ensure the security of a military force irrespective of its form, location or function. Sometimes called by other names, such as "duty officer's duties," rounds are essential to the safety and fighting capability of a force and therefore, in whatever form, are as old as the military profession itself. An officer a century ago came close to the mark when he defined rounds as "going round to inspect sentinels. The general visting of the decks, made by officers, to see that all is going on right."[98]

A much earlier conception of the importance of rounds is to be found in *An Abridgment of the English Military Discipline*, published in London in 1689 for the use of His Majesty's Forces: "In Garrisons that are well Guarded, the Rounds go every quarter of an hour, To the end the Rampart may never be unfurnished."[99]

So, whether the routine orders for rounds were written today or centuries ago, there are two basic purposes involved — ensuring against surprise by a hostile force, and preserving the safety and therefore the fighting capability of the force from being jeopardized by such things as fire, the elements, or conditions contributing to poor health. Consequently, rounds may range from those of the picquet thrown out round a night field position with sentries keeping watch, to the officer of the day and the duty petty officer on board ship in harbour making rounds in the mess decks before "pipe down" in the evening, to see that all is squared away and shipshape for the night.

Today, on land, the term rounds is not used as much as it once was. Seldom if ever will it be found, for example, in routine orders. It depends to some extent on the type and location of the military establishment. For example, in a barracks located in a city, the majority of Service personnel spend the night in their own private accommodation outside the barracks, resulting in much of what was called rounds being carried out by non-Service personnel, the commissionaires. But, even so, the orderly sergeant still makes his rounds in the early evening, and the duty officer still inspects hospital and guardroom facilities on a regular basis.[100]

What it really amounts to is that the time-honoured system of rounds, like so many other aspects of Service life today, has been adapted to suit a variety of situations. There is little of the uniformity which once prevailed. On some bases, the battalion orderly sergeant supervises rounds as of old. On others, particularly within a regiment's lines, members of the unit, called regimental policemen, carry out this duty. On yet other bases, there are no rounds on foot at all; reliance is placed on the cruiser rounds of military police.

All of this, of course, reflects changing attitudes in society at large. Indeed, some say it is one more aspect of the "civilianization" of the military. For example, in the forces today, "hotel system" and "inn-keeper" are commonly used terms. Hotel system refers to the fact that troops in barracks no longer live in dormitories, but two or four to a room, or even one to a room. It means male and female Service personnel sharing the same barrack buildings. Very few people are required to live on base. To do so, except in training establishments, is a matter of individual choice. One hears the rejoinder, "You don't make rounds in married quarters, why would you in single quarters?" The inn-keeper is the NCO responsible for keeping the block clean but not for the disciplining of its residents.

Flexibility in routines is, of course, essential in the context of a variety of situations. For example, during a prolonged exercise in the field, there are many occasions when picquets must be thrown out and sentries posted, requiring some form of rounds, however temporary the need may be.

On the other hand, in HMC ships, when the pipe "clear up messdecks and flats for rounds" is heard, all hands know that in short order the officer of the day and the duty petty officer in harbour, or the executive officer and the coxswain at sea, will soon be briskly walking through all the messdecks and all the spaces from forepeak to tiller flat, keeping a weather eye for any irregularity which might interfere with the safety and fighting capability of the ship. The captain's rounds are normally made once a week.[101]

There is one aspect of rounds in the army tradition which has survived very much in a ceremonial form, and that is the mounting of a quarter guard in honour of a visiting officer of high rank, say to a military encampment. Such a guard consists of some ten to fourteen men, depending on the number of posts to be manned, for a period of some twenty-four hours. Issuing from the quarter guardroom, the men would be fallen in in two ranks, and pay appropriate compliments to the visiting dignitary. Then over a specified period the men would man sentry posts and perform the time-honoured ritual of the challenge and response, and of the new sentry taking over from the old.

Something of the timelessness of this ceremonial ritual may be seen in the standing orders of the old Toronto unit, the Governor-General's Body Guard a century ago:

> A sentry should consider his duties as a sacred trust . . . . After watchsetting, on any one approaching he will challenge, 'Who comes there?' and port his arms. If the answer is satisfactory, he will say 'Advance, friend, all's well;' should the answer be 'Rounds,' he will demand 'What Rounds?' If he is posted at the guardhouse, and the reply is 'Grand Rounds' or 'Visiting Rounds,' he will call 'Stand, Grand (or Visiting) Rounds, Guard turn out.' If posted anywhere else, he will say, 'Pass, Grand (or Visiting) Rounds, all's well.' If there is a countersign, he will command them to 'Advance one and give the countersign.'[102]

In a typical eighteenth century satire, there are these references to rounds in the form of advice to the major:

> When it is your turn to be field officer of the day in camp, be sure to keep the picquets waiting as long as you can, particularly if it should rain: this will accustom the soldiers to stand the weather, and will make them glad to see you.
>
> "In going the rounds in the night, do not fail to keep the serjeant and escort in a good round trot. This will prevent their catching cold, and may be done without the least inconvenience, if you are on horseback."

To the private soldier:

> If you are sentinel at the tent of one of the field officers, you need not challenge in the forepart of the evening, for fear of disturbing his honour, who perhaps may be reading, writing, or entertaining company. But as soon as he is gone to bed, roar out every ten minutes at least, 'Who comes there?' though nobody is passing. This will give him a favourable idea of your alertness; and though his slumbers may be broken, yet will they be the more pleasing, when he finds that he reposes in perfect security. When the hour of relief approaches, keep constantly crying out, 'Relief, relief!' it will prevent the guard from forgetting you, and prove that you are not asleep.[103]

She and Her

Ships are regarded as feminine and in the parlance of sailors are referred to as "she" and "her." This custom is centuries old but how it came to be is not known. There has been, of course, much conjecture, but much of this sounds contrived, for example, that "she's hard to manage," or "she's unpredictable."

Yet, there is no doubt that the custom is very much alive in expressions, such as "the eyes of her," that is, the fore end of the ship near the hawse pipes through which the anchor cables are paid out. Or "to meet her," as used when the rudder has been put over in altering course and it is necessary "to meet her" with opposite rudder to prevent the ship swinging too far.[104]

The suggestion that ships are referred to as "she" because most bear feminine names does not hold water, for thousands have been given masculine names. Similarly, while most carved figureheads adorning the stems of ships were female forms, many were not.

The most likely explanation for ships and boats being referred to as feminine is the traditional belief of sailors that a ship is very close to being a living entity, endowed with spirit and a distinct personality, demanding respect and, given proper consideration, most dependable. And, somehow, through some curious alchemy in the mind of the seaman in the days of sail, often away from the land for months on end, this near-human being took on the beauty and mystique of a woman.

Whatever the origin, there can be no doubt about the antiquity of this custom of speech. In a Spanish deposition regarding a South Pacific raid by Drake in the *Golden Hind*, there is this statement:

On Friday, February thirteenth, 1578, . . . the ship of some English Corsairs, with a pinnace and skiff arrived at the port of Callao de Lima. Entering between the ships that lay at anchor there, the Corsairs enquired for the ship of Miguel Angel, ... On boarding her they found . . . she did not contain the riches they expected, for the silver had not yet been carried aboard.[105]

Similarly, in a letter written in 1610 by a young sea officer to the vice-admiral at Plymouth and referring to an inquiry about a particular ship, he wrote: "Concerning the ship the case thus standeth: Shee was taken by one Captaine Walmer whom we had like to have taken at our first arrivall in Ireland."[106]

The Ship's Bell

Despite the inevitability of changing customs, functions and technology, the ship's bell remains, like the binnacle, one of the focal points of the ship. It continues to be one of the most valued pieces of the ship's original equipment. Indeed, it is often all that is left long after the ship herself has vanished. The reasons for this feeling toward a piece of highly polished, fine bronze are many and varied.

Traditionally, the bell is engraved with the ship's name and the year of her build. For example, the bell of HMCS *Provider* displays below the name in bold characters, 1963. The size of a ship's bell varies with the dimensions of the ship.

For centuries, the ship's bell was used primarily to indicate the hour, and therefore, in a sense, controlled the ship's routine. In the days of sail, when most of the people on the lower deck were illiterate and certainly carried no time-piece, the ringing of the ship's bell to mark the changing of the watch was of great importance.

Until Harrison invented the marine chronometer in the late eighteenth century (the first versions of which may still be seen in the National Maritime Museum, Greenwich, England), the measurement of time was achieved by the half-hour sand-glass kept near the binnacle on the quarter-deck. It was the duty of one of the ship's boys to turn the glass, under the watchful eye of the quartermaster of the watch, and ring the ship's bell, the number of bells rung corresponding to the time elapsed, there being eight bells to each four hour watch.

This function of the ship's bell has now largely disappeared in HMC ships owing to the fact that the same information may be heard by means of the pipe over the ship's broadcast. Also, of course, everyone wears a watch, although it is not many years ago in the Royal Canadian Navy that the wearing of watches and rings, et cetera, by people engaged in gunnery, torpedo and cable work was forbidden by regulation to prevent physical injury.

Another use of the ship's bell which has given way to modern means of communication is as an alarm, as in the case of fire. For centuries at sea, the rapid ringing of the bell brought the swift attention of the whole ship's company to the receiving of orders. An illustration of this and what it meant when fire occurred in a lone ship far from outside help may be seen in the case of HMS *Menai*, frigate. She was on passage from her station at St. Helena, where she had been keeping a weather eye on the exiled Napoleon over that empty stretch of ocean to the Cape of Good Hope, a century and a half ago.

The boatswain's yeoman had removed the candle from a lantern, left it burning by a beam, and forgot it when going to his supper. "[We] soon heard a murmur rising from the lower deck and then the awful cry of 'Fire' . . . The fire-bell rang out; all went to their stations to fight the fire, which had broken out in the boatswain's store room, separated only by a double bulkhead from the powder magazine."[107] The ship's bell brought prompt action, and superb discipline saved the ship.

But the primary purpose of the ship's bell, today, is to help avert collisions between ships. *The International Regulations for Preventing Collisions at Sea* requires that a vessel at anchor in fog, in harbour, or in a roadstead must ring her bell rapidly for five seconds at intervals of one minute. This practice is a very old one and well illustrated in the seventeenth century diary of Chaplain Teonge, Royal Navy.

Describing a convoy passage from Deal to Tangier in 1675, under the escort of the frigate *Assistance*, Teonge recorded one of the convoy instructions to the masters of the merchantmen. "If it prove foggy weather by night or day, we must ring our bells, and fire a musket now and then. And in dark nights each ship to carry a light." And, again, in 1678, this time from the Captain of the *Royal Oak*, 64 guns, "So great a fog that we are fain to ring our bells, beat drums, and fire muskets often, to keep us from falling foul one upon another."[108]

A visitor to the Parliament Buildings, Queen's Park, Toronto, may notice that a ship's bell occupies an honoured place there. It is the bell of the cruiser, HMCS *Ontario*. A closer look will reveal the names of children inscribed on the bell, children who were baptized on board the *Ontario*. Traditionally, in Her Majesty's ships, children of members of a ship's company may be christened by a chaplain using the ship's unshipped bell inverted as a baptismal font. Afterwards, the consecrated water is returned to the sea by the chaplain and the side is piped during this part of the ceremony. The child's full name is then inscribed on the bell.[109]

Today, in Stadacona Chapel, CFB Halifax, the permanently fitted baptismal font is the bell of HMCS *Uganda* bearing the date 1944. Inscribed on it are the names of children baptised during the cruiser's periods in commission.

Splice the Main Brace

Even though the daily issue of rum in HMC ships was abolished in 1971, current regulations authorize seamen to receive a special issue of spirits in exceptional circumstances. Soldiers and airmen may receive the same treatment when performing their duties "under unusual and difficult conditions . . . ."[110]

There is a long Service tradition behind the special issue of spirits, as may be seen in an order issued by James Wolfe as he faced the task of taking Quebec in the summer of 1759: "When rum is to be issued out to the troops on account of the badness of the weather, or their having suffered extraordinary fatigues, any soldier who is known to have disposed of his allowance to another . . . shall . . . be struck entirely out of the roll when rum is to be delivered out . . . ."[111]

Similarly, a century and a half after Wolfe, the Royal Canadian Dragoons in their fighting march against the Boers from Bloemfontein toward Johannesburg and Pretoria braced themselves against the bitter cold with "the thrice-weekly issues of rum — two and a half ounces. This warmed the stomachs and brightened the outlook. . . . "[112]

Today, in the navy, there is a relatively rare issue of rum which is made on the order "splice the main brace," when every officer and man in the ship's company receives two and one half ounces of spirits. Such an occurrence is usually related to victory in battle, such as V-E Day, 1945, or observance of some happy occasion of national significance.

Such an occasion was celebrated on board HMCS *Ontario*, cruiser, in the port of Seattle, Washington, in August, 1950. The crash of the saluting guns shattered the windows in the dockyard and the local residents, streaming down to the jetty-side to see what the noise was all about, happily joined the ship's company on the fo'c's'le and quarter-deck for the splicing of the main brace. It was the announcement of the birth of Her Royal Highness the Princess Anne. The order, splice the main brace, may be given only by Her Majesty, the Queen or other member of the royal family, His Excellency the Governor-General, or the chief of the defence staff.[113] Governor-General Roland Michener gave the order in HMCS *Preserver* at Antwerp in 1971 and Governor-General Leger did so in HMCS *Terra Nova* at Victoria in 1974.

The expression itself has an interesting origin and is related to the theme of duty well done in exceptionally arduous conditions.

In a square-rigged ship, as most sailing men-of-war were, the mainsail, the largest sail carried, was set on the mainyard at right angles to the mainmast. This great mainsail had an important part in the application of windpower to drive the ship ahead. To exert the desired wind force, the yard with its sail had to be trimmed to a particular angle relative to the direction of the wind and the course to be steered. This was done by hauling on the main brace, a very important part of the rigging. To splice the main brace, that is, to repair or replace this heavy piece of rigging, required great skill and speed on the part of the ship's company, a strenuous task even in good weather, a dangerous one in foul weather.

It is said that the expression, splice the main brace, in the sense of a special issue of spirits, dates from Captain James Cook's tiny squadron of 1773, when Lieutenant James Burney, commanding HMS *Adventure*, in reporting additional allowances of spirits, recorded amounts of rum consumed under "splice the main brace."[114]

Submariners

Submariners are probably the most unorthodox people in the Service with respect to dress, particularly once their boat has slipped from the buoy or the jetty. It is something of a paradox that the function, design and environment of their vessel has, over the course of some seven decades of submarine development, produced one of the toughest systems of self-discipline side by side with the least formal officer-man relationship in the Service today. These are factors essential to "fighting the ship" in the depths of the sea, as well as to the preservation of the boat and her company.

Space to live and work, and even to stow gear, is extremely limited, as is fresh water for bathing and laundering. A submariner must live, often for weeks on end, in very confined quarters and the informality of his attire at sea is one of the ways in which the underwater sailor comes to terms with his duties and environment.

One mark of the submariner is his high-necked white sweater, a good buffer against the elements while standing watch on the open bridge atop the conning tower. The submariner's sweater has been in vogue since the early days of submarines in the Royal Navy prior to the First World War, and Canada's first underwater craft, the CC boats of 1914 at Esquimalt.

The normal rig-of-the-day in HMC submarines at sea is called "pirate rig," a wide variety of scruffy clothing, sometimes of quite an imaginative bent, often jeans and T-shirts bearing colourful designs and slogans.

Another effective garment of the submariner, particularly for duties on the exposed casing running the length of the pressure hull, is the "poopy suit," a snug coverall that clings to the ankles and wrists, and is so-named because of the necessity of removal to do the necessary.

Finally, in respect to submariner's dress, one must experience a mess dinner in the wardroom of a submarine to believe it. At first glance, it seems incongruous that in this space, little more than nine feet by ten feet, some seven officers not only live and dine, but enjoy an occasional mess dinner, properly served and using fine crystal, china and plate. But once again, it is attire that sets the submariner apart. At such a mess dinner, any kind of rig is quite acceptable providing the diner wears a tie. And one can only imagine the weird and wonderful forms of neckwear which can be and are fashioned by the ever resourceful submariner.[115]

Sunset Ceremony (The Tattoo and the Retreat)

Given the glorious colour of approaching sunset, and then, the gathering darkness; given the spirited movements of the troops and the mood of martial music; given the beautiful physical settings both natural and man-made with which Canada abounds — there is a sense of mystery and magic in the drama called the sunset ceremony. Simple duties of centuries ago, such as closing the

Naval gun's crew practising for the sunset ceremony, Parliament
Hill, Ottawa, June, 1971.

gate, troops returning to their quarters for the night, and the setting of the watch, all to the beat of the drum, have in the course of time evolved into a beautiful ceremonial tradition reflecting our people's long military heritage.

The sunset ceremony in all its colourful, smooth-flowing pageantry encompasses three happenings — the tattoo, the retreat and the lowering of the national flag of Canada. A full presentation may involve as many as one hundred officers and men. Basically, the detachment consists of a guard and band, and guns' crews.

An interesting characteristic of the ceremony as laid down in regulations is that it can be carried out in grand manner, as is done occasionally on Parliament Hill, Ottawa, or on a reduced scale, as in a jetty-side presentation by a ship's company in a foreign port.[116]

The portion of the sunset ceremony called the tattoo is of ancient origin. The word itself is of interest. In the historical sense, tattoo is defined as "Beat of Drum, or bugle call, at 10 p.m., recalling soldiers to quarters." In the seventeenth century, the word usually appeared as "tap-too," reflecting its Dutch origin, *tap-toe*, meaning to shut off the tap or spigot.

In the days before permanent barracks, troops in garrison or on the march were billeted on the town, sometimes in private houses but more often in inns and ale-houses.[117] After the day's duty, the place of resort for most soldiers was the inns and taverns of the town. The signal to get the troops back to their billets for the night was by beat of drum through the various districts of the town where the ale-houses were located. The beat of the tattoo conveyed two messages — one to the innkeeper, ordering him (originally in the Dutch tongue, *doe den tap toe*,) to turn off his taps and serve no more ale or spirits; the other to the soldiers "to retire to their chambers, to put out their fire and candle, and go to bed."[118]

An officer, a sergeant and a file of men followed within minutes the drummers, sometimes augmented by fifers, and woe betide the innkeeper who did not obey, for his premises would soon be declared out-of-bounds and therefore out of business. An indication of what befell the tardy tippler is to be found in orders issued by Major James Wolfe in 1748/49* when he forebade

any man to appear out of his quarters, without a written leave from his officer, from half an hour after tattoo is beat till the reveille; any man who shall presume to disobey this order, and shall be discovered, to be put the next morning into the dungeon, and confined there for four days upon bread and water.[119]

*For a short time in the mid-eighteenth century, the year was written "old style" or "new style" when an adjustment was made in the number of days to bring the current calendar into line with solar time.

There is an interesting record of the meaning of the beating of the tattoo at Halifax, Nova Scotia, in the eighteenth century. In May, 1758, a mighty fleet of ships of war and troop transports lay in Halifax harbour under the command of Edward Boscawen, Admiral of the Blue, preparing for the assault on the fortress of Louisbourg. The admiral's order read in part:

> No petty officer, non Commissioned [Officer] of the Troops, Soldiers or Seamen to have leave to go on shore but on some very particular occasion, and that Leave to be given in writing by the Captain of his Majesty's ship, or the Commanding Officer of those embarked on board the Transports.
> All the Boats belonging to his Majesty's ships, and all those belonging to the Transports, to return on board their ships at the beating the Taptoo.[120]

From the original lone drummer, the gradual increase of more drums, and then flutes or fifes, until the latter part of the eighteenth century when bands appeared in the regiments, the small but authoritative procession in the evening beating the tattoo has taken on the aura of marching entertainment, the elaboration of which has become the tattoo as most people know it today.

Another aspect of beating the tattoo that is still with us to this day is the "Last Post" sounded on a bugle or trumpet. Something of the Serviceman's feeling for those notes rendered on the night air may be gathered from a trooper's description of life in a militia camp near Sussex, New Brunswick, before the outbreak of war in 1914:

> When it got dark you could look around the camp and you'd see row after row of tents, on the flats and up on infantry hill, and every tent was like a little triangle of light. They used candles to light them. At 10 o'clock you'd hear the bugles sound lights out. . . .
> Then you'd hear the Last Post. Everybody would get quiet when the bugler played the Last Post. It's strange the sort of hush there is in that music. You'd always get a feeling way down inside when it came across the camp there in the night.[121]

"Post" here is used in the sense of a soldier's station, as in sentry post. In beating the tattoo, the drummers marched from post to post in the town or camp, the first post would be the signal of their having taken up position to begin their round, while the last post indicated they had completed the round.[122] (One can readily see here the symbolism of the "Last Post" at military funerals).

After the tattoo portion of the sunset ceremony, comes that part derived from the historic "beating the retreat." Perhaps it should be said here that down through the centuries, both in practice and in the literature, there is apparent confusion between the two routines, the tattoo and the retreat.[123] However, it seems quite clear that, basically, the retreat signified the closing of the gate at sunset and the setting of the watch, and the tattoo was the signal for soldiers to return to their billets for the night, which was after darkness had fallen, usually at 10 p.m.

The latter is the origin of *le couvre-feu* (the curfew) which is signalled by the booming report of a 105 mm gun at 9:30 every evening at the Citadel of Quebec. Like the noon-day gun so familiar to generations of the citizens of Quebec, the *couvre-feu* is fired daily by the Royal 22e Régiment from its station in the old fortification overlooking the St. Lawrence River and the Plains of Abraham — a reminder from long ago that it is time for members of the garrison to return to their quarters for the night.

Another point of interest here is that in the eighteenth century a dozen different drum-beats were used to convey orders, and these different rhythms or beats were well understood by every soldier. There were two retreats; one was the retreat at sundown in garrison or camp; the other was the tactical manoeuver in battle.[124] This latter was known in the Royal Navy and probably had to do with grappling and boarding an enemy ship. There is an amusing incident described whereby Midshipman Jackson, aged about fourteen years, was mastheaded for his sins, in HMS *America*, 44 guns, on the Pacific Station in 1844. This item appears in Moresby's diary:

Jackson mastheaded during church-time at Callao, for telling the drummer to beat a retreat from division without orders. As church was rigged on the upper deck, Jackson occupied the position of the sweet little cherub that sits up aloft, and some ladies who had come on board manifested the extremest sympathy. . . . [125]

But the beating of the retreat, which is associated with the setting sun, is likely sixteenth century in origin and we have an early example, primitive but practical, in our own pioneer development. In 1642, the infant settlement of Montreal, then called Ville-Marie, was founded within a tiny stockade by Maisonneuve and a band of brave men and women known as *Messieurs et Dames de la Société de Notre-Dame pour la conversion des Sauvages de la Nouvelle-France*. These early settlers were almost constantly threatened by the Iroquois. Yet, in spite of the danger, the men gradually cleared a field for cultivation, toiling from dawn to dusk under the watchful eyes of a sentinel or two, posted at the edge of the clearing. In the gathering darkness, a bell would ring out from the stockade and the workers from the fields would wend their way to the safety of the barred gate.[126]

A good eighteenth century description of beating the retreat by a British regiment reads:

> Half an hour before the gates are to be shut, which is generally at the setting of the sun, a Serjeant and four men must be sent from each port to the main-guard for the keys; at which time, the Drummers of the port guards are to go upon the ramparts, and beat a Retreat, to give notice to those without, that the gates are going to be shut, that they may come in before they are. As soon as the Drummers have finished the Retreat, which they should not do in less than a quarter of an hour, the Officers must order the barriers and gates to be shut, leaving only the wickets open; after which, no Soldier should be suffered to go out of the town, though port-liberty should be allowed them in the day-time.[127]

It was, of course, at beat the retreat that the piquets were formed and the watches set. In the modern sunset ceremony, allusion is made to this ancient routine in the section drill.

There follows the firing of a feu-de-joie, then the band commencing the thoughtful and familiar strains of an evening hymn. Finally comes the stirring rolls of the drums, the majestic rendition of "O Canada" and "God Save the Queen," and the lowering of the national flag of Canada.

Thus has unfolded down through the centuries, from simple military routine duties, this colourful and moving sunset ceremony.

And out of the same traditions have come the countless military tattoos, which have given such joy to countless thousands, from those of the militia at Camp Niagara in the 1920's (where the troops would rush from the field to catch the last steamer to Toronto); to that of the Royal 22e Régiment at that superb site, the Citadel of Quebec; through the peerless performances at Aldershot and Edinburgh Castle, where many Canadian units have taken part; to that magnificent blend of pageantry, humour and stirring drama that was the Canadian Forces tattoo in celebration of our nation's centenary in 1967.

TGIF

An air force custom much enjoyed over the past quarter century, and one that has now spilled over into civilian life, is TGIF (Thank God It's Friday). TGIF is essentially a "beer call" heard in most air force messes every Friday afternoon at the end of the day's work.

Where and when TGIF first began is uncertain. But what is certain is that it is RCAF in origin and it was observed in the early days of Canadian commitment to NATO in Europe, specifically at Marville, France, in the mid-1950s.[128]

TGIF, a gathering in the mess, marked the end of the flying week, a time to chat over a friendly glass about the past week's operations, a time to compare notes about this aircraft and that mission or manoeuvre. The popularity of TGIF became even more pronounced as the five-day week rapidly became a reality in the 1950s.

The Wedge Cap

Current dress regulations of the Canadian Forces include this rather uninspiring, matter-of-course item: "Cap, wedge, green (optional) — worn on the right side of the head . . . one inch above the right eyebrow."[129]

Yet, the fact is that the wedge cap is a good example of how a tradition was born some sixty years ago and thrives to this day — the airman's affinity for this type of head-dress.

It all began when the Royal Flying Corps was established just before the Great War of 1914-1918, a force in which Canadians played a prominent part. The field service cap, as it was then called, was adopted by the RFC along with a tunic with a high, stand-up collar and secured by buttons at the far right side of the chest. With the cap cocked well over to the right, this uniform with its jaunty air became synonymous with the daring new fighting man, the airman. The head-dress, designated wedge cap in 1941,[130] continued to be worn throughout the life of the Royal Canadian Air Force, 1924-1968, and is still the preference of many airmen in spite of the availability of the forage cap and the beret. There is little doubt that in the days when goggles and leather helmets were worn in open cockpits, the field service cap lent itself to handy storage in a pocket ready for use on return to base.

But the wedge cap is somewhat older than airmen and aircraft. It is of army origin and dates from the nineteenth century. Indeed, the airman picked up the field service cap during a lull in its use by the army.

This head-dress, first called the Austrian pattern field cap, came into official use in the British army in 1890 for other ranks and 1896 for commissioned officers.[131] This was the head-gear worn by Canadian soldiers embarking for service in South Africa at the turn of the century. The army largely switched to the peaked forage cap in 1904 and stayed with it until the Second World War when a reversion was made to the wedge-type cap until use of the beret became general in 1943.

Today's wedge cap, as every boy who served in the old school cadet corps knows, is a little different from the old field service cap, though they look very much alike. The older one was a rather ingenious garment, fairly cool to wear when perched on the side of the head, but capable of being unfolded to cover the nape of the neck, the ears and the chin. Today's version is sewn so that it does not unfold. But even so, the green wedge cap of today looks very much like those worn by the air crews standing proudly beside the Avro 504s, Sopwith Camels and SE5As of the old Royal Flying Corps.[132]

Weepers

According to the dictionary, weepers were persons hired to mourn at a funeral, but, today, weepers is a highly popular thirty year old naval institution at Halifax. First begun in the wardroom in Admiralty House, HMCS *Stadacona*, about 1947, weepers is a gathering of maritime command officers after duty on Fridays. The significance of the term itself enjoys two versions: "to weep in one's beer" in the traditional "wailing wall" fashion, airing the problems of the week; and the glint-in-the-eye allusion to supposedly weeping wives waiting at home for their wayward sailor spouses.

8
Mascots

Picture the sun-drenched but troubled island of Cyprus in the summer of 1974, and a sand-bagged observation post of the Canadian Airborne Regiment on the Confrontation Line in Nicosia under the pressure of advancing Turkish forces, when who waddles into view but a beautiful white duck, head high in the air, and resplendent in bright orange bill and gaiters. Promptly dubbed Petty Officer Wilbur Duck, no doubt as much for his sea-going gait as for his webbed feet, the new arrival at once becomes the focal point of good humour and affection, a foil to tension and a relief to boredom — in other words, a mascot![1]

The traditional buoyant spirit of the Serviceman and the nature of his calling explains the fact that mascots have been around as long as fighting formations have existed. What is generally not known, though, is that a mascot may not necessarily be, dare it be said, an animate being. Examples abound.

There is Old Blue, the magnificent golden buck's head which occupies a place of honour on a bulkhead in HMCS *Fraser*, destroyer, the "living" symbol of the spirit of the Frasers, as the ship's company is known.[2]. Old Blue, of course, was inspired by the golden buck's head in the ship's badge (the ship was named for the river honouring Simon Fraser), which is derived from the crest of the Fraser arms, and the ship's colours, gold and blue.[3]

Also inspired by a ship's badge is the much travelled wardroom mascot of HMCS *Terra Nova*, Percy the Penguin. Stuffed and highly decorated, Percy has been the center of many an amusing adventure in sixteen years of sailing the oceans of the world.[4]

Another famous mascot of this non-breathing variety was the much travelled Little Chief of the Hastings and Prince Edward Regiment, a pewter Indian, eleven feet tall, which once stood in solemn silhouette against the evening sky on the roof of the canning factory in Picton, where the regiment mustered for drill back in 1939. However, the stoical Little Chief was lost when the "Hasty P's" were hastily evacuated from Brittany through Brest when the attempt to stem the German tide failed in June, 1940. Nevertheless, a second Little Chief, this time seven feet tall and carved from solid pine, eventually joined the regiment in the European theatre of war, and today enjoys a prominent place in the regimental headquarters at Belleville.[5]

Also fashioned of metal is the well known yet seldom seen Cecil the Snake of 444 Tactical Helicopter Squadron. The device on the squadron badge is the hooded cobra and many years ago, in Germany, a fine likeness of this fierce reptile was acquired in a shop. From then on, he was called Cecil the Snake. But because visitors from other squadrons have been known to cast covetous glances at Cecil, the cobra has been entrusted to the care of the junior officer on the squadron, there being dire penalties awaiting this gentleman should anything happen to Cecil. As a result this unusual mascot emerges from his secret refuge only for very special occasions in the mess.[6]

But perhaps the most cherished and the most coveted of the long parade of inanimate mascots which led truly charmed lives in the Canadian Forces was the Greater Yellow-Legs of Ottawa's No. 2416 Aircraft Control and Warning Squadron of the Royal Canadian Air Force in the 1950s, which when glasses were raised in the squadron mess, brought forth the solemn toast, "the Honoured Twillick!"

So great was the fame of this bird that it was essential, for his own security, that he spend most of his quiet hours bound by a huge chain in a strong wrought-iron cage. For this mascot was no ordinary Twillick bird. Not only did he occupy the honoured position of being the major device on the squadron's official badge, but he dominated the scene of every mess function. Unknown to the uninitiated, the Twillick bird was fitted with an uncommonly capacious holding tank, together with a spigot concealed in the feathers just abaft the landing gear. With a flourish, the Twillick-Master would give a twist to the spigot and proceed with the ceremonial "Charging of the Noggins" with a brew which defied normal analysis, but which always evoked the lusty toast, "Up the Twillick!"[7]

The origin of the custom of maintaining regimental mascots is not known, but it was well established two centuries ago. A curious little book written and published by a British officer in New York for the express purpose of aiding, by the book's sale, the dependents of the soldiers "butchered that day" of Concord, and of those "that gloriously fell in their country's cause at Bunker Hill" (1775), gives this picture of a mascot in the North America of that day.[8]

The royal regiment of welch Fuzileers has a privilegeous honor of passing in review preceded by a Goat with gilded horns, and adorned with ringlets of flowers; . . . the corps values itself much on the ancientness of the custom.

The author went on to describe the regiment's observance of St. David's Day at a mess dinner with the richly caparisoned goat ridden by a drummer boy being led three times round the mess table by the drum-major to the tune of "The Noble Race of Shenkin," when the mascot took off at a furious rate, unseating his rider, bound for his quarters in Boston with all his elegant trappings, "to the no small joy of the garrison and populace."

Mascots also flourished in garrison life in the Canada of colonial times. In 1843, one of the units on garrison duty in Upper Canada was the 83rd Regiment of Foot. A water-colour in the Public Archives of Canada portrays a company of the 83rd shooting the Lachine Rapids bound for Quebec and return to England. The vessel shown is a typical forty-foot bateau of the period running free with her single squaresail set and there, firmly secured in the bows in a seated position, is the regimental mascot, a large bear.[9]

A few years earlier, there was a mascot with the garrison at the Citadel at Quebec who rejoiced in the name, Jacob the Goose, and who regularly did sentry-go with the picquet. A century later, the lieutenant-colonel commanding, Coldstream Guards, wrote:

Jacob the Goose was enlisted at Quebec in 1838. He came to England with the 2nd Battalion of the Regiment in 1842 and died on detachment at Croydon in 1846. He had been awarded one Good Conduct Ring. His head is preserved in a glass case at Regimental Headquarters, and it is adorned with a gorget as worn by officers of the Regiment in the early nineteenth century. . . . I feel that eight years is probably a very reasonable life for an enlisted goose.[10]

A few glimpses of mascots in the Canadian army of the period of the Great War, 1914-1918, are to be seen in regimental histories. The home station of the Royal Canadian Dragoons at St. Jean, Quebec, was also the home of the regimental mascot, Peter the Goat, whose chief claim to fame was his popularity with the local populace and his ability to collect small change to provide comforts for the RCDs at the front. After the war, Peter shared his stable accommodation and pasture with a pair of pit ponies, named for the current comic strip characters, Maggie and Jiggs, which had been acquired by a detachment of the regiment during a spell of duty at Sydney, Nova Scotia.[11]

There is little doubt that the most colourful mascot of the period was that of the Royal Newfoundland Regiment. Presented to the regiment at Ayr, Scotland, in 1917, Sable Chief was a magnificent Newfoundland dog, weighing in at some two hundred pounds. The pride of the regiment and the delight of the surrounding countryside, Sable Chief marched with dignity on parade and romped with the troops on sports days. Killed in an accident later in England, his surprisingly life-like figure is still to be seen today in St. John's.[12]

It is during periods of hostilities, with their attendant stresses and strains, that mascots make their most valuable contribution to Service life, and the Second World War, 1939-1945, was no exception. There was that big, sad-eyed St. Bernard, Wallace, of the Canadian Scottish Regiment from Victoria. His namesake, Wallace III, still serves with the regiment today.

Another was a little Aberdeen terrier affectionately known as Heather. It seems there was some small bother about regulations and when the pipe band of the Calgary Highlanders was outward bound for embattled Europe, Wee Heather made some of the more difficult parts of the passage in the big bass drum![13]

The most enduring mascot tradition of the Canadian Forces began on a battlefield in wartime Italy and continues to the present day. This is the story of Princess Louise and, most appropriate for a former cavalry regiment, the Princess was and is a very beautiful horse.

It all began on the slopes above the Besanigo River not far from the Adriatic Sea after the capture of the town of Coriano in September, 1944. Darkness had come to the valley. Fitters and mechanics of what is now the 8th Canadian Hussars (Princess Louise's), were out recovering damaged Sherman tanks. During a lull in the enemy shelling, a plaintive cry was heard. A search revealed a very young and wounded filly beside the remains of its mother. Emergency rations of a stimulating nature and the dressing of her wounds back at the Hussar lines started the young mascot, for such she had become, on the road to recovery. She was promptly named Princess Louise.

The tales of the Princess's wartime adventures are legion, some of which are true. She made the transfer to north-west Europe by being smuggled in an army lorry specially fitted with a false front in the cargo area. The war over, it seemed as though the whole town of Hampton, New Brunswick, turned out to welcome Princess Louise after her voyage in a Dutch liner to New York, thence by rail to her regimental quarters. The spirit of the homecoming is to be seen in the quaint language of the welcoming address: "Know all men by *these here present,* that the Royal Lady . . . is entitled to roam at will . . . and to devour and partake of that which she pleaseth . . . ."[14]

The Princess foaled in 1954 and after years of regimental duties was retired in 1971, aged twenty-seven years, to pasture. The new filly, of course, became Princess Louise II and in 1958 was presented to the newly formed Regular Force component of the regiment at Camp Gagetown. There followed some three years service with the regiment in Germany. At Petawawa, in 1966, Princess Louise III came along but succumbed to an infection four years later. But the second Princess, elegant in her richly embroidered saddle cloth, continues to carry out her ceremonial duties, the beloved embodiment of a regimental tradition spanning more than three decades.[15]

Sea-going mascots are rather scarce in our forces' story, but the Korean War brought forth an incident involving the bitch Alice. In November, 1951, HMCS *Cayuga,* before proceeding on patrol to the northward of Inchon, took on fuel out at sea from a tanker, an evolution that almost ended in tragedy. Alice, whose seniority dated from July, 1950, when she joined ship at Guam, fell overboard between *Cayuga* and the tanker. But Alice was no novice; she'd been over the side twice before. She struggled valiantly in spite of the towering hulls on either side. Also, it is said that the pipe "Alice overboard!" evoked an even quicker response than the sounding of "action stations!"[16]

Most sailors have at one time or another witnessed the timeless little drama of the sea when a shore bird, driven far from the land by the gale, falls exhausted on the deck of a ship. Such was the origin of the mascot of HMCS *Gatineau,* on passage from New Zealand to her home port, Esquimalt, late in 1972. Much pampered by the ship's company, pigeon Tom was named for the destroyer's captain.[17]

A mascot from the wide open spaces of the prairie has attained something approaching immortality in that his mask is the central device on the badge of his unit, the Loyal Edmonton Regiment.

The old 101st Regiment, of Edmonton, raised several battalions for service in the Canadian Expeditionary Force in the First World War. One of these was the 49th and, during the journey by troop train to the east coast, a coyote puppy was presented to the battalion at Lestock, Saskatchewan. The coyote was dubbed Lestock.

Though coyotes generally do not possess the best of reputations, Lestock made friends everywhere he went, and soon became the pride of the Edmonton battalion. Many were his adventures before he eventually wound up in Regents' Park Zoo in London when the battalion embarked for France in the fall of 1915.

It was early in 1916 that the 49th Battalion was to receive a new cap badge. A strong case was put forward to have Lestock's head as the major device. The battalion's wish was granted, even though the authorities said the much-maligned coyote had "no heraldic standing" and the official blazon called Lestock a wolf. Today, that coyote pup of sixty years ago graces the badge of the Loyal Edmonton Regiment.[18]

Back in 1957, there was a goat mascot at RCAF station Camp Borden. Impeccably groomed and turned out in a tasselled coverlet of silk bearing three chevrons, Sergeant W. Marktime graced all inspection parades of a training school on the base.[19] And so the story of mascots in the Canadian Forces comes full circle, for the goat is the focal point of the military mascot tradition.

It is generally agreed that the earliest regimental mascot, properly maintained and accoutred, and with a long record of service, was the goat of the Royal Welch Fusiliers in the eighteenth century, the one that saw service in the American Revolution (see page 127). And a goat of the Canadian Forces today is a product of that tradition, Batisse of the Royal 22e Régiment.

In Britain there is a royal herd of white goats, the result of a presentation of a pair of goats by the Shah of Persia to Queen Victoria.[20] In 1955, by permission of Her Majesty the Queen, colonel-in-chief of the regiment, a goat was selected from the herd and presented to the "Van Doos," a thousand strong, on the Plains of Abraham, Quebec, by the then Governor-General, the Right Honorable Vincent Massey. The mascot of the Royal 22e Régiment was at once given that familiarly affectionate French-Canadian name, Batisse.

Richly caparisoned and with gilded horns and a specially engraved silver shield on his forehead, Batisse, attended by the traditional goat-major, was on his best behaviour as His Excellency spoke to the Honorary Colonel, Major General Georges Vanier and his regiment:

> Acts of bravery of a Regiment such as yours can only come from a deep-rooted *esprit de corps* and a sense of tradition . . . . You are affiliated with a very famous British Regiment. It is important, I feel, that you should share with The Royal Welch Fusiliers a tradition which has been theirs for centuries — that of having a Royal Goat as a member of your Regiment . . . . [21]

Batisse II was presented to the Van Doos in 1964 by His Excellency the Governor-General, General Georges Vanier. However, this goat died without issue. Now Batisse III, presented to the regiment in 1972 by the Governor-General, the Right Honourable Roland Michener, is the pride of the regiment. At the same time a suitable mate was provided, and the succession of mascots for the Royal 22e Régiment seems assured, an important link in a Canadian Forces' tradition already well established.

The Right Honourable Vincent Massey, Governor-General of Canada, addressing the Royal 22e Régiment on the occasion of the presentation of the goat mascot, Batisse, a gift of Her Majesty the Queen. The mascot was accepted by the Honorary Colonel of the Regiment, Major General Georges Vanier who eventually succeeded Mr. Massey as Governor-General. The presentation occurred at Quebec, November, 1955.

9
Launching and Commissioning
of HMC Ships

When man first fashioned a vessel and put to sea in it is not known. But it is known that for centuries and centuries the launch of a ship has been a very popular event, and one usually attended by considerable ceremony, just as it is today.

When crowds of people gather in the shipyard, there is an air of cheerful excitement and expectation, not just in witnessing the product of master craftsmen rushing down the ways to meet the element for which it was designed, but also in feeling some of the sense of adventure and enterprise, and wondering what the future holds for this creature about to swim for the first time. This seems to be why people gather for the launch, and why, to this day, the beginning of life for one of Her Majesty's Canadian ships, is such a gala occasion.

The other aspect, the ceremony, has a deeper significance and therefore, traditionally, is of a religious nature. There is the deep-felt need for divine protection for the ship in future encounters with wind and weather, and with the enemy, and divine guidance for the ship's company that they may measure up to the challenges in store and to the traditions of the sailors who have gone before. Over the years it is these needs which are expressed in the formal words and prayers used in the religious services.

Ceremonies relating to the building of a ship, by custom, take place at the laying of the keel, the launch and naming, and the commissioning.[1] However, while each of these functions is essential, conditions sometimes dictate flexibility so far as ceremony is concerned.

In wartime, for example, the keels of most corvettes and frigates were laid without ceremony because of the demands for speed and the nature of production line techniques. Similarly, at Sorel in 1954, HMCS *Assiniboine* was launched in winter in an "unspectacular and laborious" manner using a marine railway. She was named and commissioned in a dual ceremony on a sunny day in August, nearly two years later.[2]

The keel-laying ceremony is usually quite an informal affair and most of the arrangements are made by the builders. After the arrival of the guests, a brief address is delivered by a representative of the yard, the keel section is lowered into place on the blocks by crane, and the sponsor declares the keel of the unnamed ship (usually referred to by the builder's hull number), "well and truly laid," much as the cornerstone of a building is laid. The long process of construction has begun.

The second ceremony is the christening or naming, and the launching. Because of the long period of fitting out yet to come, the ship is still the responsibility of the builders, including the actual launching. At the appointed time, the crowd gathers, usually reinforced by the shipyard workers out in force to see the result of their labours, and the guests assemble on the platform erected close to the decorated stem of the vessel. Ships and boats in harbour stand by with their whistles and horns ready to join in the celebration. Often, a band is in attendance.

The ceremony itself traditionally consists of these basic elements: a short address by the ship's builder; the blessing of the ship by specially appointed clergy; and the naming or christening by the sponsor, now almost always a lady, using the traditional words: "I name you Her Majesty's Canadian ship (name of ship). God bless this ship and all who sail in her." With flags flying, the band playing and the roar of many voices, the new ship starts down the ways for her appointment with the sea.

In ancient times the ritual performed at the launching of a vessel was built around the idea of making a sacrifice to appease the gods who, it was believed, controlled the destiny of the ship and all her future voyages. From these pagan beginnings has come the modern blessing of the ship by the officiating clergy and prayers for divine guidance and protection for the ship and her company. Many writers see in the traditional smashing of the bottle of wine on the ship's bow a parallel with the concept of baptism.[3] While religious observances have had a prominent place in the launching ceremony for a very long time, a standard order of service, originally written by the Archbishop of Canterbury, has been in vogue in the Royal Navy only since 1875.[4]

Although the term "christening" is gradually being replaced by the word "naming," in the former can be seen the idea of baptism. An example of its use in eighteenth century North America is the case of the giant raft built by Amherst's forces to carry heavy artillery during the campaign of 1759 on the Lake Champlain route. "In the afternoon [29 September 1759] the Radeau

The launching of HMCS *Algonquin*, destroyer, at Lauzon, Quebec, April, 1971.

was Launched & christened *Ligonier.* She is 84 feet long & 20 feet broad on the Platform, where the Guns run out she is 23 feet, & to carry six 24-pounders . . . "5

Quite a graphic description of a naming ceremony has come down to us from the campaign on Lake Ontario of more than two centuries ago. After the fall of Quebec, British forces spent the winter planning a three-way pincer concentration for the reduction of the last major French position, Montreal, the ensuing spring. Armies were to advance from Quebec, the Richelieu and Lake Ontario. To control the lake between Oswego and the St. Lawrence, two ships of war were built at Niagara during the winter of 1759-60, HM ships *Mohawk,* 18 guns, and *Onondaga,* 22 guns, (forbear of our present submarine). Launched as *Apollo,* the new ship and her consort, HMS *Mohawk,* arrived at Oswego, and Amherst reported in his journal on 1 August 1760:

> To please the Indians I desired them to christen the Snow and took all the Chiefs on board in the afternoon, as they had told Sir Wm. Johnson they would like to have her called Onondaga. I had a large flag made with an Onondaga Indian painted on it. This was hoisted just as I christened the Snow by breaking a bottle at the head. Then Gage's Regt fired a volley. The Fort fired a gun & the R[oyal] Highlanders fired a volley & the Onondaga answered it with 9 guns. All this pleased the Indians extremely & I had made them some speeches by Sir Wm. Johnson. Gave them some Punch & they were greatly delighted with the whole, promised to be fast friends & said they were ready to go with me 6

It is of interest that in the case of the naming of HM Snow *Onondaga,* the commander-in-chief himself, Amherst, did the honours. This is a reminder that in earlier times a male member of the royal household, or some other person of high station, was expected to do the duty of sponsor when a ship was to be launched. The present custom of inviting a lady to do so dates only from the nineteenth century.7

The traditional breaking of a bottle of wine by smashing it against the bow of the ship, now usually achieved by a mechanical contrivance to avoid faulty aim and possible "misfire," stems from the old practice of drinking a toast of prosperity for the ship from a silver cup, which was then cast into the sea, and no doubt salvaged by some enterprising soul. Towards the end of the seventeenth century, this custom gave way to the present practice.8

Finally comes the day of commissioning, when the vessel, built, launched and completely fitted out as a fighting ship — stored, munitioned, fuelled and manned — becomes one of Her Majesty's Canadian ships in commission, ready to join the fleet. Behind these procedures are centuries of tradition in which the captain was the ship and the ship was the captain, so much so that the captain was often called, by signal, by the ship's name.

A couple of centuries ago, then, when a ship was to be commissioned, it really meant the commanding officer being handed his commission to place the ship herself in service. Such an officer, ashore, was, in a sense, no longer a sea officer even though he had had many years of service as a sea officer; he was simply commissioned to carry out a particular mission, and when the mission was completed he reverted, to all intents, to civilian status again.

The captain would be summoned to the admiralty in Whitehall and be presented with a formal document, which, in essence, ordered him to proceed to a particular port, such as Portsmouth, to bring a ship out of ordinary (that is, out of reserve), and to put that ship into a sea-going condition. This was a job of formidable proportions. It was the captain's duty personally to see that the vessel, practically a bare hulk in maintenance reserve, was brought forward. He personally saw to it that the ship was fitted with masts, spars and sails; completely out-fitted with guns, ammunition, stores and victuals, and provided with a ship's company, whether they be volunteers or coerced by his own press-gang.[9]

But before any of this could be legally carried out, the captain, on arrival at Portsmouth, would have a boat take him out to the anchored hulk, climb the accommodation ladder and — even though his only audience, other than the ship's warrant officers, might be a couple of ship-keepers and a few dockyard mateys, and they were probably quite indifferent to the proceedings — stand on the quarter-deck and in a great voice read out the terms of the commission that had been handed to him at Whitehall. With the ensign lashed to a jury-staff, and the pennant at the masthead, the ship was now in commission.[10]

Today, the commissioning ceremony for HMC ships is a very moving experience, both for the general public and for the ship's company. The observances usually take place within the building yard, with the ship, freshly painted, secured alongside at the company's jetty. Invited guests occupy a specially constructed seating area with a good view of the proceedings, and the ship's company are fallen in as for Sunday divisions at the jetty-side, adjacent to the ship.

Addresses are delivered by representatives of the builder, the department of supply and services responsible for the letting of construction and equipment contracts, and the department of national defence. There follows a ceremonial signing of acceptance of the ship by high-ranking officers of the two departments and the Canadian Forces, and by the officer appointed to command the new ship. A symbolic presentation of "keys to the ship" is made to the captain by an officer of general officer's rank.

The guard and ship's company mustered on the jetty for the commissioning of HMCS *Preserver*, operational support ship, at Saint John, New Brunswick, July, 1970.

Then comes the commissioning service normally conducted by the two chaplains general from national defence headquarters. It is at this point that the commanding officer orders Her Majesty's Canadian ship to be commissioned. Immediately, the ensign and jack are hoisted and the ship's pennant is broken out at the masthead. It is a dramatic moment; those who "go down to the sea in ships" know that, barring calamity resulting "from the dangers of the sea, and from the violence of the enemy," the ship's pennant will stream from aloft for a good twenty years.

The keynote address for the occasion is then delivered by the guest of honour, perhaps a cabinet minister or a general officer. (The term flag officer is no longer used in the Canadian Forces.)

There follows a brief address by the ship's commanding officer, largely directed to the ship's company assembled on the jetty. He concludes with the order: "Man Her Majesty's Canadian Ship (name of ship)." As soon as the ship's officers and men have taken over the ship, the commanding officer exercises his traditional prerogative and is piped on board. He in turn greets all the guests who repair to the hangar space for the reception to follow.

The religious service which takes place mid-way through the commissioning ceremony has, through the centuries, held great meaning for sailors about to embark on long voyages in dangerous waters to possibly hostile shores. Typical of a modern twentieth century commissioning service was that conducted jointly by the chaplains general (Protestant and Roman Catholic) for HMCS *Athabaskan* in 1972 at Lauzon, Quebec:

The Commissioning Service

The Exhortation

Brethren, seeing that in the course of our duty, we are set in the midst of many and great dangers, and that we cannot be faithful to the high trust placed in us without the help of Almighty God, let us unite our prayers and praises in seeking God's blessing upon this ship and all who serve in her, that she may sail safely under God's good providence and protection.

Hymn: (Tune: Melita)

O Father, king of Earth and
    Sea,
We dedicate this ship to
    Thee;

In faith we send her on
    her way,
In faith to Thee we humbly
    pray,

O hear from Heaven our
sailors' cry,
And watch and guard her
from on high.
And when at length her course is
run,
Her work for home and country
done;

Of all the souls that in her
sailed,
Let not one life in Thee have
failed;
But hear from Heaven our
sailors' cry,
And grant eternal life on
high.

Psalm 107 (Verses 23 to 31, 43) to be read responsively.

23. They that go down to the sea
in ships, that do business
in great waters;

24. These see the works of the
Lord, and His wonders in the
deep.

25. For He commandeth, and
raiseth the stormy wind, which
lifteth up the waves thereof.

26. They mount up to the Heavens,
they go down again to the
depths; their soul is melted
because of trouble.

27. They reel to and fro, and
stagger like a drunken man,
and are at their wit's end.

28. Then they cry unto the Lord
in their trouble, and He bringeth
them out of their distresses.

29. He makes the storm a calm, so
that the waves thereof are still.

30. Then are they glad because
they be quiet; so he bringeth
them unto their desired haven.

31. Oh that men would praise the
Lord for His goodness, and for
his wonderful works to the
children of men!

43. Whoso is wise, and will observe
these things, even they shall
understand the loving kindness
of the Lord.

Then shall the Captain of HMCS *Athabaskan* say to his ship's company
in the words of "The Gaelic Blessing":

I call upon you to pray for God's
blessing on this ship.
May God the Father bless her.

Ship's Company: Bless our ship.

Captain: May Jesus Christ bless her.

Ship's Company: Bless our ship.

Captain: May the Holy Spirit
bless her.

Ship's Company: Bless our ship.

Captain: What do ye fear seeing that God the Father is with you?

Ship's Company: We fear nothing.

Captain: What do ye fear seeing that God the Son is with you?

Ship's Company: We fear nothing.

Captain: What do ye fear seeing that God the Holy Spirit is with you?

Ship's Company: We fear nothing.

Captain: Our help is in the name of the Lord.

Ship's Company: Who hath made Heaven and Earth.

Captain: The Lord be with you.

Ship's Company: And with Thy Spirit.

Amen.

Let us Pray

O Eternal Lord God, who alone spreadest out the heavens and rulest the raging of the sea; who has compassed the waters with bounds until day and night come to an end; be pleased to receive into Thy Almighty and most gracious protection the persons of us Thy servants, and the Fleet in which we serve. Preserve us from the dangers of the sea and from the violence of the enemy; that we may be a safeguard unto our most gracious sovereign Lady, Queen Elizabeth, and her Dominions, and a security for such as pass on the seas upon their lawful occasions; that the inhabitants of our Commonwealth may in peace and quietness serve Thee our God; and that we may return in safety to enjoy the blessings of the land, with the fruits of our labours; and with a thankful remembrance of Thy mercies to praise and glorify Thy Holy Name; through Jesus Christ Our Lord.

Amen.

Almighty and Eternal God, the strength and support of those who put their confidence in you, be pleased, we beseech you, to bless this ship which is being commissioned today; guard and protect her from all danger and from all adversity; protect her against the visible and invisible snares of the enemy that she may defend the paths of justice and overcome, with your help, the powers of the enemy. Pour into this ship, the officer who commands her, and all her officers and men the richness of your blessing, guidance, and protection. May they ever be inspired by your Holy Law. May they grasp with their minds, cherish in their hearts, and carry out in their actions the teachings that lead to the safe haven of eternal life; through Christ Our Lord.

Amen.

The Blessing

Go forth into the world in peace; be of good courage; hold fast to that which is good; render unto no man evil for evil; strengthen the faint hearted; support the weak; love the Brotherhood; fear God; honour the Queen.

And the blessing of God Almighty, the Father, the Son and the Holy Ghost be upon you, and remain with you always.

Our Father, Who art in heaven, hallowed be Thy name; Thy kingdom come; Thy will be done on earth as it is in heaven. Give us this day our daily bread; and forgive us our trespasses as we forgive those who trespass against us; and lead us not into temptation, but deliver us from evil. For thine is the kingdom, the power and the glory, for ever and ever.

Amen.[11]

10
Some Distinguishing Marks

A badge is a sign, a symbol, a distinctive mark, intended to identify its bearer. The origins of this concept of identification are lost in the mists of prehistoric times. However, the system of badges and other identifying symbols employed in the Canadian Forces has come down to us through our European heritage. In the days of chivalry, knights fully armed and helmed needed signs on their shields to indicate their identity, just as the famed standards had done, more than a thousand years before, for the legions of the Roman Empire. Thus it is that the badges and other marks used in the Canadian Forces today are inextricably bound up with the history and traditions of the units of the Service they identify. Some of these symbols are only months old, others go back to the very beginnings of the nation and beyond.

The four-arrowhead breast pocket insignia of Mobile Command dates from the year of unification of the Forces, 1968. The thunderbird of 426 Squadron was born of wartime service in 1943. HMCS *Skeena*'s leaping salmon, cast in bronze, appeared on the destroyer's after canopy just after her commissioning in 1931. The bounding springbok of the Royal Canadian Dragoons had its origin in an incident of the Boer War in 1900. The Royal Hamilton Light Infantry (Wentworth Regiment), established in 1862, shares with regiments such as the Brockville Rifles, the North Saskatchewan Regiment, and Princess Patricia's Canadian Light Infantry, the well known eighteenth century device, the tasselled bugle-horn of the skirmisher. These unit badges number in the hundreds,[1] visual symbols of the magnificent achievements of Canada's military forces in peace and war over the years of our storied past. They are also a constant inspiration to the men and women of the forces who proudly serve the Canadian people today.

In addition to unit badges, there are several symbols used in the forces, each of which serves to identify and each of which has an origin of considerable interest. One of these is the roundel, which shows the identity of Canadian Forces aircraft.

When the first aeroplanes of the Royal Flying Corps arrived in France in 1914, their pilots soon found out how necessary it was to be able to identify themselves as British. They were fired upon by friend and foe alike! Several markings were tried, including the Union flag which, at a distance, unfortunately, looked very much like the cross device used by the enemy.

Eventually, the RFC turned to their French allies who had already devised a roundel of concentric red, white and blue circles inspired by the tri-colour flag of France. The British simply reversed the colour order, placing the blue on the outside and the red in the centre. The roundel used in the Canadian Forces has evolved from that of the French through the adaptation made by the Royal Flying Corps and the Royal Naval Air Service.[2]

In 1921, the short-lived Canadian Air Force was permitted to use, as its own, the light blue ensign of the Royal Air Force which displayed the roundel in the fly. Three years later, on 1 April 1924 the Royal Canadian Air Force came into being and its identifying mark continued to be the British roundel used throughout the empire to identify military aircraft.

It was in 1940, during the Second World War, that the RCAF was authorized to replace the inner red circle with the red maple leaf. However, this step was delayed until after the close of hostilities. Canadian military aircraft began to wear the maple leaf roundel in 1946.[3] Finally, it was in a decision of 1965 that the eleven-point, stylized maple leaf of the new national flag became the centre-piece of Canada's roundel.[4]

The adoption of the maple leaf as an emblem of the people of Canada became more and more popular commencing early in the nineteenth century. Gradually over the years it has become very well known the world over by a variety of avenues, not least of which being its display in HMC ships. A current regulation reads: "Ships are to wear a red maple leaf in the form of a metal badge . . . on each side of the funnel, (or) on the side of the hangar for DDH 280 Class (that is, the new Tribal Class destroyers such as HMCS *Iroquois*)."[5] The wearing of the maple leaf badge on the funnels of Canadian warships is a tradition stretching back some six decades.

In November, 1917, four wooden patrol vessels of the Royal Canadian Navy, called drifters, put to sea from Halifax escorted by HMCS *Shearwater*, sloop, bound eventually for service in the Royal Navy off the west coast of Africa. Manned mainly by Canadian sailors, it was not long before these tiny ships sported bright green maple leaves on their funnels.[6]

During the Second World War, the wearing of the green maple leaf as a funnel badge was officially authorized by the Naval Board. In those days, all of His Majesty's ships, from whatever country of the Commonwealth, proudly flew the white ensign. The maple leaf badge readily identified a ship of the Royal Canadian Navy. This symbol carried over into peacetime, but the colour of the maple leaf was changed from green to red, much as it appears today.

The maple leaf on the funnels of HMC ships points up a tradition bridging a century, the funnel band to designate ships of a particular force or formation. Today, destroyers and lesser ships are organized in squadrons, yesterday in flotillas or groups. In the Second World War in the Atlantic, some frigate groups displayed a numeral on the maple leaf funnel badge to indicate a numbered escort group. But perhaps the best remembered funnel band of the Royal Canadian Navy in the long Atlantic battle was that of C-5 Group of the Mid-Ocean Escort Force, at first called the Newfoundland Escort Force.

When merchant ship losses to the German submarine "wolf packs" became extremely serious in 1941-42, part of the antidote lay in the provision of port-to-port close escorts of convoys, including the great middle gap of the Atlantic between the Grand Banks of Newfoundland and the western approaches to Britain. The destroyers, corvettes and later, the frigates providing that protection were organized into C groups. One of these was the C-5 group. The funnel of this group sported red and white slanted stripes, and C-5 was promptly dubbed "The Barber Pole Brigade."

There was already an established tradition that when the new Canadian corvettes first put to sea, they were ushered on their way, appropriately enough, to the tune of "The Road to the Isles." It was then only a matter of time when the barber pole funnel marking and the melody that expressed so well the swelling sweep of the Atlantic seas, should come together as the "Barber Pole Song," penned by Surgeon Lieutenant W.A. Paddon, RCNVR, of HMCS *Kitchener*, corvette.

To this day, some thirty-five years later, the red and white barber pole band graces the mast structure or the radar pedestals of the ships of the Fifth Canadian Destroyer Squadron, inheritor of a proud tradition. And the "Barber Pole Song" is still sung with great spirit wherever sailors gather to the familiar tune, "The Road to the Isles." Here is the first verse and the chorus:

> It's away outward the swinging
> fo'c's'les reel
> From the smoking seas' white glare
> upon the strand

It's the grey seas that are slipping
    under keel
When we're rolling outward bound
    from Newfoundland.

Chorus
From Halifax or Newfiejohn or Derry's
    clustered towers
By trackless paths where conning
    towers roll
If you know another group in which
    you'd sooner spend your hours
You've never sailed beneath the Barber
    Pole!
It's the grey seas that are slipping
    under keel
When we're rolling outward bound
    from Newfoundland.

One badge in the Service today has enjoyed the spotlight of good-natured controversy. It concerns the breed of the bird with wings spread as depicted in the badge of the air operations branch of the Canadian Forces, adapted from the insignia of the Royal Canadian Air Force. The debate has continued for generations and surfaces in the press to this day — and this despite the clarity of the evidence. Indeed, so familiar is the topic among airmen that the focal point of the discussion is invariably termed "the bird."

It all started back in 1914 when the British admiralty issued a regulation saying that officers of the newly established Royal Naval Air Service (RNAS) would wear an eagle above the gold rank lace on the left sleeve of their uniform jackets. An eagle was also to replace the anchor on the officers' cap badges and jacket buttons. But during the war at sea, the flying sailors of the RNAS, large numbers of whom were Canadians, somehow developed the conviction that no sailor worth the salt in his blood could possibly display anything but "a proper seagoing albatross."[7]

Then, in 1918, the Royal Flying Corps (RFC) and the RNAS were combined to form the Royal Air Force (RAF). The rank insignia and the bird of the RNAS were adopted by the new RAF. In due course, the Royal Canadian Air Force (RCAF) was firmly established in 1924 and the dress regulations for the new air force made it clear that the bird *was* an eagle. But, sure enough, RNAS veterans in the RCAF soon spread the word about the dastardly conspiracy and "the fact" that the badge of the RCAF was really an albatross.[8] Even the official word of the College of Arms, "an eagle *volant affronté*, the head lowered and to the sinister," approved by King George VI in 1943, had little effect on those who proclaimed "it isn't an eagle at all, but — as any clot can plainly see — an albatross!"[9]

There is an intereting side-light to the bird. It is a well known custom in military circles that the major device on collar dogs and lapel badges, if not symmetrical, must always face inwards. For example, to be caught wearing the stag of the Grey and Simcoe Foresters facing outwards is to invite dire sanctions at the bar or extra duty.[10] Yet the eagle of the air operations branch lapel badge is correctly worn facing outwards, and the reason again goes back to 1914. In the Royal Naval Air Service badges the eagle faced to the sinister, that is, to the wearer's left, the design, it is said, having been inspired by a lady's brooch of the time. When these naval officers were required to wear the eagle on the left sleeve, the bird, of course, faced aft. It still does.[11]

While the badges of all air squadrons, the majority of regiments, and all bases and stations, are surmounted by the royal crown, the badges of HMC ships are all contained within a rope surround surmounted by the naval crown, a device of great antiquity. Somewhat similar to the rostral crown of Roman origin, this symbol consists of a circlet bearing the sterns of four ships-of-the-line, each with three poop lanterns, and four squaresails, each spread on a mast and yard and fully filled and sheeted home. The hulls and sails are positioned alternately around the circlet. The naval crown is also to be found in the fly of the Canadian Forces Naval Jack authorized in 1968.

An eighteenth century author stated that the naval crown was given as a mark of commendation "to Officers & who first grapled or Board[d] an Enemy's Ship."[12] Like the laurel wreaths of ancient times, the naval crown can be traced back to the Romans where it was known as the *corona navalis* or *rostrata* (which may have been two distinct degrees of recognition; both are mentioned in Virgil's *Aeneid*) and was given to the sailor who first boarded an enemy's vessel. In more recent times, the naval crown has been granted as an honourable augmentation to the armorial bearings of outstanding naval officers, for example, Earl St. Vincent and Lord Nelson.[13]

Another heraldic device used in the Canadian Forces is the astral crown, a symbol of quite recent origin. The badge of air command was approved in 1975, the year the command was established, and consists of an eagle rising out of a Canadian astral crown. This latter device may be described as a circlet displaying eight stars around the base and bearing four maple leaves each set within a pair of elevated wings.[14] Inspired by the astral crown of the Royal Air Force, the Canadian design was approved by Her Majesty the Queen in 1975.

Something of an enigma is the ancient badge of mariners the world over —
the foul anchor. A dictionary definition a century ago made no mistake
about the connotations of the expression: "An anchor is said to be foul, or
fouled, either when it hooks some impediment under water, or when the ship,
by the wind shifting, entangles her slack cable a turn round the stock, or round
the upper fluke thereof. The last from its being avoidable by a sharp lookout,
is termed the seaman's disgrace."[15] If the foul anchor insignia does, in fact,
illustrate one of the worst examples of poor seamanship, no one has ever
found the explanation for the badge's highly cherished prestige.

The great age of this badge is not disputed. There is clear evidence in Roman
stone, on an English seal of 1601, on a British admiral's flag in 1695, as well as
on the arms of various Lords High Admiral and printed title pages.[16] The foul
anchor was the major device of the official badge of the Royal Canadian
Navy. It was proudly worn on the sleeves of petty officers and leading seamen,
as well as on the shoulders of naval officers in full dress uniform. The foul
anchor, true to its long tradition, enjoys an honoured place in the Service
today: Canadian Forces badge (1967) and ensign (1967); badge of Maritime
Command (1968) and the Naval Jack (1968); and badge of the Naval Operation's Branch (1973).

Still, there is no hard evidence of why "the sailor's disgrace" has occupied
such a prominent place in the affairs of seamen and the sea. Perhaps it is
simply a matter of design. Some early artist may have shown a remnant of
cable bent to the anchor's ring. Then another may have made the device what
he thought was more decorative by taking turns with the rope or cable round
the stock and shank — artistic license not unlike that of the heraldic device,
the "rudder ancien," forming the badge of HMCS *Bytown*, in which the tiller
is backwards on the rudder head, to make a better design.

The badge of the Canadian Forces, which came into use at the creation of
the unified force in 1968, is a *mélange* of the major devices taken from the
badges of the former Royal Canadian Navy, Canadian Army, and Royal
Canadian Air Force. It is described heraldically:

Within a wreath of ten stylized maple leaves Gules, a cartouche Azure edged Or,
charged with a foul anchor Or, surmounted by Crusaders' Swords in saltire Argent
and Azure, pommelled and hilted Or; and in front an eagle volant affronté head to
the sinister Or, the whole ensigned with a Royal Crown Proper.[17]

The army's contribution to this design is, of course, the crossed crusaders'
swords. The origin of this device is an interesting one.

In 1935, an officer in the War Office in London, Captain Oakes-Jones, was commissioned to design a badge to represent the British army for inclusion in a stained glass window of Ypres Cathedral honouring the memory of Belgium's beloved wartime commander, Albert, king of the Belgians. The main device of that badge was the crossed swords and after slight modification, the design became the official badge of the British army in 1938.

Shortly after the Second World War, when it became desirable to have a single badge to represent the Canadian army, the major device, the swords in saltire, were taken from the British badge to symbolize the historic ties between the two forces. Also, the swords were altered in design to represent crusaders' swords in recognition that the Crusades of the Middle Ages had in the Christian view elevated warfare to the dignity of a sacred trust where the sword is drawn only in defence of that which is morally right and of the weak against the strong. The Canadian army badge was approved by King George VI in 1947.[18]

These crossed swords, together with the navy's foul anchor and the air force's flying eagle, within a wreath of maple leaves, the whole under St. Edward's Crown, forms the badge of the Canadian Forces today.

11
Music and Verse

Music has been a part of military life from very early times. Long before airs and melodies were developed, musical sounds were used, and still are to this day, to convey messages and pass orders in the field and at sea. A writer of nearly two centuries ago expressed it this way: "Military musick, before the introduction of fire arms, served to animate the soldiers in battles and assaults of places, as well as for the purpose of signals for the different manoeuvres and duties in camp and garrison; wherefore it cannot be doubted but it was used in our antient armies."[1]

The trumpet and fife, and horns of a wide variety of shapes and sizes, have come down from very remote times. But perhaps the instrument of greatest interest, and one that has been known to many primitive societies, is the drum. The number and variety of the messages conveyed by the drum beat have, through the centuries of human history, been limited only by the extent of man's ingenuity.

A military dictionary of the eighteenth century lists ten distinct drum beats, each of which was fully understood by the soldier on the battlefield.[2] Much depended on the drummer's skill and unflagging courage under fire in making those beats heard above the din of battle. Mention has been made elsewhere in this work about the beating of reveille, the retreat and the tattoo.

One drum beat that was well known to the soldier and civilian alike was the alarm, the beat to arms. On the last day of the year 1775, in the pre-dawn darkness on the ramparts of Quebec, an officer of the Royal Highland Emigrants saw suspicious lights. As it turned out, these lights, sighted intermittently through the falling snow, signalled the coming attack on Quebec by rebel forces from the American colonies. With the drums beating and the bells of the town ringing out the alarm, the whole garrison were soon at their posts ready to repel the invaders.[3]

Some twenty years after these events at Quebec, strange lights again brought a garrison out at the double. It was at Port Royal, Jamaica. The watch on deck in HMS *Blonde,* frigate, heard the drums ashore beating to arms. Three boats with armed landing parties were at once sent to assist the apparently beleaguered garrison. "The adventure produced much laughter at the expense of the piquet who had given the alarm . . .," for the mysterious lights above the town turned out to be clouds of fireflies![4]

Another long-time use of the drum, and the meaning is seen in the civilian expression of "drumming up business," was recruiting by beat of drum. In that troubled summer of 1775 in British North America, the *Quebec Gazette* of August 3 reported that a recruiting party had begun "beating up for volunteers" for the Royal Highland Emigrants, a regiment specially raised for the defence of Canada.[5] However, at times, volunteers did not come readily to hand. The famous Secretary at the Admiralty, Samuel Pepys, was, as he said, always anxious to avoid "offence to the country," particularly in times of peace, when he instructed recruiters "to invite seamen by beating of drums in the place usual" rather than compel them to serve in the Royal Navy. But in 1652 during the First Dutch War, at Sandwich, when beat of drum brought only one man, the press gang promptly went into action and "signed up" fourteen more.[6]

Today, in the Canadian Forces, the term, "the drums," means a corps within a unit consisting of drums, fifes, and bugles or trumpets, or, in some units, "the pipes and drums" is the expression used, particularly in Scottish regiments. Often, the beats employed by the drums today, particularly in ceremonial situations, reflect the beats used in earlier times. The roll, depending on how it is rendered, may be reminiscent of the ruffles accorded flag officers on boarding a ship of war, or of the dreaded "hands to witness punishment." Then there was the call to church and the beat of the drum during foggy weather at sea.

The "drums beating" is an important part of a unit's exercising its right of freedom of the city, just as the granting of permission to march out of a fortified place with drums beating was a mark of respect for a gallant foe by a generous victor. Such was the case when Fort Beauséjour by the Bay of Fundy was surrendered to a British amphibious force in 1755. An article of the instrument of capitulation stated: "The Commandant, staff officers in the (French) King's service, and the garrison of Beauséjour shall march out with their arms, baggage and drums beating" the honours of war.[7]

A widely used drum beat, called the chamade, or the parley, was the means of communication between enemies prior to a flag of truce being sent to arrange, for example, a cease-fire to permit burial of the dead, or the evacuation of non-combatants. The drummers who beat the firing signals for the batteries of Louisbourg in Nova Scotia in 1745 beat the chamade asking General Pepperrell and Commodore Warren to hold their fire prior to drawing up the articles of surrender.[8]

One use of the drum which is common to both ancient and modern times is the measured beat of marching in cadence, setting the pace and helping the troops to keep in step. In the days before personnel carriers, it was important that commanders be able to estimate accurately the time necessary for an army to cover a specific distance. Under ordinary field conditions, once the length of the step and the number of paces per minute were known, it was simple arithmetic for commanders to have their troops reach a certain fortified town or suitable campground in a given length of time. Also, the rhythm of the marching cadence has often kept tired troops going until their objective was reached. This has been particularly the case since the arrival of the military band and the music of the march.

A Canadian infantry sergeant has recorded an example of what band music can do for tired troops, especially where soldiering is based on a strong regimental spirit.

It was early June, 1900, and the capital of the Boer Republic, Pretoria, had fallen. The troops of the Empire had campaigned all the way from Cape Town. They were now about to enter the city, the commander-in-chief himself taking the salute. The Canadian sergeant wrote:

> It was the climax of the campaign, even if it was not the end of the war. I shall never forget that parade. Ragged and tanned, footsore and weary, dirty and gaunt, we trudged along the western road leading into the square . . . . As we wheeled round the corner the band struck up "The Boys of the Old Brigade." I thought it was the sweetest music I had ever heard. We squared our shoulders, chucked out our chests, and put all the ginger we could into our step. I hope everyone else felt as much stirred up as I did; if so, they experienced a sensation they will not forget in many days. Out of a regiment of 1,150 men, we entered Pretoria with 438. We had marched 620 miles on scant rations since being brigaded on February 12th, had assisted in the capture of ten towns, had fought in ten general engagements and on many other days, and had stood shoulder to shoulder all through with British regiments of long and great tradition . . . It was one of those unique moments which only come to a man occasionally during a lifetime. It will never be forgotten. If anyone asks me what I consider the greatest occasion in my life, I say that it was when I marched past Lord Roberts in Pretoria, June 5th, 1900, with the Royal Canadian Regiment.[9]

Band music not only lifts the spirit of weary troops on the march, it also minimizes the monotony and stiff-leggedness of having to stand still over long periods of time. During the Second World War, HMCS *Cornwallis*, on the shores of Annapolis Basin, was said to be the largest naval training establishment in the Commonwealth. Certainly, the fourteen thousand sailors and wrens at Sunday divisions on the parade square made an impressive sight. But it meant long periods of standing while the captain inspected the numerous divisions. However, once the band started to play, the effect was striking. There was a barely perceptible, yet very real, swaying of those thousands to the rhythm of the music, particularly to the strains of "Oh, What a Beautiful Mornin.'"[10] Fatigue and boredom were forgotten.

A musical tradition of long standing is associated with the departure of units on active service. In the past it was men marching down the road, or boarding troop trains and troop ships. Today, such departures are more likely to be by air. But, traditionally, a band was there to cheer them on their way. Such was the case of HMCS *Magnificent* in 1956 when she sailed from Halifax for service as headquarters ship at Port Said, Egypt, in the United Nations Emergency Force. The official history states:

> The carrier with 406 army personnel and supplies for UNEF slipped her lines on 29 December to the accompaniment of a rendition of "Auld Lang Syne" given fortissimo by three bands, HMCS *Stadacona*, the Royal Canadian Artillery and the pipes and drums of the Royal Highland Regiment of Canada (Black Watch).[11]

There is one marching song inseparably linked with regiments leaving their station for distant parts. For over two centuries many a tear has been shed as the troops swung down the road to the tune, "The Girl I Left Behind Me."[12] Indeed, in many a garrison town, the local belles felt sorely neglected if the departing soldiers failed to make this final musical tribute.

In February, 1813, a detachment of the 104th Regiment of Foot, originally raised in New Brunswick and Nova Scotia as the New Brunswick Regiment of Fencible Infantry, was ordered overland from Fredericton to Quebec and Kingston. The United States had declared war the previous year. On the day of departure, the temperature was in the vicinity of twenty degrees below zero (fahrenheit). One soldier reported in his diary about the low spirits of himself and his companions until "our bugles struck up the merry air 'The Girls We Leave Behind Us.'"[13]

A musical instrument unique in its construction and sound, and profound in its influence on military affairs through the ages, is the bagpipe. Played in many lands and known as far back as Roman times, the bagpipe is a reed instrument having a leather bag as an air reservoir, enabling the piper to continue the melody while taking a breath.

Today, the bagpipe is recognized as the national instrument of the Scottish people and revered by transplanted Scots and others the world over whose hearts quicken at the skirl of the pipes.[14]

The notes of the piper have brought mind's-eye pictures of the "hills of home" to many a lonely Canadian settler, to others, comfort in time of sorrow. In battle, on many a field, the piper has encouraged his comrades in the thick of the fight, sounding the charge, or onset, in the same tradition as Piper James Richardson, VC, of Victoria's 16th Battalion (Canadian Scottish).

In October, 1916, in the attack on the "Regina Trench" in the Battle of Ancre Heights, the battalion was pinned down at the barbed wire defences by heavy machine gun fire. Piper Richardson, just eighteen years old, with complete disregard for his own safety, strode up and down playing his pipes in the time-honoured way and so inspired the battalion that they stormed the wire and pressed on to their objective.[15]

While military calls by drum and horn have been used since the earliest days of organized war operations, which pre-date written history, the military band as it is known today came from the continent to the British army in the mid-eighteenth century.[16] The use of the flute, drum and trumpet by troops on the march was known in medieval times, but it is evident that there was little coordination of effort music-wise. The main object seems to have been the production of the greatest possible amount of noise. This is to be seen in Chaucer's *Canterbury Tales*, in "The Tale of the Knight."

Similarly, while the troubadours who wandered over the land and the minstrels who visited the great houses of Europe kept alive melodies that would otherwise have been lost, they performed largely as individuals. The development of the multi-instrumented, musically co-ordinated band was dependant on the evolution of the instruments themselves, and this was a very slow process. So that while Louis XIV's court saw significant growth in this direction in the France of the seventeenth century, it was the time of the conquest of Canada in the eighteenth century before regiments of the British army were beginning to produce regimental bands. Indeed, it was not until 1857 that the War Office removed the confusion in organization and musical procedures in British army bands, by the formation of the Royal Military School of Music at Kneller Hall, Twickenham, England.[17]

In the Canadian Forces today, there are more than 125 officially approved marches in use by units, commands and branches.[18] There are, of course, many duplications. For example, eight Scottish regiments lay claim to the well known Scottish air, "The Highland Laddie," while five regiments march to

"Bonnie Dundee," four to "Blue Bonnets over the Border," and three each to "A Hundred Pipers" and "The Piobaireachd of Donald Dhu." These and "March of the Cameron Men" give some idea of the strength of the Scottish tradition in the militia.

Some marches show the geographical region of the unit concerned, for example, the Royal Newfoundland Regiment's "The Banks of Newfoundland"; the Royal New Brunswick Regiment's, "The Old North Shore"; and "Red River Valley" of the Fort Garry Horse. The title of the march of the Rocky Mountain Rangers comes from the site of the regimental headquarters at Kamloops, meaning "The Meeting of the Waters," the confluence of the North and South Thompson Rivers in British Columbia.

The quick march of Princess Patricia's Canadian Light Infantry shows the regiment's First World War origin, the musical score being a medley of "Has Anyone Seen the Colonel," "Tipperary," and "Madamoiselle from Armentières," while the old song, "Vive la Canadienne," is most appropriate for the Royal 22e Régiment. Four of the older regiments march proudly to the tune, "British Grenadiers."

It is said that music seals friendship. Certainly the march in common is one of the ties which has so successfully bound regiments in alliance, often over a period of many years. Because of the long, proud record of many British regiments, the Canadian units with which they are allied have been honoured by being invited to march to the music of the older regiments. An example is the march, "The Buffs," of the Queen's Own Rifles of Canada, allied with the Queen's Own Buffs, the Royal Kent Regiment. Some will recall the stirring lines telling of the lone soldier of magnificent courage, awaiting barbaric execution rather than be broken by his captors, as given in Sir Francis Doyle's *The Private of the Buffs.*

Three regiments of the militia — the Elgin Regiment, the British Columbia Regiment (Duke of Connaught's Own), and the Hastings and Prince Edward Regiment — have the same quick march, "I'm Ninety-Five." The tune has an interesting origin. In 1816, the 95th Regiment of Foot, in recognition of its outstanding service in battle, was removed from the list of numbered line regiments and given the title, the Rifle Brigade. But the unit's marching song continued to be "I'm Ninety-Five." The three-stanza lyric, of a comic strain, followed re-arrangement of the music into a proper march. Once Queen Victoria showed her enthusiastic approval, the tune grew steadily in popular esteem, so much so that other units, not necessarily rifle regiments, adopted it. [19]

One mark of a good marching song is the combination of a relaxed, swinging tempo and that hard-to-define quality of a tune that immediately lifts the spirit. Such is the march of Lord Strathcona's Horse (Royal Canadians), "Soldiers of the Queen." It was written at the close of Queen Victoria's reign and enjoyed great popularity.[20]

An example of a very old tune used as a quick march in the Canadian Forces today, is that of the 1st Canadian Signal Regiment, "Begone, Dull Care." As a march it originated in the Royal Corps of Signals, but as a tune it dates from 1687 when it was known as "The Buck's Delight."

> Begone, dull Care! I prythee begone from me!
> Begone, dull Care! You and I shall never agree.[21]

"Ça Ira," the regimental march of the Royal Montreal Regiment, is of considerable antiquity and, at first glance, a curious choice of tune for one of the queen's loyal regiments. Blood thirsty and revolutionary, its selection represents one of those odd twists of human nature.

In the Napoleonic Wars it was not unusual for bands of British regiments to play French revolutionary tunes in derision, such as "Ça Ira" ("It will succeed") and "Marche des Marseillois," interspersed with "Rule Britannia" and "The British Grenadiers," a form of psychological warfare.[22] At Famars, in 1793, the 14th Regiment of Foot was repulsed by the fanatical revolutionary soldiers of France. But once regrouped, the commander of the 14th ordered the band to strike up "Ça Ira," and with the blood-curdling notes of the tune that had accompanied the nobility of France to the guillotine, ringing in the ears of the 14th, the regiment swept on to victory.[23]

The 14th Regiment of Foot with great zest took "Ça Ira" for their own march, and later became the West Yorkshire Regiment (the Prince of Wales Own). The Royal Montreal Regiment, which perpetuates the 14th Battalion, Canadian Expeditionary Force of 1914-18, has been allied with the West Yorkshires for more than half a century. And that is why "Ça Ira" is heard in the streets of Montreal.

Since the unification of the forces in 1968, some formations have disappeared and new ones have been established. This in turn has provided an opportunity for new marches to be composed and adopted. For example, the official march for all Service battalions, "Duty Above All," composed by Captain B.G.M. Bogisch, was approved in 1973. The well known "CA-NA-DA," written by Bobby Gimby in the year of the centenary of Confederation, 1967, was re-arranged by Major J.F. Pierret and approved as the regimental march of the Canadian Airborne Regiment in 1974. The communications and electronics branch has for its quick march "The Mercury March," composed and arranged by Captain A.C. Furey, and officially approved in 1975.

Most of the marches used in the Canadian Forces today belong to the army, and their richness in variety and tradition is the result of the decentralizing effect of the former corps system and the presently retained regimental system. Quite different is the heritage of the naval and air forces. Each had, before unification, a single service organization and concept in which identities and loyalties were not focused primarily on units, but rather on the Royal Canadian Navy and the Royal Canadian Air Force, respectively. This is still reflected in the marches of sailors and airmen today.

"Heart of Oak" is the quick march of the naval operations branch and maritime command. The words, commencing "Come cheer up, my lads, 'tis to glory we steer," were written by David Garrick and set to the music composed by William Boyce. It was first heard on the London stage in a production called "Harlequin's Invasion," in celebration of the "Year of Victories" (Minden, Quiberon Bay, and Quebec), 1759.[24]

Similarly, all airmen in the Canadian Forces march to a single tune, "RCAF March Past." This musical score, known in Britain as "The Royal Air Force March Past," was written originally by Sir Walford Davies shortly after the formation of the RAF in 1918, and later was re-arranged and altered by Sir George Dyson.[25] It was in 1943, when the RCAF was so heavily engaged in the air war over Britain and Germany that permission was granted for the RCAF to use the march and, today, "RCAF March Past" continues to be the quick march of the air operations branch and air command.[26]

Article II of the 1757 edition of *Regulations and Instructions Relating to His Majesty's Service at Sea* laid down that:

> The Commanders of His Majesty's Ships are to take care, that Divine Service be performed twice a Day on Board, according to the Liturgy of the Church of England, and a Sermon preached on Sundays, unless bad Weather, or other extraordinary accidents, prevent it.

Things have changed since that day. Owing to many factors, including the five-day week and the family-oriented nature of Service routines in peace time; the three-shift system on operational bases; the current trend of the majority of single personnel living off-base; and the general decline of religious observances in civilian life; divine service in the Canadian Forces is reduced largely to small voluntary attendance, or selected personnel required to attend for a special occasion. However, it is worth noting that in operational situations such as exercises in the Arctic or on United Nations service abroad there is a good voluntary turn-out. Certainly, in HMC ships at sea, where there is no way of avoiding the round-the-clock watch system, seven days a week, attendance at divine service, though voluntary unless accompanied by Sunday divisions and captain's inspection, is still normal routine.

At such a service on board ship, the Naval Hymn is invariably part of the worship and is sung with spirit as it has been for over a hundred years. "Eternal Father" was written by William Whiting, a clergyman, in 1860 after passing through a fierce gale on passage through the Mediterranean Sea. It was set to the tune "Melita" by John B. Dykes in 1861.

The Naval Hymn

Eternal Father, strong to save,
Whose arm hath bound the restless wave,
Who bidd'st the mighty ocean deep
Its own appointed limits keep:
  O hear us when we cry to Thee
  For those in peril on the sea.

O Christ, whose voice the waters heard,
And hushed their raging at Thy word,
Who walkedst on the foaming deep,
And calm amid the storm didst sleep:
  O hear us when we cry to Thee
  For those in peril on the sea.

O Holy Spirit, who didst brood
Upon the waters dark and rude,
And bid their angry tumult cease,
And give, for wild confusion, peace:
  O hear us when we cry to Thee
  For those in peril on the sea.

O Trinity of love and power,
Our brethren shield in danger's hour;
From rock and tempest, fire and foe,
Protect them wheresoe'er they go:
  Thus evermore shall rise to Thee
  Glad hymns of praise from land and sea.[27]

Interestingly enough, this composition, in this case called "The Navy Hymn," was adopted by the United States Naval Academy, Annapolis, in 1879, and so has been in use there for nearly a century.[28]

Also traditional to divine service on board HMC ships is the Naval Prayer, the beautiful language of which has remained unchanged these 300 years. It was published in the Book of Common Prayer in 1662, shortly after the Restoration of King Charles II.

The Naval Prayer

O Eternal Lord God, who alone spreadest out the heavens, and rulest the raging of the sea; who has compassed the waters with bounds until day and night come to an end; be pleased to receive into thy almighty and most gracious protection the persons of us thy servants, and the Fleet in which we serve. Preserve us from the dangers of the sea, and from the violence of the enemy; that we may be a safeguard unto our most gracious Sovereign Lady, Queen Elizabeth, and her Dominions, and a security for such as pass on the seas upon their lawful occasions; that the inhabitants of our Empire may in peace and quietness serve thee our God; and that we may return in safety to enjoy the blessings of the land, with the fruits of our labours, and with a thankful remembrance of thy mercies to praise and glorify thy holy Name; through Jesus Christ our Lord. Amen[29]

Church service in the air force usually includes the hymn, "O Thou within whose sure control." The words were written for "travellers by air" by Kathryn Munro in 1928 and set to the same tune as "The Naval Hymn," "Melita," composed by John B. Dykes in 1861.[30]

O Thou within whose sure control
The surging planets onward roll,
Whose everlasting arms embrace
The sons of every clime and race:
    Hear Thou, O Lord, a nation's prayer
    For these Thy children of the air!

Thou at the impulse of whose will
A troubled Galilee grew still,
Thy chart and compass shall provide
Deliverance from storm and tide:
    Hear Thou, O Lord, a nation's prayer
    For these Thy rangers of the air!

Across the ocean, dread and deep,
Above the forest's lonely sweep,
Or when through serried clouds they rise
And hidden are from mortal eyes;
    Hear Thou, O Lord, a nation's prayer
    For Thy crusaders of the air!

Uphold their shining argosies
Upon the vast ethereal seas;
Encompass Thou their valiant wings
In all their brave adventurings:
   Hear Thou, O Lord, a nation's prayer
   For these Thy children of the air!

Many regiments have over the years devised their own distinctive order of service on church parade, including a regimental prayer. Typical is that of the 8th Canadian Hussars (Princess Louise's), written expressly for the regiment by the Bishop of Fredericton, the Right Reverend Harold L. Nutter, in 1972.[31]

Almighty God, who has revealed thyself in mercy and justice, we pray that our service to Queen and country may always be characterized by those qualities.

Keep all who serve in this Regiment loyal to Thee and to those with whom they serve. Shelter them in the day of battle, and ever keep them safe from all evil.

We remember before Thee with thanksgiving the courage and fellowship of those who have died in the cause of righteousness and peace, and all those who have shared with us in the life of this Regiment.

We pray that we may be guided always to serve as seeing Thee who art invisible:

Through Jesus Christ Our Lord

Amen

The Regimental Collect of the Queen's Own Rifles of Canada was prepared for the regiment by Honourary Major F.H. Wilkinson, Bishop of Toronto.[32]

O God, whose servant David put off his armour the better to prevail against his enemy, grant, we beseech thee, that we, thy servants of the Queen's Own, who were chosen of old to obey with speed and to fight unburdened, may lay aside every weight and every besetting sin and run with patience the race that is set before us by Jesus Christ our Lord, and this we ask for His Name's sake.   Amen

Finally, there is a piece of poetry which in three decades has become almost a legend. The sonnet, "High Flight," was written by a nineteen-year old pilot officer of the Royal Canadian Air Force just months before he was killed in 1941.

John Gillespie Magee, Jr., (1922-1941) was born of American parents in

China and received some of his education at Rugby in England. In 1940, he crossed the border to "do his bit" with the RCAF. He received his "wings" in June, 1941, and, shortly after, joined 412 Squadron. He flew several operational missions in his Spitfire fighter. Four days after Pearl Harbour, on 11 December 1941 Pilot Officer Magee, while flying through cloud during a convoy patrol, was killed in collision with another aircraft.[33]

In language reminiscent of Francis Thompson's "The Hound of Heaven," Magee expressed the exhilarating, boundless sense of spiritual freedom and awe on escaping the earth to soar high across the great dome that is the sky.

High Flight

Oh! I have slipped the surly bonds of earth
And danced the skies on laughter-silvered wings;
Sunward I've climbed, and joined the tumbling mirth
Of sun-split clouds — and done a hundred things
You have not dreamed of — wheeled and soared and swung
High in the sunlit silence. Hov'ring there
I've chased the shouting wind along, and flung
My eager craft through footless halls of air.

Up, up the long, delirious, burning blue
I've topped the wind-swept heights with easy grace
Where never lark, or even eagle flew —
And, while with silent lifting mind I've trod
The high untrespassed sanctity of space
Put out my hand and touched the face of God.

John Gillespie Magee

12
Flags and Colours

The flag, a piece of coloured cloth, is among the oldest of symbols, and at the same time one of the most up-to-date. Dipped in blood and lashed to a pole overhead, it cowed the vanquished in remote times of human conflict. Planted in the lunar dust, it proclaimed the simple courage and faith of men and one more instance of the mastery of his environment. Spanking on a stiff breeze, like a sail before the wind, it is a thing of aesthetic beauty. Draped against a wall, it can mean hope and succour to the suffering, or dread to the fearful.

It is hard to visualize a world without flags because they serve man so effectively. They symbolize his feelings, achievements and aspirations. They identify. They send messages or, as the sailor says, they make signals. They are so practical — a red flag to warn the motorist of road repairs, or to keep clear because ammunition or fuel is being embarked; or the yellow flag of quarantine indicating the presence of infectious disease; or the "Blue Peter" at the fore truck saying: "This ship is about to sail."

Flags convey abstract yet strongly felt ideas, often with emotional impact — perhaps the symbol of some political philosophy, or the sorrow of the meaning of the flag at half-mast, or the joy of seeing the queen's personal Canadian flag floating over Rideau Hall when Her Majesty is in residence there.

The most common use of a flag is to show nationality, to identify a people. It is said that the oldest national flag, unchanged in design, is the Dannebrog, the red flag with the white cross which has flown over Denmark since 1219.[1] In comparison, the Royal Union Flag as it is known in Canada today and which was approved by Parliament in 1964 "as a symbol of Canada's membership in the Commonwealth of Nations and of her allegiance to the Crown," dates in its earliest form from 1606.[2] The national flag of Canada, the Maple Leaf

Flag, was adopted by Parliament and proclaimed by Her Majesty the Queen on 15 February 1965.

Because the national flag symbolizes sovereignty, loyalty to the Crown, the laws and institutions of the nation, the authority of Parliament and the proud heritage of the people, it demands respect, and that respect, together with affection, is expressed in custom and tradition, for example colours and sunset.

At Canadian Forces bases and establishments, colours in this context means the hoisting of the national flag normally at 0800 hours. It is lowered at sunset. Proper marks of respect are paid by all persons in the vicinity. In most cases the hoisting and lowering is carried out by a designated non-commissioned officer, sometimes by a commissionaire. Regrettably, an elaborate ceremony is much more likely to be observed with respect to Canada's national flag at a headquarters like Colorado Springs than at Canadian operational bases, even to the parading of a guard and band. Several reasons are given for this: shortage of personnel; the fact that most people live off the base; and, perhaps, the tendency in modern times to down-grade patriotism.

In training establishments, the story is quite different. For example, at the Royal Military College, Kingston, the national flag is hoisted and lowered with impressive ceremony daily by a detachment of five cadets called "the fire picquet." Off to the side, the proceedings are observed by the cadet duty officer and the duty staff officer, a member of the senior staff. At sunset, a piper contributes to the solemnity of the occasion.[3] A similar daily routine is carried out at le Collège Militaire Royal de Saint-Jean, Quebec, and at Royal Roads, Esquimalt, British Columbia.

At Canadian Forces Base Chilliwack, British Columbia, a training base, colours and sunset are accompanied by the appropriate bugle calls and the playing of the national anthem, all controlled electronically from the guard house.[4]

In HMC ships, the national flag is known as the ship's ensign. This conforms with naval practice in French and United States warships where the country's flag is worn as the naval ensign, whereas in ships of the United Kingdom and the Soviet Union, ship's of war wear a distinctive naval ensign quite different from the national flag.

When HMC ships are in Canadian ports, they generally conform to colours and sunset as performed on land bases, that is, 0800 and sunset. When the alert is sounded on the bo's'n's call, all hands on the upper deck face aft and salute. The ship's ensign in HMC ships in commission is worn at all times, day and night, when under way. The wearing of the Canadian Forces ensign in Canadian ships of war is forbidden.

It is an impressive sight when there are many ships of the fleet in their home port, either at colours or sunset. All ships act in unison, governed by the "preparative" flag hoisted on the port signal tower ashore or in the senior officer's ship afloat. The signalman reminds the officer of the day that it is "five minutes to sunset, sir." When the preparative is sharply hauled down, the officer of the day repeats the time-honoured words: "Make it so!" Should the ship's boat be in the vicinity, the coxswain orders his engine cut, comes to attention in the stern sheets, faces the stern of his ship nearby, and salutes.

Because of the nature of life afloat, flags are used much more by sailors than by soldiers and airmen, and here the pennant plays an important part in the daily routine at sea. Like the ensign at the stern and the jack at the jack staff forward, the ship's pennant at the peak of the mast is part of a ship's "suit of colours."

The ship's pennant, sometimes called the commissioning pennant or masthead pennant, is the mark of a ship in commission and the symbol of the authority of the captain to command the ship. This symbolism is of great antiquity. Mr Henry Teonge, a chaplain in the Royal Navy, wrote in his journal at Malta on 22 February 1676:

> This day we saw a great deal of solemnity at the launching of a new brigantine of twenty-three oars, built on the shore very near the water. They hoisted three flags in her . . . . Then they came out and hoisted a pendant, to signify she was a man-of-war. . . . [5]

When HMS *America*, a frigate of 44 guns, was commissioned at Devonport in 1844 for service in the Pacific to watch over the infant settlement on Vancouver Island, a naval officer recorded: "The pennant hoisted, the first lieutenant and master remained to fit the ship for sea, . . . and, with the aid of flaming posters, to attract a ship's company."[6]

In HMC ships, the pennant is six feet long and only three inches wide at the hoist, tapering to a point at the fly. Though a new masthead pennant has been designed with three equal vertical panels, white-red-white, HMC ships continue to fly the ancient white streamer with the red St. George's Cross at the hoist. It is broken at the mainmast head at the time of commissioning and is flown continuously throughout the ship's commission.[7]

Closely associated with the ship's commissioning pennant is the paying-off pennant. It is traditionally flown when leaving a fleet or squadron and when entering home port for the last time prior to paying-off (not "de-commissioning"). This pennant and the ritual associated with it have long been dear to the sailor's heart, for they meant going home and at long last receiving his pay.

While a destroyer today may spend her whole life of say twenty-five years in a single commission, in earlier times a ship of war was usually paid off after say three years to be refitted or laid-up "in ordinary" in the dockyard of her home-port. HMS *Victory* of Trafalgar fame was launched in 1765 and is still in commission at Portsmouth today. In her life time, she has served many commissions.

Also in earlier times, members of the ship's company had most of their pay withheld until the end of the commission. So that in addition to the ship her-self being paid-off, the seamen were literally paid-off. The passage home was therefore a generally happy one. One of the ways the sailors celebrated was in the making of the paying-off pennant and hoisting it at the mainmast head. Custom ordained that in a normal commission, the length of the pennant equalled the length of the ship. But if, as often occurred, a commission had been extended, the pennant was increased in length proportionately.[8] Many a ship has come home with her paying-off pennant streaming well astern of the taffrail, the tail-end kept afloat by a skin bladder!

One of the most aesthetically attractive bits of bunting still used at sea today is the church pennant. It is divided into a red St. George's Cross on a white field at the hoist, and three horizontal stripes, red, white and blue, in the fly. Hoisted at the mainmast peak or at a yardarm halyard, it means that the ship's company is attending divine service or is at prayers. (This used to be a bit con-fusing to the landsman for, depending on where in the rigging the church pen-nant was hoisted, it could mean the recall of all boats or "I am working my anchors").

There is an interesting legend attached to the church pennant. It dates from the seventeenth century Dutch Wars, the sea battles of which usually took place in the North Sea and the English Channel. Before the engagement com-menced, it was customary for divine service to be conducted in the ships of both the Royal Navy and the Dutch fleet. So that such devotions would not be interrupted in that more chivalrous age, the ships of both fleets hoisted the church pennant, a combination of the British St. George's Cross and the Dutch tricolour. When the last pennant fluttered down, all hands went to action stations![9]

Divine service at sea illustrates how customs change. The church pennant may be used as an alter cloth or to drape a podium. During the Second World War the white ensign was often used for this purpose, covering a ready-use ammunition locker or some other convenient upper deck facility. But just as often, flag "negative" was used, simply because it was white and had five black-crosses on it. One sailor of the Second World War describing life in a destroyer on Atlantic patrol wrote: "Church is held on the Seamen's Mess

The HMCS *Huron*, Tribal class destroyer, first commissioned in 1943. She is seen here returning to Halifax in April, 1963, flying her paying-off pennant. The length of the pennant, representing a long time in commission, is fitted with bladders to keep afloat.

Deck. . . . The black and white negative flag is draped over the stove . . . . the Ship's Bible is placed on the flag-draped stove."[10]

However, by the 1950's, the old code of naval flag signals had been superseded for purposes of standardizing communications in combined fleets and the old familiar flag negative with the crosses had disappeared.

Before the advent of the Maple Leaf national flag in 1965, HMC ships flew as a jack the Canadian blue ensign. Today, the jack is a white flag with the Maple Leaf Flag forming the upper canton at the hoist, and a device in blue consisting of an anchor and eagle surmounted by a naval crown, in the fly. Normally the jack is flown only in harbour and always at the jackstaff in the bows of the ship. In 1975, authorization was given for parading the Naval Jack of the Canadian Forces on shore by units of maritime command.[11]

Jacks were first flown at the masthead but in a short time, judging by the numerous marine paintings of the period, it was shifted to the sprit topmast, a short stump mast fixed to the bowsprit at the bow. The jack has remained at the bow ever since. As long as ships were square-rigged, this was a handy arrangement for this important means of identifying a king's ship. But when fore-and-aft rig came into vogue, with foresails and jibs, the jack often fouled the rigging. As a result, it became the custom for the jack to be flown only in harbour. This is still the case today.[12]

The origin of the term jack is open to considerable conjecture. In British tradition, as in the Union Jack, the word is associated with the flag that gave visible evidence of the union of the crowns of England and Scotland. The sovereign at that time was King James VI of Scotland who became James I of England, and who, in signing state documents, sometimes used the French form *Jacques*. The story goes that this is the source of the term jack.

However, there is much evidence that jack, in the sense of identification, long pre-dates the early seventeenth century. In feudal times the mounted knights and soldiers on foot in the field wore an over-garment extending from the neck to the thighs called a surcoat or jacque (whence our word jacket). On this tunic was sewn a cross or other device to identify the wearer's allegiance to a liege lord or king in the same way as nationality would be shown today. These surcoats or jacks came to be known as the jacks of the various nations and were worn also by the sailors in the ships used to transport the soldiers. It was only one short step in the progression to see a sailor's surcoat or jack lashed to a pole and suspended out over the bow as a means of a ship showing her colours.[13]

From the time of the establishment of the Royal Canadian Navy in 1910 until the arrival of the Maple Leaf national flag in 1965, HMC ships wore the white ensign, and naval shore parties on the march carried the white ensign. It was a white flag with a red St. George's Cross overall, with the Union Flag in the upper canton at the hoist. It was identical to that worn by ships of the Royal Navy and other navies of the Commonwealth. This storied flag still exists in the Canadian Forces in the form of the queen's colour of the Royal Canadian Navy which is kept in a special display cabinet in the wardroom of Canadian Forces Base, Halifax. Another, identical in appearance, is held at Canadian Forces Base, Esquimalt.

The queen's colour of the naval service has never officially been laid up or retired, yet it cannot be recognized as the queen's colour of maritime command for it does not contain the Maple Leaf national flag. However, at time of writing, a new queen's colour in the form of a white ensign, and containing the Maple Leaf Flag, is being designed for the naval forces.

The sovereign's or first colour, usually called the queen's colour, of the navy, is of recent origin compared to that of the army. First designated "the king's colour" in regulations dated 1747 in the reign of George II,[14] the sovereign's colour as approved for British regiments pre-dates those of the Royal Navy and the Royal Air Force by nearly two centuries.

The king's colour of the Royal Navy was approved for the first time by George V in 1924,[15] and for the Royal Canadian Navy in 1925.[16]

Some idea of the financial stringencies under which the armed forces of the twenties struggled to stay alive may be gleaned from this first king's colour of the RCN.

Approved by the king in 1925, Commodore Walter Hose, director of the naval service, as much as he wanted the new colour for the navy, could not scrape up the necessary sixty pounds from his budget until 1927. And then, too, there were only two destroyers in commission, HMC ships *Patrician* and *Patriot*, one on each coast. A ship's company was essential for the presentation ceremony, for there were not enough seaman ratings ashore, and a ship in harbour just never seemed to coincide with a visit by the Governor-General. So George V's colour never was presented to the Royal Canadian Navy. Today, the one in Halifax is laid up in St. Mark's Church, the one at Esquimalt in the Church of St. Andrew, HMCS *Naden*, now Canadian Forces Base Esquimalt.

The presentation of the king's colour to the RCN had to await the first visit of the reigning sovereign to Canada. In a memorable ceremony just before the outbreak of war in 1939, George VI presented his colour to the navy at Beacon Hill Park, Victoria. Today, this colour is laid up in St Paul's Naval and Garrison Church, Esquimalt. Carried out on 24 May 1960, the site chosen for the laying-up seems most fitting, for St. Paul's has been closely associated with all the ships and sailors who have come and gone at Esquimalt for over a hundred years.

George VI's colour at Halifax, considered to have been presented at the same time as that of the Pacific Command, was laid up on Trafalgar Day, 21 October 1959 in the Church of St. Nicholas, HMCS *Stadacona*, now Canadian Forces Base Halifax.[17]

The present queen's colour of the Royal Canadian Navy was presented by Her Majesty the Queen at Halifax on 1 August 1959, and the one at Esquimalt was deemed to have been presented at the same time. During the course of her address to the sailors assembled, the queen said:

> This is a solemn moment in the history of the Navy. You are bidding farewell to one Colour and are about to pay honour to another . . . .
>
> I have no boubt that my Colour is in very good hands . . . . During the Second World War, and particularly during the Battle of the Atlantic, you most admirably fulfilled your responsibilities to the Crown, to your country, and to the free world.
>
> I now commend to your keeping this Colour. I know that you will guard it faithfully and the ideals for which it stands, not only in war but also during the peace, which we all hope so sincerely will ever continue. Remember always that, although it comes from me, it symbolizes not only loyalty to your Queen but also to your country and service. As long as these three loyalties are in your hearts, you will add lustre to the already great name of the Royal Canadian Navy.[18]

The Royal Canadian Air Force received its only sovereign's colour in 1950 together with the colour of the RCAF, the latter being comparable to a regimental colour. Both were consecrated and presented in the name of King George VI on Parliament Hill, Ottawa, on the king's birthday, 5 June 1950, by the Governor-General, Viscount Alexander of Tunis. The RCAF was the first of the Royal Air Forces to be granted, as a service, the privilege of carrying the king's colour. Those presented earlier were to particular components of the Royal Air Force.[19]

Besides being the only sovereign's colour the air force has ever had, it having been designated "queen's colour" in 1952 in spite of its bearing the royal cypher of the recently deceased King George VI, it is of unusual design for an air force sovereign's colour.

The Royal Air Force ensign of light blue with the Union Flag at the hoist and the red-white-blue roundel in the fly was authorized in 1920. The Royal Canadian Air Force inherited the same privilege for its establishment in 1924. When the Royal Air Force began to receive its series of king's colours in 1948,

The colours of the Royal Canadian Air Force and the colour guard are paraded before the Memorial Gates at RCAF Station Trenton, July, 1951. The gates, a gift of the people of the United Kingdom, Australia and New Zealand, were presented in honour of the RCAF's part in the wartime British Commonwealth Air Training Plan, in September, 1949. (Note that the queen's colour still bears the cypher of her father, King George VI. Note, also, the guards on the tips of the bayonets to protect the colours from damage in the wind, and that, in the air force, swords are no longer in use.)

the design was based on that of the ensign, that is, the Union Flag at the hoist, the royal cypher in the centre and the roundel in the fly, all on a field of light blue. But the Royal Canadian Air Force chose to have its king's colour designed in the army tradition, the Union Flag with the crown and royal cypher in the centre, thus adhering to the regulations first set down in 1747. The second colour of the RCAF is a light blue flag bearing the crown-and-eagle badge of the air force in the centre and a golden maple leaf in each corner.

These colours are still extant today after more than a quarter century. Each of the three stands of colours occupies an honoured place: one in the RCAF Officers' Mess, Gloucester Street, Ottawa; one in the Officers' Mess of Air Command, CFB Winnipeg; and the third in the Black Forest Officers' Mess, Canadian Forces Europe, at Lahr, Germany.

Unlike the air force and the navy, this situation did not arise in the army, organized as it was, and is, on a regimental basis, each unit having its own customs, traditions and colours. In 1968, Her Majesty approved the issue of new colours "to all Canadian infantry units and guards regiments which are entitled to carry them."[20] This process has been going on apace ever since, with the queen's colour being based on the design of the Maple Leaf Flag, replacing the Union Flag design traditionally employed for infantry units other than guards regiments. This reflects the custom established for infantry line regiments in the mid-eighteenth century whereby the sovereign's colour is based on the design of the national flag.[21]

The queen's, or first, colour symbolizes the unit's loyalty to the crown. Authorization to possess a queen's colour can be granted only by the reigning sovereign and may be presented to a unit, command or Service only by the sovereign or her representative. The term itself first appeared in the British army in "Regulation for the Uniform Clothing of the Marching Regiments of Foot, their Colours, Drums, Bells of Arms, and Camp Colours, 1747," which stated: "The Kings or First Colour of every Regiment or Battalion is to be the Great Union."[22]

The second, or unit, or regimental colour is probably the most cherished possession of a fighting force. This is because it embodies a whole spectrum of ideas, beliefs and emotions which together may be characterized as "the spirit of the regiment." The regimental colour symbolizes in a very visible way the pride a man feels in serving in a unit whose reason for being is one of worth, the proud heritage of those of the regiment who have gone before, and the record of achievement of the regiment, perhaps enshrined on the colour in the battle honours displayed within its folds. There is a mystique about the colours which constantly reminds every officer and man how dependant he is on his comrades-in-arms and makes it extremely difficult for him in battle to fail in his duty, and as often as not spurs him on to undreamed of exploits of valour.

Something of what the regimental colour means to the soldier may be gathered from an account given in the memoirs of James II, telling of the assault on Etampes in 1652 in the time of Louis XIV of France:

> ... Turenne's own regiment went on in the face of both armies ... ; and without any manner of diversion, or so much as one cannon-shot to favour them, they came up to the attack. Notwithstanding the continual fire that was made at them, both from the work and the wall of the town, they marched on without firing one single shot; the captains themselves taking the Colours in their hands, and marching with them at the head of their soldiers till they were advanced to the work ... ; and then at one instant poured in their shot and came up to push of pike with so much gallantry and resolution, that they beat out the enemy, and lodged themselves upon the work.... It was universally confessed by all who were then present, that they never saw so daring an action. Marshal Turenne himself, and the most experienced officers of the army, were all of opinion, that it had been impossible for them to have done so much, if their Colours had not been always in their view.[23]

In the journal of a seventeen-year-old ensign of the 34th Regiment of Foot a glimpse is seen of what the colours meant when Wellington met Napoleon's army in Portugal in 1811:

> Our gallant and worthy general, riding along our front, said, 'Are you all ready?' 'Yes, sir.' 'Uncase your colours and prime and load.' ... As I took the King's colour in charge being senior ensign, the major said, 'Now my lads, hold those standards fast, and let them fly out when you see the enemy.'[24]

The forerunners of colours may be traced to the distant past when primitive men identified their leaders and forces in war with some form of totem on a staff or pole. The same purpose is to be seen in the elaborate eagle standards of the Roman legions. In the Middle Ages, the leaders in war were generally noblemen and, in their garb of mail or armour, identified themselves with banners and pennons bearing marks or devices from their coats of arms.

By the early seventeenth century the traditionally basic units, the companies, each with its own colour, were being gathered into regiments often called by the name of the colonels who raised them. Each regimental officer irrespective of rank also commanded his own company in the regiment and the company colours bore devices derived from the colonel's arms. Individual company colours still remain in guards regiments today. It was not until the regulations of 1747 that a colonel of the British army was forbidden to place "his Arms, Crest, Device or Livery on any part of the Appointments of the Regiment under his command."[25]

The colours, when carried in battle, served two practical purposes — identification and place of concentration. A military writer nearly two centuries ago explained the reason for carrying the colours in the field:

> Flags, banners, pencils, and other ensignes, are of great antiquity; their use was, in large armies, to distinguish the troops of different nations or provinces; and in smaller bodies, those of different leaders, and even particular persons, in order that the prince and commander in chief might be able to discriminate the behaviour of each corps or person; they also served to direct broken battalions or squadrons where to rally, and pointed out the station of the king, or those of the different great officers, each of whom had his particular guidon or banner, by which means they might be found at all times, and the commander in chief enabled from time to time to send such orders as he might find necessary to his different generals.[26]

With the advent of more advanced weaponry, the long-established custom of carrying regimental colours in action, ceased. In the Zulu War in 1879, casualties in defence of the colours of the 24th Foot (the South Wales Borderers) brought public condemnation of the practice. Two years later, a similar situation arose for the 58th Foot (the Northamptonshire Regiment) in the engagement at Laing's Nek, South Africa. This was the last time in the forces of the British Empire that regimental colours were carried in action, with one exception — Princess Patricia's Canadian Light Infantry.[27]

When the clouds of war rolled over Europe in the summer of 1914, Canada as a loyal member of the Empire responded to the threat. One response was the raising of a new regiment, Princess Patricia's Canadian Light Infantry, named for the popular daughter of the Governor-General, the Duke of Connaught. Princess Patricia, appointed honorary colonel of the regiment, personally fashioned a colour of red and royal blue, fringed in gold, technically a camp colour, but one which soon took on the full character of a regimental colour. There is probably no more famous colour in the Canadian Forces.

In August, 1914, before the regiment proceeded overseas, Princess Patricia presented her colour to her regiment at Ottawa, and the commanding officer promised that it would be guarded "with their lives and that it would always remain with the regiment."[28] That promise was most faithfully kept.

The colour, now affectionately known as the "Ric-A-Dam-Doo," was carried to France in December, 1914, and always flew over regimental head-

The roundel marking of aircraft of the period of the Great War, 1914-1918, as displayed on a restored Sopwith Pup here landing at CFB Ottawa (Rockcliffe), 1975.

The modern roundel identifying Canadian military aircraft, in this case a CF-101 Voodoo of 425 (Alouette) Squadron, 1973.

The pipe band from CFB Ottawa, wearing the tartan of the Royal Canadian Air Force, being inspected by His Royal Highness the Prince Philip, Duke of Edinburgh, on the occasion of presentation of squadron standards at Baden, Germany, May, 1973. The national flags are those of nations of the North Atlantic Treaty Organization.

The cadet choir preparing for the annual Christmas carol service, a long tradition at the military college, Royal Roads, Victoria.

The drumhead consecration of the colours of the Canadian Airborne Regiment, Edmonton, June, 1973. The presentation was made by the Honourable Grant MacEwan, lieutenant governor of Alberta.

The consecration of the standards prior to their presentation to 421, 439 and 441 Squadrons by His Royal Highness the Prince Philip, Duke of Edinburgh, Baden, Germany, May, 1973.

The presentation of new colours to regiments of the Canadian army by Her Majesty the Queen on Parliament Hill, Ottawa, during the royal visit in the year of the centenary of Confederation, 1967.

The queen's colour of the Royal Canadian Navy with armed escort, Halifax, 1959. The ratings are of the gunnery branch and the chief petty officer is armed with a cutlass.

His Royal Highness the Prince Philip, Duke of Edinburgh, presenting new colours to the Royal Canadian Regiment, Parliament Hill, Ottawa, 1973.

The Canadian Forces ensign.

Maritime Command

QUEEN'S COLOUR

National Defence Headquarters
January, 1977 Director of Ceremonial

The queen's colour of Maritime Command.

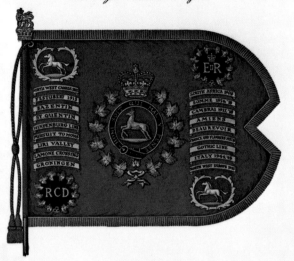

The guidon of the Royal Canadian Dragoons.

12e Régiment Blindé du Canada

GUIDON DU RÉGIMENT

Canadian Forces Headquarters
January 1969

Director of Ceremonial

The guidon of the 12e Régiment Blindé du Canada.

Aproved

Elizabeth R

Royal 22e Régiment

DRAPEAU DE LA REINE

The queen's colour of the 1st Battalion, Royal 22e Régiment.

The Governor General's Foot Guards

REGIMENTAL COLOUR

Canadian Forces Headquarters
June, 1970

Director of Ceremonial

The regimental colour of the Governor-General's Foot Guards.

The regimental colour of the Black Watch (Royal Highland Regiment) of Canada.

The Colour of Air Command

National Defence Headquarters
January, 1977

Director of Ceremonial

The colour of Air Command.

The squadron standard of 400 Squadron.

quarters. Early in May, 1915, those headquarters were in front-line trenches and it was in that exposed position that the colour was torn by shrapnel and small arms fire. But the inspiration of the Princess's colour to the troops that day "enabled them to hold out against terrible odds with no support on either flank."[29]

In January, 1919, at Mons, Belgium, this colour, which had survived five years of trench warfare, and on the march in France was always carried by an officer with an appropriate escort and with proper marks of respect paid by all troops met, was consecrated as the regimental colour. A month later, at Bramshott, England, Princess Patricia, now colonel-in-chief, presented a laurel wreath of silver gilt to be borne on the regimental colour. It bears this inscription:

> To The P.P.C.L.I.
> From the Colonel-in-Chief
> PATRICIA
> In Recognition Of Their Heroic
> Services in the Great War 1914-1918

The laurel had been won at a frightful cost; only forty-four of the 1,098 originals were on parade that day.[30]

> The Ric-A-Dam-Doo, pray what is that?
> 'Twas made at home by Princess Pat.
> It's Red and Gold and Royal Blue;
> That's what we call the Ric-A-Dam-Doo.[31]

It was the introduction of standing armies in the seventeenth century and their basic organization into regiments which led to the widespread use of regimental colours. In the British army it was the regulation of 1747 which set the pattern of both design and usage as they stand today.

There were three distinct kinds of regimental banners — standards, guidons and colours. Standards are authorized for household cavalry and dragoon guards only. The Governor-General's Horse Guards, of Toronto, which enjoys the status of dragoon guards, is the only regiment in the Canadian Forces today that carries a standard. The standard was a very large flag flown by armies in medieval times. It was not intended to be carried in battle but rather to stand or be planted before the commander's tent, hence the name, standard.

The guidon, derived from the old French word *guydhomme*, the flag borne by the leader of horse, was authorized for regiments of cavalry such as dragoons, and is swallow-tailed. A dictionary of 1780 defined the word as, "a French term for him that carries the standard in the guards, or 'Gens d'Armes', and signifies likewise the standard itself. It is now become common in England. He is the same in the horseguards, that the ensign is in the foot."[32] Today guidons are used by armoured regiments, the successors of cavalry. Like the horse guards' standard, the guidon is made of crimson silk damask.

The regimental colour, the one specifically mentioned in the regulation of 1747, and which together with the sovereign's colour forms a stand of colours, was for foot guards and infantry line regiments. In the eighteenth century, it was known simply as the second colour. Although it soon took on the sobriquet regimental colour, this expression was not officially recognized until 1844.[33]

A point of interest here is that for infantry line regiments, the old tradition of George II that the sovereign's colour should be based on the design of the national flag (in the regulation of 1747, this meant the Grand Union Flag, commonly called the Union Jack), while the regimental colour should reflect the hues of uniform facings, has been maintained. But also in the tradition of the British army, it is the reverse for regiments of foot guards. In the latter case, the queen's colour is crimson, and regimental colour is similar to the Maple Leaf Flag, and the battle honours are displayed on both.[34]

Flying squadrons of the Canadian Forces, after completion of twenty-five years service, or having earned the sovereign's appreciation for especially outstanding operations, are eligible to carry a squadron standard. An air force standard is a rectangular flag of light blue silk and bears the battle honours won by the squadron. Its institution came about in this way. During the Second World War, in 1943, the Royal Air Force marked its twenty-fifth anniversary. To commemorate the milestone, King George VI inaugurated the award of squadron standards, and thirty squadrons of the Royal Air Force were honoured in that wartime anniversary year.[35]

In 1958, the award of flying squadron standards was extended to the Royal Canadian Air Force. The first unit to qualify was the 400 Squadron and the presentation took place at RCAF Station Downsview by the lieutenant-governor of Ontario, the Honourable J.K. MacKay on 10 June 1961.[36]

In a general way this is the story of the development of queen's and second colours in the Canadian Forces, following as they do in the wake of the much longer established customs of the British Services. However, as is to be expected, many diversions and exceptions to established practice have occurred, and some of these anomalies are of long standing.

The Royal Regiment of Canadian Artillery carries no colours, in the usual

The colours of 2nd Battalion, Princess Patricia's Canadian Light Infantry, being marched on board a Boeing CC 137 transport aircraft at Winnipeg as the battalion proceeded on peacekeeping duty in Cyprus, 5 October 1972. Note the silver-gilt laurel wreath honouring the regiment for its gallantry in the Great War, 1914-1918, presented by Her Royal Highness the Princess Patricia, colonel-in-chief, in 1919. The ribbon is that of the United States presidential Distinguished Unit Citation, awarded for the Patricia's fight at Kapyong, Korea, in April, 1951.

sense of the word. The guns are its colours. On ceremonial occasions the guns are accorded the same marks of respect as the standards, guidons and colours of other units. The reason behind this long-held tradition is related to the gunners' motto, *ubique*, meaning everywhere, that is, that the artillery has been present in just about every campaign.

The custom of the guns being the colours dates from the eighteenth century and the Royal Artillery's practice of that time of designating the largest gun of an artillery train as the flag gun, that is, the piece accorded the honour of bearing the equivalent of the sovereign's colour. This evolved into the guns themselves being regarded as the colours of the artillery.[37]

Regiments of infantry with a rifle tradition, that is, the rifle regiments, also have no queen's nor regimental colours, but for a different reason emanating from their historic role in the field. The rifles, who wore green uniform clothing with black buttons and black cross belts, did so to keep as low a profile as possible, the better to blend into the environment. As sharpshooters and skirmishers out ahead of the infantry of the line, it was their task to take advantage of every vestige of cover in rapid advance. Hence, no colours were carried in battle to advertise their presence. Today, the rifles still do not carry colours; battle honours won are displayed on the drums,[38] and, in some units, on the cap badges.

Occasionally, a unit finds itself contravening the established order of colours as in the case of the Algonquin Regiment of Northern Ontario. This unit, though an infantry regiment, is the proud possessor of a guidon presented about the same time in 1965 as the regiment was converted from the armoured role.[39]

Although units take great pains to ensure the safety of their colours, accidents sometimes do occur. On 6 December 1917 when the ammunition ship *Mont Blanc* collided with another ship in Halifax harbour, there was great loss of life in the city. A side-light of the tragic explosion was the damage sustained by Wellington Barracks above HMC dockyard where the colours of the Royal Canadian Regiment were buried in the rubble. They were recovered.[40]

In the church of St. Mary Magdalene, Picton, Ontario, a sovereign's colour is laid up together with the bare pike which once held a second colour. In 1960, the regimental colour of the Hastings and Prince Edward Regiment was stolen from its case in the officers' mess. It has not been recovered.[41]

On 18 April 1975 at Fort York Armoury, Toronto, a stand of colours was handed over to the Queen's York Rangers by the lieutenant-governor of Ontario, the Honourable Pauline M. McGibbon. Both colours have a badge with a shield for the main device bearing the words "QUEEN'S RANGERS

1ˢᵗ AMERⁿˢ" These are the oldest colours still extant in Canada, which belonged to a forbear of a regiment active in the Canadian Forces today, the Queen's York Rangers (1st American Regiment).

These are the colours that were carried by the Queen's Rangers (1st Americans) commanded by Lieutenant-Colonel John Graves Simcoe in the War of the American Revolution (1775-1783). Known as the Simcoe Colours, they may have been used by a later unit of the Queen's Rangers after the war when Simcoe became the first lieutenant-governor of Upper Canada. These ancient colours, now carefully restored, spent the better part of two centuries in the Simcoe family home, Wolford Lodge, in Devon, England, where they were acquired by interested Canadians some fifty years ago.[42]

During the life of a colour, there are three basic ceremonies — consecration, presentation, and laying-up or depositing of the colours. Because of the meaning of the colours, these ceremonial occasions are always carried out with dignity and reverence, and with colourful military precision and pageantry, usually out of doors.

On Dominion Day, 1972, the Governor-General's Foot Guards were presented with new colours on Parliament Hill by the Governor-General, the Right Honourable Roland Michener, who was also honorary colonel of the regiment. The regiment was drawn up on the lawn beneath the Peace Tower. Detachments of the Canadian Grenadier Guards of Montreal, and the Cameron Highlanders of Ottawa, were also on parade. After the royal salute and His Excellency's inspection of his foot guards, the old colours were trooped and then marched off the parade ground to the tune of "Auld Lang Syne." This was followed by divine service in which the new colours were consecrated. The following order of service is typical of the ceremony of consecration of the colours in the Canadian Forces.[43]

The Service of Consecration of Colours

Commanding Officer: Reverend Sir, on behalf of the Governor-General's Foot Guards, we ask you to bid God's blessing on these Colours.

Chaplain: We are ready to do so.

Chaplain: Forasmuch as men at all times have made for themselves signs and emblems of their allegiance to their rulers, and of their duty to uphold those laws and institutions which God's providence has called them to obey, we, following this ancient and pious custom, are met together before God to ask His blessing on these Colours, which are to represent to us our duty towards our Sovereign and our Country. Let us, therefore, pray Almighty God of His mercy to grant that they may never be unfurled, save in the cause of justice and righteousness, and that He may make them to be to those who follow them, a sign of His presence in all dangers and distresses, and so increase their faith and hope in Him, who is King of Kings and Lord of Lords.

Let us pray

Our help is in the Name of the Lord.

Response: Who hath made Heaven and Earth.

Chaplain: The Lord be with you.

Response: And with Thy spirit.

Chaplain: Almighty and everlasting God, we are taught by Thy Holy Word that the hearts of Kings are in Thy rule and governance, and that Thou dost dispose and turn them as it seemeth best to Thy Godly wisdom, we humbly beseech Thee so to dispose and govern the heart of Elizabeth, Thy Servant, Our Queen and Governor, that in all her thoughts, words and works, she may ever seek Thy honour and glory, and study to preserve Thy people committed to her charge in wealth, peace and Godliness. Grant this, O merciful Father, for Thy Son's sake, Jesus Christ our Lord. Amen

O Lord our God, who from Thy throne beholdest all the Kingdoms of the earth, have regard unto our land, that it may continue a place and a people who serve Thee to the end of time. Guide the governments of our great Commonwealth and Empire, and grant that all who live beneath our flag may be so mindful of that threefold cross, that they may work for the good of others, according to the example of Him who died in the service of men, Thy Son, our Saviour, Jesus Christ. Amen

Remember O Lord what Thou has wrought in us, and not what we deserve, and as Thou has called us to Thy service, make us worthy of our calling through Jesus Christ our Lord. Amen

Then shall the Commanding Officer lead the Regiment in an Act of Dedication.

Commanding Officer: To the Service of God and the hallowing of His Holy Name.

Response: We dedicate ourselves afresh.

Commanding Officer: To the maintenance of honour and the sanctity of man's plighted word

Response: We dedicate ourselves afresh.

Commanding Officer: To the protection of all those who pass to and fro on their lawful occasions

Response: We dedicate ourselves afresh.

Commanding Officer: To the preservation of order and good government

Response: We dedicate ourselves afresh.

Commanding Officer: To the hallowed memory of our comrades, whose courage and endurance and undying lustre to our emblems

Response: We dedicate our Colours.

Commanding Officer: In continual remembrance of our solemn oath and in token of our resolve faithfully and truly to keep it to the end

Response: We dedicate our Colours.

The Act of Consecration.
Chaplain: (Laying his hands on the Colours): In the Name of the Father and of the Son and of the Holy Spirit, we do consecrate and set apart these Colours, that they may be a sign of our duty towards our Queen and our Country in the sight of God. Amen
Let us Pray

All: Our Father who art in Heaven, Hallowed be Thy Name, Thy Kingdom come, Thy will be done, on earth as it is in Heaven. Give us this day our daily bread. And forgive us our trespasses, as we forgive them that trepass against us. And lead us not into temptation. But deliver us from evil, for Thine is the Kingdom, the power and the glory, forever and ever. Amen.

Chaplain: O Lord, who rulest over all things, accept we beseech Thee our service this day. Bless what we have blessed in Thy Name. Let Thy gracious favour rest upon those who shall follow the Colours now about to be committed to their trust.
Give them courage and may their courage ever rest on their sure confidence in Thee. May they show self-control in the hour of success, patience in the time of adversity; and may their honour lie in seeking the honour and glory of Thy great Name.
Guide the counsels of those who shall lead them, and sustain them by Thy help in time of need. Grant they may all so faithfully serve Thee in this life, that they fail not finally to obtain an entrance into Thy heavenly Kingdom through the merits of Thy Blessed Son, Jesus Christ, our Lord. Amen

The Blessing
May God who has called you to this service enable you to fulfil it; may the Father make you strong and tranquil in the knowledge of His love; may the Lord Christ bestow upon you the courage of His gentleness and the steadfastness of His brave endurance; may the Holy Spirit grant you that the self-control which comes from the gift of His wisdom, and may the Blessing of God, the Father, the Son and the Holy Spirit, be upon you now and always. Amen

Following the actual presentation, the personage making the presentation (normally the sovereign or her representative), customarily addresses the assembled troops. The thoughts expressed usually take the form of a charge to the unit and it is here that the recruit begins to understand the true meaning of the colours.

On 21 October 1953 the Royal Newfoundland Regiment received new colours from the hands of their honorary colonel and lieutenant-governor of the province, Sir Leonard Outerbridge. These were the first colours to be presented to a Canadian regiment in the reign of Queen Elizabeth II. Sir Leonard's address ended with this admonishment: "Guard them well and carry them proudly as the symbols of the great traditions and honours which have been won by those who have gone before you."[44]

A century earlier, on 12 July 1849, a ceremony took place at Winchester Barracks, England, which shows the timelessness of the presentation of the colours. The regiment being honoured, the Royal Welch Fusiliers, had just returned from more than a decade of service in British North America, having been stationed at places as far apart as Halifax and Annapolis, Quebec and Montreal, and Kingston and London in Canada West. The presentation of new colours was made by Queen Victoria's consort, Prince Albert. The drill of that day sounds very much as it does today:

> The regiment, being drawn up in line with the old colours in the centre, received His Royal Highness with the usual honours, the flank companies were then brought forward so as to form three sides of a square, to the centre of which the new colours were brought under escort and piled on an altar of drums.[45]

After the consecration service conducted by the chaplain-general, Prince Albert proceeded to give his charge to the regiment in the language of his day:

> Soldiers of the Royal Welch Fusiliers! — The ceremony which we are performing this day is a most important and to every soldier a most sacred one; it is the transmission to your care and keeping of the colours which are henceforth to be borne before you, which will be the symbol of your honour and your rallying points in all moments of danger.
>
> Receive these colours — one emphatically called 'The Queens,' let it be a pledge of your loyalty to your Sovereign and of obedience to the laws of your country; the other — more especially the 'Regimental' one — let that be a pledge of your determination to maintain the honour of your regiment. In looking at the one you will think of your Sovereign; in looking at the other you will think of those who have fought, bled, and conquered before you![46]

It is a symbol of the continuity in the affairs of men that more than a century later, the prince consort's great-great-granddaughter, Queen Elizabeth II, would be presiding over a similar presentation. It was a happy coincidence, too, that the regiment she honoured on the Plains of Abraham 23 June 1959 is the Canadian regiment allied to the Royal Welch Fusiliers, the Royal 22e Régiment.

In a very moving ceremony Her Majesty, as colonel-in-chief, spoke to her French-speaking regiment in a way that is still remembered with affection by the "Van Doos" on parade that day. These were her words:

Commanding Officers, Officers, Non-Commissioned Officers and Privates:

I am pleased to be in Quebec City with my French Canadian regiment; I am proud of the regiment and take pleasure in presenting it with new colours.

I am aware of your history which dates back to the beginning of the First World War. French Canadians decided at that time to form a regiment recalling their origins. The regimental insignia bears the motto *Je me souviens* (I remember). It is a moving tribute to the country of your forebears.

On the colours that I have just presented to you are inscribed the names of French towns in whose liberation you participated. What emotion you must have felt in liberating people of your own blood, and what joy they must have felt in welcoming the descendants of the French men and women who three centuries before had set sail for Canada.

You have had a short but glorious history. During the two world wars and the operations in Korea the regiment forged a noble tradition of honour, courage and sacrifice.

I have been able to see today that in peacetime you maintain the same laudable tradition of discipline and dress, for which I warmly congratulate you.

I know that my father, King George VI, had the highest regard for his French Canadian regiment. He clearly proved this by becoming its colonel-in-chief in 1938, and I took pleasure in succeeding him in this position.

I thank you with all my heart for the faithful dedication that you have shown me in the past and on which I know I can always rely.

The alliance that exists between you and the Royal Welsh Fusiliers, another brave regiment of which I am colonel-in-chief, gives me great joy.

I entrust these new colours to you with complete confidence. Your past makes me certain that you will defend them as your predecessors defended the old colours — fearlessly and faultlessly.[47]

Colours are the embodiment, the visual symbol, of loyalty to the crown, to the nation, and to the unit in which one serves. But, in spite of the aura of veneration and mystique which surrounds the colours, they are at the same time material things and their use does come to an end. In earlier times, they were subject to capture by the enemy as in the case of the defending forces at Louisbourg, some of whose surrendered colours are to be seen in St. Paul's Cathedral in London to this day. Since colours are no longer carried in battle, and barring loss by fire or theft, they are eventually disposed of by laying-up or by depositing them in some safe place, perhaps a church. Whatever the case, colours go into retirement always with great respect and appropriate ceremony.

Closely related to the traditional laying-up and depositing of the colours is the regimental church. From coast to coast in Canada, there have grown up over the years very close bonds between individual units and particular congregations.

After the Great War of 1914-1918, the colours of the old 79th Cameron Highlanders of Canada were marched off to the tune, "The March of the Cameron Men," and laid up in First Presbyterian Church, Winnipeg. This is the spiritual home of Winnipeg's Queen's Own Cameron Highlanders of Canada where "the people" and the regiment share the beauty and the meaning of the Cameron Memorial Chapel and the Cameron stained glass memorial window.[48]

The laying-up ceremony occurs when a colour becomes no longer serviceable and is to be replaced by a new colour. Once a colour has been laidup, it is not brought back into service again.

On the other hand, the ceremony of depositing a colour takes place when a unit is disbanded, or made dormant, or transferred to the supplementary order of battle. Such colours remain the property of the crown and may be recovered should the unit be reconstituted in its former status.[49] A good illustration of the two procedures is the case of the Regiment of Canadian Guards who had one stand of colours laid up, and another deposited, in the span of a few short years.

Formation of this regular force regiment was authorized in 1953. The colours of the 1st Battalion were presented in 1957 by the Governor-General, the Right Honourable Vincent Massey, those of the 2nd Battalion in 1960 by Mr. Massey's successor, General the Right Honourable Georges P. Vanier.

In the course of a few years the colours, fashioned of fine silk, needed replacement, largely owing to being paraded daily by the public duties detachment of the regiment while performing the celebrated ceremony, the changing of the guard, on Parliament Hill, Ottawa. The Regiment of Canadian Guards

The colours of the 1st and 2nd Battalions, Black Watch (Royal Highland Regiment) of Canada, being paraded for the last time prior to the regiment reverting to reserve status, CFB Gagetown, June, 1970.

carried out this duty each summer for eleven years commencing in 1959. On 5 July 1967 on Parliament Hill, as part of the celebration of Canada's centenary of confederation, Her Majesty the Queen, colonel-in-chief of the regiment, presented new colours to both guards' battalions in a joint ceremony in which guidons and colours were also presented to four other units — the Ontario Regiment, the Sherbrooke Hussars, the 1st Hussars, and the Cameron Highlanders of Ottawa.

In due course, the old, worn colours of the guards were laid-up in impressive ceremonies. In August, 1969 they were marched to their respective sanctuaries, the colours of the 1st Battalion on August 31 to Christ Church Cathedral and those of the 2nd Battalion, a week earlier, to Notre Dame Basilica, both in Ottawa. On both occasions the ancient ritual of gaining entry to a sacred sanctuary was exercised — the troops already inside the church, the colour party approached the door and the parade adjutant with drawn sword used the hilt to strike the door the traditional three times. The clergy on the inside answered the summons and bid the colour party enter, the armed escort leaving their bearskins on their heads to leave their weapon hands free to defend the colours in the ancient manner.[50] From the chancel steps, the colours were received by the clergy and placed on the altar. The old colours of the Regiment of Canadian Guards were now laid-up.[51] But within the year, the new colours too, would be retired, this time by being deposited, rather than laid-up.

In an army reorganization of 1970, the Canadian Guards were removed from the regular force. On the anniversary of the invasion of Normandy, 6 June 1970, to the tune of "Soldiers of the Queen," the guards marched to Parliament Hill to troop their colour for the last time. After hearing a message from their colonel-in-chief, the queen, they marched off to Rideau Hall on Sussex Drive in Ottawa where the wife of the Governor-General, Mrs. Roland Michener, had personally selected the place in Government House where the colours of the regiment were to repose, the foyer. The ceremony and divine service now over, the colours of the Regiment of Canadian Guards are said to be deposited, rather than laid-up, in the hope they will one day see service again.[52]

Another occasion when colours are deposited is when they are temporarily lodged for safekeeping during the time a unit is away on active service. One sunny day in March, 1940, large crowds, sensing an historic occasion in the life of their city, gathered outside Mewata Armouries, Calgary, to see the colours of the Calgary Highlanders emerge from the barracks to be escorted to a church sanctuary "for the duration." Once formed up, the battalion swung along Seventh Avenue with fixed bayonets guarding the colours. A capacity

An officer of the 2nd Battalion, the Regiment of Canadian Guards, performing the ancient ceremony of striking the door of the sanctuary with the hilt of his sword requesting admittance to lay up the old colours of the regiment, Notre Dame Basilica, Ottawa, August, 1969.

congregation saw the regiment deposit its colours in the Anglican Cathedral of the Redeemer. In handing over the colours to the church authorities, the words of the commanding officer, followed by the placing of the colours on the altar, the "present arms" and the playing of "God Save the King," as recorded by the regimental historian, somehow communicated the significance of that impressive ceremony to all ranks — "These consecrated Colours, formerly carried in service of King and Empire, I now deliver into your hands for safe custody within these walls for the duration of the war."[53]

There is little doubt, however, that what is best known about the colours is that most stirring of ceremonies, trooping the colour. From very early times, the colours or standards, or their more primitive equivalents, led armies into battle and were the rallying points in time of danger. It was essential that the soldier know what the colour looked like so that he would know his duty almost instinctively. He soon learned to look upon and treat the colour with the highest respect. To do so, the soldier had to see his colour at close range, and that is what trooping the colour is all about. It is the ceremonial parading of the colour with armed escort slowly up and down before the regiment drawn up for the purpose. Every soldier of the regiment, or of the company before there were regiments, took a good look at the colour so that he would recognize it in the din and heat of battle and so know his place and rallying point.[54]

Trooping the colour can be traced to the sixteenth century and a simple routine known as lodging the colour. Lodging in this sense is still used today. Just as the queen's and regimental colours are kept today (sometimes cased in a leather container, sometimes on display behind glass) in the officers' mess, so in earlier times the colours were lodged for safekeeping in the ensign's quarters or lodging at the end of the day's parade or, during a campaign, at the end of the day's fighting. With the colours under armed escort, this rather informal ceremony was carried out before the troops with dignity and respect. The same was true when the colours were "sent for" the next day. Simple as the ceremony of lodging the colour was, it evolved into a much more elaborate ritual until, in 1755, it became by British army regulation part of the regular guard mounting drill.[55] The term trooping gradually replaced lodging and is derived from "the troop," a beat of the drum ordering the troops "to repair to the place of rendezvous, or to their colours."[56]

In the ceremony of trooping the colour, only one colour is carried, except at the presentation of new colours where it is customary to troop the old sovereign's and regimental colours together before they are marched off the parade ground. The queen's colour is trooped only when a guard is mounted for Her

Majesty, members of the royal family, the Governor-General, or a lieutenant-governor, or in a ceremonial parade in honour of the queen's birthday.

The trooping of the second or regimental colour is carried out on a great variety of occasions in Canada today. For example, on 6 June 1970, at CFB Gagetown, two battalions of the Black Watch (Royal Highland Regiment) of Canada, trooped their colours to mark their departure from the regular order of battle. On several occasions the 48th Highlanders of Canada have performed the ceremony at the Canadian National Exhibition Stadium and Maple Leaf Gardens in Toronto for capacity audiences, the proceeds being donated to worthy charitable organizations.[57] The guidon of the British Columbia Dragoons, presented in 1967 by Her Royal Highness, Princess Alexandra of Kent, is trooped annually in one of three cities of the Okanagan Valley, Vernon, Kelowna and Penticton.[58]

Finally, to return to the meaning of the colours, this is brought home in a very special way to the officers and men of one militia regiment. Every year, in the spring, the Royal Montreal Regiment reconsecrates its colours in the regimental church, St. Matthias, Westmount, "to the memory of all our war dead."[59]

Appendix
Calendar of Anniversaries
Observed by the Canadian Armed Forces

January   Each year since 1970, in January, the Royal Military College, Kingston, and the United States Air Force Academy, Colorado Springs, compete in a two-game hockey series. In the odd-numbered years, the USAFA team visits Kingston; in the even, the reverse.

January 1   Traditionally, New Year's Day is celebrated widely throughout the Canadian Forces. Many units enjoy activities, the nature of which are peculiar to a particular base, station or unit, and these are mentioned elsewhere in this book. But most consist of the warm geniality of inter-mess visiting and levees. (See page 94)

January 16   On 16 January 1863, the forbear of the Princess of Wales Own Regiment, the 14th battalion, Volunteer Militia Rifles, Canada, was formed. The regiment observes the day annually with a ceremonial parade at Montreal Street Armoury, Kingston.

January 25   Burns Night. The birth of Robert Burns, 25 January 1759. The Pipes and Drums of the Canadian Scottish Regiment (Princess Mary's) hold their annual Burns Night Dinner on the Saturday nearest January 25 in traditional Scottish fashion.

January 25   The Black Watch (Royal Highland Regiment) of Canada celebrates Burns Night at a mess dinner in the sergeant's mess.

February   Annually, usually in February, the CFB Petawawa Military Engineers' Pigspiel is held on the base and is open to all military engineers and their civilian colleagues throughout the Canadian Forces. This curling bonspiel culminates in a grand banquet.

February   Each year, in the first week of February, the officers of the Canadian Scottish Regiment (Princess Mary's), at Victoria, entertain their ladies at dinner in the mess.

February 1   The Queen's Own Cameron Highlanders of Canada dates from 1 February 1910 when the 79th Highlanders of Canada was authorized. This anniversary is observed by the regiment on the first Sunday of February with a church parade to the regimental church, First Presbyterian Church, Winnipeg.

February 15   A joint mess dinner is held in Côte des Neiges Armoury by the Royal Canadian Hussars and 2nd Field Regiment, Royal Canadian Artillery, Montreal.

February 16   On this day, the King's Own Calgary Regiment commemorates the mobilization of the regiment, 16 February 1941, with an informal dinner dance. It is called the Mobilization Dinner.

February 27   Paardeberg Day. The Royal Canadian Regiment observes this day to commemorate the surrender of Boer forces to the regiment at Paardeberg, South Africa, 27 February 1900. The celebration takes the form of field games between all-ranks teams, the emphasis being on fun rather than serious contest. Traditionally, with the 1st Ballalion, it is broomball. But for the 3rd Battalion in the deep snows of CFB Petawawa, it is tug-of-war and soccer on snowshoes! These hilarious events are immediately followed by regimental gatherings, usually in the junior ranks messes.

March   Each year, early in March, the cadets from the Royal Military College, Kingston, and the United States Military Academy, West Point, New York, meet for a week-end of friendly rivalry in a variety of activities. In the odd-numbered years, RMC cadets travel to West Point, in the even years, the reverse. Highlights of the week-end are the traditional hockey game first played in 1923, and the annual debate.

March   The Goose Bay Annual NATO mess dinner. Each year at Canadian Forces Station Goose Bay, Labrador, the senior non-commissioned officers of the Royal Air Force, the United States Air Force, and the Canadian Forces stationed there, hold a mess dinner which over the years has become the major social event of the year. Sponsored on a rotating basis by the warrant officers and sergeants of the three forces representing three signatory powers of the North Atlantic Treaty Organization, this annual mess dinner is honoured by the presence of a general officer as guest of honour and music is provided by the North American Air Defence Band.

March
In mid-March the Queen's York Rangers (1st American Regiment) observe York County Night, a custom of a hundred years. In 1878, the warden of York County, Ontario, and his council presented the regiment with a stand of colours. To return the compliment, it became a custom for the rangers to give the colours back each year at the first session of the council. This annual return of the colours carried out with impressive ceremony has been celebrated each year for almost a century and the evening filled with colourful pageantry, is known as York County Night.

March 17
St. Patrick's Day. As a special tribute to the character of the united counties in eastern Ontario, the Stormont, Dundas and Glengarry Highlanders celebrate St. Patrick's Night in the officers' mess.

March 17
This was the birthday of the Lady Patricia Ramsay, until her death in 1974, the colonel-in-chief of Princess Patricia's Canadian Light Infantry. As Princess Patricia of Connaught, this granddaughter of Queen Victoria sponsored the founding of the regiment in 1914, and her birthday, 17 March 1886, was for nearly six decades celebrated as the birthday of the regiment. Today, the anniversary is known as regimental day. It is the occasion for battalion parades, all-ranks luncheons, and mess dinners. A long-time feature of the day is the annual broom-i-loo tournament between the sergeants and the officers played outdoors irrespective of weather conditions, using a soccer ball and corn brooms.

March 24
The official birthday of 12e Régiment Blindé du Canada (regular force) based at CFB Valcartier is the date the unit was established, 6 May 1968. The Regimental Day of le Régiment Blindé du Canada (Militia), based in Trois-Rivières, is March 24, commemorating the day in 1871 when four independent companies were brought together to form the Three Rivers Provisional Battalion of Infantry.

March 30
On this day, at Sarcee Barracks, Calgary, Lord Strathcona's Horse (Royal Canadians) celebrates the anniversary of the regiment's famous cavalry charge at Moreuil Wood, near Amiens, France, 30 March 1918. Spread over a three-day period, the observances take the form of

a ceremonial parade including the regimental guidon, and divine service for which the centre-piece is the Memorial Gong, in service since 1929 in commemoration of those members of the regiment who gave their lives for king and empire during the Great War, 1914-18. Moreuil Wood Day is also the occasion for the presentation of the Hessin Sword, awarded annually since 1961 to the subaltern of the regiment who, in the judgement of his fellow officers, has displayed the highest qualities of leadership, integrity and ability.

Each spring, the Lake Superior Scottish Regiment holds its Annual Military Spring Ball.

April   400 Air Reserve Squadron, Toronto, holds the 400 Squadron Annual Ladies Night, formerly the Red and Silver Ball, for all ranks, the first Friday evening in April.

April   Each spring, the cadets of Collège Militaire Royal de Saint-Jean and their guests attend the Annual Sports Dinner in the cadet mess. The guest of honour, usually a well known professional athlete, officiates at the presentation of athletic awards.

April   Le Collège Militaire Royal de Saint-Jean, on the first Sunday of April, is the scene of the cadets' annual "Assault at Arms." Attended by a general officer as guest of honour, the day-long occasion consists of a ceremonial parade, demonstrations of precision drill and gymnastics, a luncheon in the officers' mess, and a tea attended by all the cadets and their guests.

April 1   Anniversary of the establishment of the Royal Canadian Air Force, 1 April 1924.

April 1   The Loyal Edmonton Regiment was founded 1 April 1908, as the 101st Regiment. Annually on this day there is a ceremonial parade and a reunion with the 49th Battalion Association in honour of the regiment's part in the Great War, 1914-18.

April 1   The Fort Garry Horse was founded on 1 April 1912. At suitable intervals, this anniversary is celebrated by the regiment on the weekend closest to April 1.

April 1   The regimental birthday of the British Columbia Dragoons is 1 April 1911, when the 1st Regiment British Columbia Horse was formed. Annually, the regimental guidon is trooped in one of three major communities of the Okanagan — Vernon, Kelowna and Penticton.

April 1	The Rocky Mountain Rangers, with headquarters at Kamloops, celebrates the regiment's birthday, commemmorating the formation of the 102nd Regiment on 1 April 1908.
April 1	The Calgary Highlanders observes the regiment's birthday, 1 April 1910.
April 4	Regimental birthday of the 8th Canadian Hussars (Princess Louise's). On this day in the year 1848, eleven troops of cavalry were formed into a regiment called the New Brunswick Yeomanry Cavalry, making the militia component of the 8th Canadian Hussars the oldest, though not the senior, cavalry, now armoured, regiment in the Canadian Forces. The anniversary observances include a ceremonial parade and drumhead church service, sports in the afternoon, and mess dinners and dances in the evening.
April 8	Although officially formed on 8 April 1968, the Canadian Airborne Regiment's regimental day is celebrated on June 6 in commemoration of that day in 1944 when the regiment's forbear, the 1st Canadian Parachute Battalion, made its first jump to engage the enemy, at the invasion of Normandy.
April 9	On the Sunday nearest this day, the battalion of the Royal 22e Régiment in garrison at the Citadel parades with veterans of the regiment to the wooden Croix de Vimy near the chapel on the heights of Quebec. There, divine service is conducted in memory of those members of the regiment who fell at the Battle of Vimy Ridge, France, in 1917.
April 9	On the Saturday nearest this day, the Seaforth Highlanders of Canada and the regimental association dine in remembrance of the victory of Vimy Ridge, 9 April 1917.
April 9	Annually, on April 9, les Fusiliers du St. Laurent holds a regimental dinner. Also, the regiment has its Annual Regimental Ball.
April 22/ April 23	St. Julien Day. On this day, the sergeant's mess of the Canadian Scottish Regiment (Princess Mary's) dines in commemoration of the gallant part played by the 16th Battalion (Canadian Scottish) in the Battle of St. Julien Wood, 1915.
April 22/ April 23	Annually on the weekend closest to this date, the Calgary Highlanders honours the heroic stand of the 10th Battalion (Calgary Highlanders)

during the first German gas attack, Battle of St. Julien Wood, 22/23 April, 1915. The weekend observances include the officers' St. Julien Mess Dinner, the all-ranks dinner with the 10th Battalion Calgary Highlanders Association, and a church parade.

April 22/
April 23

The 56th Field Regiment, Royal Canadian Artillery, annually, on the Sunday after April 22, holds a parade at St. Catharines, Ontario, to honour the gallant stand of the 10th Battery at the Battle of St. Julien (2nd Battle of Ypres 1915), the first German gas attack. The survivors of that day have an honoured place in this parade.

April 23

Birthday of HMCS *Malahat,* 23 April 1947. Even though this shore establishment functioned as a naval recruiting centre during the Second World War, its birthday is considered to be its commissioning as a naval division, 23 April 1947. This day is observed either by a reception or by a mess dinner.

April 23

St. George's Day. Annually, on the weekend closest to April 23, the King's Own Calgary Regiment observes St. George's Day to mark its alliance with the King's Own Royal Border Regiment. The observance takes the form of a church parade, an all-ranks luncheon, a sergeants' mess dinner, and the "passing of the Wassail Bowl" at the officers' mess dinner.

April 23

St. George's Day is observed by the Canadian Grenadier Guards.

April 25

There is a celebration annually in the officers' mess, Canadian Forces Station, Sydney, marking the founding of the unofficial Royal Cape Breton Air Force in 1956.

April 25

"Kapyong Day," commemorating the battle fought in Korea in which Princess Patricia's Canadian Light Infantry participated, is observed by the regiment, particularly the 2nd Battalion, with mess dinners and regimental balls, decorations for the latter featuring oriental motifs. Kapyong Barracks is located at Winnipeg.

April 26

On this day, the Queen's Own Rifles of Canada celebrates the founding of the regiment, 26 April 1860.

April 29

Although the regular component of the old Canadian Engineer Corps dates from 1 July 1903, military engineers consider their natal date the day they were designated the Corps of Royal Canadian Engineers, 29 April 1936. On this day, or close to it, a variety of reunions of military engineers occur. One of these takes place annually when some fifty parachutists of the First Airborne Engineer Field Squadron of the Canadian Airborne Regiment, from Edmonton, literally drop into the School of Military Engineering, CFB Chilliwack, British Columbia.

April   A popular and growing custom in the fleet occurs on Easter Sunday when the families of members of the ships' companies are invited on board for dinner.

May   Annually, early in May, the officers of the Royal 22e Régiment dine those officers leaving the regiment. Each departing officer receives a plaque and a letter of appreciation from the commanding officer.

May   On a selected day in mid-May, le Régiment de Maisonneuve parades a guard of honour for the observance at the Maisonneuve monument commemorating the founding of Montreal by Maisonneuve in 1642.

May   The regimental dinner of the Royal Canadian Hussars is held each spring, usually in May.

First
Sunday
in May
    On the first Sunday in May, the Royal Montreal Regiment holds its annual church parade to St. Matthias' Church, where the regimental colour is re-consecrated to the memory of the regiment's war dead, with particular reference to the heavy losses at Ypres and St. Julien in the spring of 1915.

First
Sunday
in May
    On "Battle of the Atlantic Sunday," commemorative services are held from coast to coast and in HMC ships at sea. The national ceremony is held at Halifax, where the men of the fleet parade to the naval memorial at Point Pleasant. In HMCS York, the naval division at Toronto, a wreath is cast upon the waters of Lake Ontario. A similar ceremony is performed at Victoria Pier, Montreal, by HMCS Donnacona.

May   Graduation, better known as Grad Day, at le Collège Militaire Royal de Saint-Jean, occurs annually early in May. The trooping of the college colour takes place in the afternoon, followed by the Graduation Ball at night. The all-night party is concluded at dawn next day with a group photograph out on the parade square of the cadets and their partners who are then served breakfast prepared by the college commandant, staff officers and their ladies.

May   Annually, in early May, at several major land force bases, field engineer squadrons sponsor a week-end of festivities called a "Milly Reunion." It replaces a similar celebration formerly associated with the birthday of the old Corps of Royal Canadian Engineers. Attended by military engineers, active and retired, and their families, the three-day event includes a ceremonial parade, a candle-light dinner and all-ranks dance, and, on the Sunday, an old-fashioned family-style picnic.

May | First Saturday of the month. The Battle of Cut Knife Hill, associated with the regiment's first battle honour, North-west Canada 1885, is observed by the Governor-General's Foot Guards with an annual mess dinner in the sergeant's mess.

May 4 | Anniversary of the establishment of the Royal Canadian Navy, 4 May 1910.

May 6 | The official birthday of le 12e Régiment Blindé du Canada (regular force) based at CFB Valcartier, is the date the unit was established, 6 May 1968. The regimental day of le 12e Régiment Blindé du Canada (Militia), based at Trois-Rivières, is March 24, commemorating the day in 1871 when four independent companies were brought together to form the Three Rivers Provisional Battalion of Infantry.

May 6 | A close relationship has grown up between the chief and petty officers of HMCS *Star,* and United States Naval Reserve units in the Lake Ontario region. Each spring and fall, visits are exchanged with the USNR at Rochester, and also at Oswego, New York. The Battle of Oswego occurred 6 May 1814, when Commodore Yeo's squadron of the Royal Navy successfully attacked the port.

May 8 | The ceremony of trooping the colour is performed by Princess Patricia's Canadian Light Infantry in commemoration of the regiment's part in the Battle of Frezenberg, 8 May 1915, particularly by the 1st Battalion. Events include all-ranks luncheons, mess dinners the preceding day, and regimental balls on May 8.

May 12 | Batoche Day. On this day, the Royal Regiment of Canada commemorates the participation of its forbear, the 10th Royal Grenadiers, in the North-west Rebellion, 1885, in particular the capture of Batoche in northern Saskatchewan.

May 24 | "Strathcona Day" of Lord Strathcona's Horse (Royal Canadians) marks the anniversary of the Crossing of the Melfa River during the

Italian campaign, 24 May 1944. Normally held at Sarcee Barracks, Calgary, the event takes the form of an all-ranks sports day and "bun feed."

May 24   The Royal Westminster Regiment Association holds its Melfa Dinner on the weekend prior to May 24, while the regiment has its mess dinner on the weekend following this date. At this commemoration of the Battle of Melfa Crossing in Italy on 24 May 1944, representatives of Lord Strathcona's Horse renew their battle association with the Royal Westminster Regiment.

May 24   Official birthday of the sovereign. A royal salute is fired at noon on the official birthday of Her Majesty the Queen, which is celebrated in Canada on the Monday immediately preceding May 25. Saluting stations for this royal anniversary observance are: St. John's, Charlottetown, Halifax, Fredericton, Quebec City, Ottawa, Toronto, Winnipeg, Regina, Edmonton and Victoria (Esquimalt).

May 26   Artillery Day. This day is celebrated by most units of the Royal Regiment of Canadian Artillery with a variety of events including special parades, sports days, mess dinners, teas, parties and open house. The founding date of the Royal Artillery was 26 May 1716.

May   Annually, during the last week-end in May, the Canadian Scottish Regiment (Princess Mary's) exercise their privilege of freedom of the city of Victoria, British Columbia.

June 1   Though formed from four independent companies in 1900, the Algonquin Regiment, based in North Bay and Timmins, Ontario, celebrates the birthday of the regiment on June 1, the day in 1903 that it was designated the 97th Regiment Algonquin Rifles. The observance takes the form of a dining-in for serving officers and associated members of the officers' mess.

June 2   The Queen's Own Rifles of Canada commemorates the regiment's first battle casualties, the Engagement at Ridgeway during the Fenian Raids, 2 June 1866.

June 2   The Lake Superior Scottish Regiment holds its Regimental Mobilization and Anniversary Dinner marking the regiment's birthday, 2 June 1885.

June 4-6   "Rome-Normandy Days" commemorate the First Canadian Special

Service Battalion's entry into Rome on 4 June 1944, and the 1st Canadian Parachute Battalion's jump into Normandy early in the morning of 6 June 1944. The three-day observances by the Canadian Airborne Regiment include a church parade, trooping of the colour, exercising freedom of the city of Edmonton, a full day of jumping at Namao, Alberta, with the families of the regiment being served lunch in the drop-zone, a tea party in the officers' mess, and an all-ranks dance.

June 6   The Regina Rifle Regiment parades on June 6 to the Cenotaph in Regina's Victoria Park in remembrance of fallen comrades in the Hooge-Ypres Salient, Belgium, 6 June 1916, and the Normandy Invasion, 6 June 1944. This is followed by a regimental mess dinner in Regina.

June 6   A regimental mess dinner is held on June 6 by le Régiment de la Chaudière, Lévis, Quebec, in commemoration of the regiment's landing in Normandy, 6 June 1944.

June 6   Annually, on this day, the Queen's Own Rifles of Canada honours the fallen in the Normandy Landing, 6 June 1944.

June 6   On the weekend closest to June 6, the Fort Garry Horse commemorates the part played by the regiment in the Invasion of Normandy, 1944.

June 6   Although officially formed on 8 April 1968 the Canadian Airborne Regiment's regimental day is celebrated on June 6 in commemoration of that day in 1944 when the regiment's forbear, the 1st Canadian Parachute Battalion, made its first jump to engage the enemy, at the Invasion of Normandy.

June 7   Birthday of the Governor General's Foot Guards, 7 June 1872. It is celebrated with a mess dinner in the officer's mess.

June 13   Sorrel Day. On the Sunday closest to this day the Royal Regiment of Canada remembers the Battle of Mount Sorrel, 13 June, 1916, in which the regiment's Forbear, the Toronto Regiment, distinguished itself.

June 14 The Service battalions from coast to coast celebrate their birthday on this day. Usually, the occasion is marked by special ceremonial parades, and battalion dances in the evening.

June 18 June 18 is the regimental birthday of the Princess Louise Fusiliers. It was on this day in 1869 that the Halifax Volunteer Battalion of Infantry was authorized. This event is commemorated by the annual officers' mess dinner.

June 30 A dinner in the officers' mess of the Royal Newfoundland Regiment is held annually on the eve of the anniversary of the heroic advance of the regiment at the Battle of Beaumont Hamel, 1 July 1916.

June Armed Forces Day. On the Saturday preceding Canada Week, which embraces July 1 (Dominion Day), the commands, bases, stations and units of the forces, at home and abroad, are "at home" so that the public may become better acquainted with the forces and their work.

July 1 Dominion Day. On the anniversary of Canada's birthday, units of all three elements perform public services from coast to coast as well as at stations abroad, in the form of ceremonial parades, gun salutes and fly-pasts.

July 1 Dominion Day. To commemorate the Confederation of Canada, 1 July 1867, twenty-one-gun salutes are fired at noon, July 1, at Canadian Forces saluting stations at: St. John's, Charlottetown, Halifax, Fredericton, Quebec City, Montreal, Ottawa, Toronto, Winnipeg, Regina, Edmonton, Vancouver and Victoria (Esquimalt).

July 1 Commemoration Day. Since 1917, units of the forces have joined with the people of Newfoundland on the Sunday nearest to July 1, a day set aside by an Act of the Parliament of Newfoundland to honour in solemn remembrance the men of the Newfoundland Regiment who fell in heroic sacrifice at the Battle of Beaumont Hamel, 1 July 1916.

July 1 The Order of Military Merit, of which His Excellency the Governor-General, Commander-in-Chief of the Canadian Forces, is Chancellor, was inaugurated on 1 July 1972. The honours lists of this first truly Canadian military decoration are announced twice yearly on a day close to July 1 and January 1.

July 3 The regimental birthday of the Stormont, Dundas and Glengarry Highlanders is 3 July 1868, when the 59th Stormont and Glengarry

Battalion of Infantry was authorized to be formed from six independent companies. Each year a day is selected for the annual regimental dinner in the officers' mess.

July 8
: The serving officers of the Highland Fusiliers of Canada observe the anniversary of the Battle of Buron in the Normandy campaign, 8 July 1944 at a mess dinner. It was at this battle that one of the regiment's predecessors, the Highland Light Infantry of Canada, suffered severe casualties.

July 10
: This day is celebrated by the Royal Canadian Regiment in honour of its landing on the Pachino Peninsula, Sicily, 10 July 1943. Highlight of the day is inter-company track and field events followed by a regimental gathering.

August
: On the first Monday of August, civic holiday, the Queen's York Rangers (1st American Regiment) celebrates Simcoe Day with military pageantry in the Borough of East York, Toronto, where the regiment enjoys the honour and privilege of the freedom of the city. (John Graves Simcoe, first lieutenant governor of Upper Canada, late in the eighteenth century, commanded a forbear of the regiment two hundred years ago.)

August 1
: Minden Day is observed by the North Saskatchewan Regiment honouring the heroic part played by its allied regiment, the King's Own Yorkshire Light Infantry at the Battle of Minden, 1 August 1759. On that day in both regiments, the White Rose of York is worn on the head-dress.

August 7
: Second Regiment, Royal Canadian Horse Artillery, celebrates its birthday on this day in commemoration of its formation at Camp Shilo on 7 August 1950, in preparation for service in Korea. In 1975, festivities included a mounted march-past, the firing of a feu-de-joie using 105 mm howitzers, and a dance attended by all ranks.

August 10
: The anniversary of 10 August 1914, the regimental birthday of Princess Patricia's Canadian Light Infantry, has an origin unique in the Canadian Forces. It is the date of the regiment's charter, the mark of a privately raised regiment. The Patricias were founded through the personal initiative and expense of Captain Andrew Hamilton Gault as a battalion of largely veteran soldiers for service in the Great War.

August 19
: Dieppe Day. The Royal Regiment of Canada observes and remembers its part in the Dieppe Raid, 19 August 1942.

August 19   On the closest Friday to this day, the Queen's Own Cameron Highlanders of Canada holds a regimental reunion.

September   On a weekend in September, "Stars," past and present, foregather in
HMCS *Star* at Hamilton for their annual reunion.

September   Towards the end of September each year, the officers of the Canadian
Scottish Regiment (Princess Mary's), at Victoria, join with the associate members of the mess for dinner.

September   The 30th Field Regiment, Royal Canadian Artillery, "the Bytown
Gunners," holds an all-ranks regimental dinner annually in September
to celebrate the founding of the original battery in 1855.

September 14   On 14 September 1866, at the time of the Fenian Raids, the 36th Peel
Battalion of Infantry was authorized. This day is observed as the
regimental birthday by the Lorne Scots (Peel, Dufferin and Halton
Regiment).

Sunday   On "Battle of Britain Sunday," commemorative services are held from
September 15   coast to coast. Until recently, the national ceremony was held at the
or first   Commonwealth Air Forces Memorial in Ottawa. Now, the Royal
Sunday   Canadian Air Force Association has accepted the sponsorship of the
following   national observance of Battle of Britain Sunday, with strong support
15 September   from the Canadian Forces. It intends to conduct this national
memorial service in Winnipeg, the home of Air Command Headquarters, and eventually in centres across the land coinciding with the
association's annual convention.

October   Each October, the officers of the King's Own Calgary Regiment hold
their Bride's Dinner and dance to honour the most recent bride of an
officer, or the wife of an officer not previously honoured by the mess.

October   Annually, in October, the Saskatchewan Dragoons troop their
guidon. The Trooping Ball is attended by all ranks.

October   Annually during October, a Sunday is designated by the Royal Westminster Regiment for church parade and the christening of children of
the regiment.

October   A day is selected each year for the annual officers' mess dinner to commemorate the part played by the Queen's Own Cameron Highlanders
of Canada at the Battle of Passchendaele, October, 1917.

October   Annually, usually early in October, the Royal Military College, Kingston, holds its highly popular and long established ex-cadet weekend. Over several days, former graduates of the college are welcomed back to dine and to witness displays of drill and sports, and to attend a special church parade and service at the Memorial Arch at the entrance to the college grounds.

October   Annually in October, the Queen's York Rangers (1st American Regiment) dine in celebration of the parts played by forbears of the regiment in two battles fought during the American Revolution and the War of 1812, the "Brandywine and Queenston Heights Dinner."

October 5   The ship's company of the destroyer, HMCS *Margaree*, celebrates the anniversary of the ship's first commissioning, 5 October 1957, at a party on board which includes beer and birthday cake.

October 8   The West Nova Scotia Regiment marks this day as Ortona Day, though the battle for Ortona, Italy, in which the regiment was heavily engaged, was waged during the month of December, 1943. (Actually, this day is the regimental birthday, its forbear, the First Regiment of Annapolis County Volunteers, having been formed 8 October 1869.)

October 21   Trafalgar Day. On the nearest Friday to this date, the officers of HMCS *Star*, past and present, commemorate Nelson's victory off Cape Trafalgar, 21 October 1805 at a mess dinner.

October 21   Trafalgar Day. This anniversary is observed in HMCS *Cataraqui* at Kingston, Ontario, with a ceremonial parade.

October 21   Trafalgar Day. The day is also marked by HMCS *Scotian*, the naval reserve division at Halifax, Nova Scotia.

October 21   Trafalgar Day in *Stadacona* wardroom, CFB Halifax, is the scene of a "super weepers" for the officers of the First Canadian Submarine Squadron, and a "penny beer" for the officers of the base.

October 21   On this day, members of the Royal 22e Régiment entertain their ladies to dinner to commemorate the birthday of the regiment, 21 October 1914, when the 22e Battalion, Canadian Expeditionary Force, was raised for war service.

October 30   The Seaforth Highlanders of Canada commemorates the capture of Crest Farm (Passchendaele) 30 October 1917, with a mess dinner in the officers' mess on the nearest Friday or Saturday.

October 31   On the weekend closest to this day, the Calgary Highlanders honour the fallen who died when the regiment led the attack in the Battle of Walcheren Causeway, 31 October — 1 November 1944. The observances take the form of a mess dinner and church parade.

October   Annually, late in October, the warrant officers and sergeants of the Royal 22e Régiment hold a dinner dance at the Citadel, Quebec, in honour of departing members of the mess.

November   Early in November, the officers of the Canadian Scottish Regiment (Princess Mary's), at Victoria, join with the associate members of the mess, and their ladies, for the annual Social and Ball.

November   On the last Friday of November, the officers of Saskatoon's naval division, HMCS *Unicorn*, hold their time-honoured AQT (Ale, Quail and Tale) Dinner. It is related to the wild game cuisine said to have been served during the only naval engagement in Saskatchewan when the SS *Northcote* was under fire in the North-west Rebellion of 1885.

November 5 The ship's company of HMCS *Brunswicker*, the naval reserve division at Saint John, attends the annual memorial service at the Jervis Bay Monument. On 5 November 1940, HMS *Jervis Bay*, an armed merchant cruiser with a close association with the city and partly manned by the Royal Canadian Navy, went down under the guns of the battleship, *Admiral Scheer*, in the epic defence of Convoy HX-84 in the North Atlantic.

November 7 On November 7, the Royal Canadian Dragoons, the oldest regular force cavalry regiment, holds a reunion of present and former members of the RCD to commemorate the day the regiment won three Victoria Crosses at Liliefontein, South Africa, 7 November 1900.

November 11 Remembrance Day. At 1100 on this day, with flags at half-mast, a twenty-one-gun memorial salute is fired at each Canadian Forces saluting station at: St. John's, Charlottetown, Halifax, Fredericton, Quebec City, Montreal, Ottawa, Toronto, Winnipeg, Regina, Edmonton, Vancouver, and Victoria (Esquimalt).

November 11 Remembrance Day dates from 11 November 1918, the armistice which brought the First World War to an end. The observance of this day honours all of Canada's war dead. Commemorative services are held from coast to coast, in HMC ships at sea, and at stations abroad. The national ceremony is conducted at the National War Memorial, Confederation Square, Ottawa.

November 11   Annually, on an evening close to this date, the Officers' Mess of the Saskatchewan Dragoons holds its Remembrance Day Ball.

November 11   On Armistice Sunday, the Royal Montreal Regiment parades to the cenotaphs at Westmount and Pointe Claire, Quebec, and to St. Anne's Military Hospital. On the Friday preceding Remembrance Day, the Royal Montreal Regiment holds its annual reunion mess dinner for both former and serving officers of the regiment.

November 11   On the Saturday preceding Remembrance Day observances, the Royal Canadian Regiment parades with the Regimental Association for Memorial Day Service. This takes place at the regiment's war memorial at the home station, Wolseley Barracks, London.

November 20   This day is celebrated as the regimental birthday of the Royal Westminster Regiment which traces its origin back to colonial times and the Westminster Volunteer Rifles of 20 November 1863.

November 20   Cambrai Day. Cambrai Day is the official regimental day of the Fort Garry Horse. On the closest week-end, the regiment celebrates the part it played in the First Battle of Cambrai, 20 November 1917.

November 21   The Canoe River Memorial Service. On this day in 1950, the Second Regiment, Royal Canadian Horse Artillery, bound for war service in Korea, suffered seventeen killed and thirty-five injured, in a railway collision near Canoe River in the mountains of British Columbia. In commemoration of this tragedy, memorial services are held on this day by the regiment and at the Canoe River Monument at the regimental depot, Shilo, Manitoba.

November 30   St. Andrew's Day. On the last Saturday nearest to St. Andrew's Day, all serving and retired officers of the Canadian Scottish Regiment (Princess Mary's) attend the annual Game Dinner consisting entirely of sea food and game procured by the officers themselves.

November 30   St. Andrew's Day is observed by the Calgary Highlanders with a mess dinner in the officers' mess.

November 30   The officers' mess of the Stormont, Dundas and Glengarry Highlanders sponsors the St. Andrews's Ball in Cornwall, Ontario.

November 30   November 30 is observed as a holiday in the Queen's Own Cameron Highlanders of Canada and all officers attend the festivities of the St. Andrews Society.

November 30   In association with the St. Andrews Society of Toronto, the 48th Highlanders of Canada, in alternate years, produces the 48th Highlanders Ball.

December   400 Air Reserve Squadron, Toronto, holds its annual Black Velvet reunion, for all former and present squadron officers, the first Friday in December. The name stems from the concoction served — stout and champagne!

December   At the annual mess dinner in the senior non-commissioned officers' mess of the Royal Westminster Regiment, the Bungled Bayonet Award is presented with much hilarity to the senior NCO who has committed during the year the greatest *faux pas*. The trophy is a CF pattern boot elegantly mounted on a mahogany shield transfixed with a Mark I bayonet.

December   About mid-month, at the end of the autumn term, the cadets of Royal Roads Military College gather on the quarter-deck in Grant Block for their Christmas carol service, complete with choir and bell ringers. This tradition began as early as 1944 in the days of the Royal Canadian Naval College, quartered in HMCS *Royal Roads*, when "Officers, Cadets, Wrens and Ratings assembled in the main hall of the Castle to sing Christmas carols." (*The Log*, HMCS *Royal Roads*, 1944-1945).

December 4   St. Barbara's Day. The day of St. Barbara, the mystical patron saint of artillerymen, is observed by units of the Royal Regiment of Canadian Artillery with church parades, sports, mess dinners and other events, even to firing salutes with miniature guns.

December 15   The Windsor Regiment celebrates its birthday on December 15, recalling its founding as the Essex Regiment (Tank) on 15 December 1936.

December 21   Birthday of the Royal Canadian Regiment, 21 December 1883. There is a regimental gathering in the junior ranks mess to commence the period of relaxed duties associated with the celebration of Christmas. The men of the regiment are served by their officers and senior NCOs in the traditional fashion. In the evening, mess dinners are held in both the officers and warrant officers/sergeants messes.

December 25   The Queen's Own Rifles of Canada celebrate the birthday of the regiment's colonel-in-chief, Her Royal Highness Princess Alexandra of Kent, December 25.

December 31   Hogmanay is celebrated by most of the Scottish regiments of the Canadian Forces in traditional highland fashion.

December 31   Other ranks of the Canadian Scottish Regiment (Princess Mary's) dine annually to honour the memory of the four members of the regiment who won the Victoria Cross.

Notes to Chapters

Notes to Introduction

1. Naval Order 112.05/3 (51) (1958).

2. Rivers-Macpherson, Colonel E.R., "The Broad Arrow," *Canadian Army Journal*, vol. 10, no. 1 (1956) pp. 70-73, 83. See also *The Journal of the Society of Army Historical Research*, vol. 1, no. 6 (Dec 1922), and vol. 9 (1930) p. 175.

3. Mackenzie-Rogan, J., *Fifty Years of Army Music* (London: Methuen, 1926) pp. 9-11. However, "The Rogue's March" has been drummed into prisoners' ears right up to relatively modern times. In the Canadian lines near Rimini, Italy, in 1944, several soldiers were summarily tried for desertion in the face of the enemy, found guilty and sentenced to hard labour. In the traditional hollow square formed by the battalion, the regimental sergeant major, wielding a knife, publicly stripped each man of his regimental insignia, and the band struck up the infamous tune as the culprits were marched off to expiate their crimes in North Africa. (Author's interview with Colonel Strome Galloway, Ottawa, 30 November 1976.) Similarly, at Hamilton Gault Barracks in Edmonton in the early 1960s, a soldier was summarily tried for theft and, within a hollow square formed by his comrades-in-arms, was stripped of his regimental insignia and marched to the gate and the arms of the civilian police. (Author's interview with officers of the 1st Battalion, Princess Patricia's Canadian Light Infantry, Currie Barracks, Calgary, 17 November 1976.)

4. Logan, H.M., "Some Courts Martial of the Past," *Canadian Defence Journal*, vol. 5 (1927-1928) p. 72.

5. Gellner, John, *Canadian Defence Quarterly*, vol. 5, no. 2, Winter (1975) pp 5-6,

40. See also Kaulback, Lieutenant-Colonel R.J.A., "The Regiment," *Journal of the Royal United Service Institution*, vol. 91 (1946) pp. 259-260.

6. Lewis, Michael, *The Navy of Britain* (London: Allen and Unwin, 1948) p. 612.

Notes to Chapter 1

1. Smith, Captain George, *An Universal Military Dictionary* (London: J. Millan, 1779).

2. Edwards, Major T.J., *Military Customs* (Aldershot, Gale and Polden, 1950) p. 164.

3. Ibid. See also Field, Colonel Cyril, *Old Times Under Arms: A Military Garner* (London: Hodge, 1939) p. 447.

4. Lowry, Lt. Comdr. R.G., *The Origins of Some Naval Terms and Customs*, (London: Sampson Low, Marston, 1930) pp. 43-45.

5. Ibid. See also L.G. Carr Laughton's article "Saluting the Quarterdeck" in *Mariner's Mirror*, vol. 12 (1926) pp. 196-204, and letters in vol. 18 (1932) pp. 205, 327; and Lovette, Vice Admiral L.P., *Naval Customs Traditions and Usage* (Annapolis, Md: United States Naval Institute, 1959) pp. 34-35.

6. Hall, Captain Basil, RN, *The Log-Book of a Midshipman* (London: Blackie & Son, 1896) pp. 91-92.

7. Willcocks, Lt. Col. K.D.H., *Customs and Traditions of the Regiment* (The Hastings and Prince Edward Regiment) Belleville, 1968, pp. 9, 20.

8. Letter to the author from the commanding officer, Les Fusiliers Mont-Royal, 9 October 1974.

9. *The Cadet Handbook: The Royal Military College of Canada*, Kingston, 1976, p. 39.

10. Walker, G. Goold, *The Honourable Artillery Company, 1537–1947* (Aldershot, Gale and Polden, 1954) p. 73.

11. *Canadian Forces Administrative Order* (CFAO) 61-8 (1972).

12.   *Regulations and Instructions relating to His Majesty's Service at Sea*, 13th ed. (London, 1790) article XX (7).

13.   Perrin, W.G. ed., *Boteler's Dialogues*, vol. 65 (London: Navy Records Society, 1929) pp. 267-268. (The title page of what is called the Sloane MS 758, reads in part: *A Dialogicall Discourse Concerning Marine Affaires...*, Collected and Penned By Captaine Nathaniell Butler, Anno 1634.) See also Oppenheim, M., *A History of the Administration of the Royal Navy and of Merchant Shipping in Relation to the Navy, 1509-1660* (London: Lane, 1896) p. 213. Also letters by Pye, E., (1956) pp. 134-5, 138.

14.   Oppenheim, M., ed., *The Naval Tracts of Sir William Monson*, vol. 4 (London: Navy Records Society, 1913) pp. 132-137.

15.   Rivers-Macpherson, Colonel E.R., "Why 21 Guns for Royalty?" *Canadian Army Journal*, vol 10, no. 2 (1956) pp. 100-101, originally published in *The Legionary*, January 1956.

16.   Mountaine, William, *The Seaman's Vade-Mecum* (London, 1778) p.v.

17.   Carr, H. Gresham, *Flags of the World* (London: Warne, 1961) pp. 20-23.

18.   Boynton, Lindsay, *The Elizabethan Militia, 1558-1638* (Toronto: University of Toronto Press, 1967) p. 164, quoting from *Papers of the Norfolk and Norwich Archives Society* (1847).

19.   Lanctot, Gustave, *Montreal under Maisonneuve, 1642-1665* (Toronto: Clark, Irwin & Co., 1969) p. 28.

20.   Simcoe, Elizabeth Posthuma, *Mrs Simcoe's Diary*, Mary Quayle Innis, ed. (Toronto: Macmillan, 1965) p. 104.

21.   Stevens, G.R., *The Royal Canadian Regiment, 1933-1966* (London, Ontario: London Printing, 1967) p. 267. See also *Part I Orders, 3rd Battalion, The Royal Canadian Regiment*, no. 34, 1 June 1953; and *War Diary, Lord Strathcona's Horse (Royal Canadians)*, 2 June 1953.

Notes to Chapter 2

1.   Much can be gleaned regarding the mess life of non-commissioned officers a century and a half ago from the standing orders governing the sergeants' messes of the 87th Regiment of Foot (1827) and the 25th Regiment of Foot (1834). See *Journal of the Society for Army Historical Research*, vol. 47 (1969) p. 120, and vol. 48 (1970) p. 61.

2.   Burney, W., ed., *Falconer's Marine Dictionary* (London, 1815).

3.   *Journal of the Society for Army Historical Research*, vol. 30 (1952) p. 9.

4.   Bell, G., *Rough Notes of an Old Soldier*, vol. 1 (London: Day, 1867) p. 38.

5.   Dyott, William, *Dyott's Diary, 1781-1845*, R.W. Jeffery ed., vol. 1 (London: Constable, 1907) p. 30.

6.   *Ibid*, p. 267. In the Royal Navy, the name is usually spelled *Fisgard*.

7.   Lewis, Michael, *The Navy of Britain* (London: Allen & Unwin, 1948) pp. 92-93.

8.   Lowry, Lieut-Cdr. R.G., *The Origins of Some Naval Terms and Customs* (London: Sampson Low, Marston, 1930) pp. 3-4.

9.   Heinl, R.D., *Dictionary of Military and Naval Quotations* (Annapolis, Md., United States Naval Institute, 1967) p. 221.

Notes to Chapter 3

1.   Booklet: "Hints for Junior Officers," Canadian School of Infantry, Vernon, B.C., 1945, p. 12.

2.   Percy, Lieutenant H.R., *Naval Customs, Traditions and Social Practices*, Ottawa, Naval Headquarters, 1963, pp. 15-16.

3.   Booklet, "Hints for Officers," Kingston, Royal Canadian School of Signals, 1959, p. 36.

4.   Author's interview with Chief Warrant Officer G.R. Heppenstall, Base Sergeant Major, CFB Kingston, 23 September 1975.

5.   While in some messes the term head table is used as in the civilian sense, others retain the view that there is no such thing as a 'head table' at a mess dinner. The Royal Canadian Regiment, Guide for Junior Officers, London, Ontario, 1974, p. 19.

6.   "The Roast Beef of Old England" was composed by a popular Covent Garden singer, Richard Leveridge (c. 1670-1758) and published in London in 1727.

7.   Hall, Captain Basil, R.N., *The Log-Book of a Midshipman* (London: Blackie & Son, 1896) p. 96.

8.   "How to Conduct a Dining-In," *U.S. Navy Medicine*, vol. 65 (March 1975) p. 26.

9.   Hering, Squadron Leader P.G., *Customs and Traditions of the Royal Air Force* (Aldershot, Gale and Polden, 1961) p. 152, and RCAF Pamphlet 4, *Notes for the Guidance of Officers*, AFHQ, Ottawa, 1964, pp. 24-25.

10.   Grubb, Commander F.E., Naval Customs and Social Usage, 1950, p. 9, and Percy, Lieutenant H.R., *Naval Customs, Traditions and Social Practices*, NHQ, Ottawa, 1963, p. 15.

11.   There are other "do's and don't's" practised in messes, but these are considered common to most. See Commanding Officer Naval Divisions, RCN(R) "Officers Divisional Course" (1955) quoted in Lovette, Vice Admiral L.P., *Naval Customs Traditions & Usage* (Annapolis, Md., United States Naval Institute, 1959) appendix D.

12.   *Standing Orders* (draft) for the Royal Regiment of Canadian Artillery, 1975, pp. 44-45.

13.   Edwards, Major T.J., *Military Customs*, Aldershot, Gale and Polden, (1950) pp. 36-38. See also Lovette, *Naval Customs Traditions & Usage*, pp. 104-9, and Dowe, Lieutenant F.S., "Gentlemen — The Queen," *Canadian Army Journal*, vol 6, no. 2 (May 1952) pp. 74-76.

14.   Dyott, William, *Dyott's Diary 1781-1845*, vol. 1 (London: Constable, 1907) p. 52.

15.   La Rochefoucault-Liancourt, François, duc de, *Travels through the United States of North America, the Country of the Iroquois and Upper Canada etc.*, vol. 1 (London, 1799) p. 287.

16.   Roach, J., *The Royal Toast Master. . . . the Seaman's Bottle Companion*, (London, 1793) frontispiece.

17.   Taylor, Lieut-Cdr A.D., *Customs of the Navy*, 1956, p. 37.

18.   Hoffman, Captain F., *A Sailor of King George: The Journals of Captain Frederick Hoffman, RN, 1793-1814* (London: Murray, 1901) p. 116.

19.   Teonge, Henry, *The Diary of Henry Teonge, Chaplain on Board H.M.'s ships Assistance, Bristol and Royal Oak, 1675-1679* (London: Routledge, 1927) pp. 40, 42, 44.

20.   Letter to the author from the commanding officer, les Fusiliers Mont-Royal, 9 October 1974.

Notes to Chapter 4

1. *Standing Orders for the Officers' Mess, The Canadian Scottish Regiment (Princess Mary's)*, Victoria, 1970, annex E.

2. Armstrong, Major W.B., "Customs, Practices and Dress of the Canadian Army," *Canadian Army Journal*, vol. 17, no. 3 (1963) p. 76.

3. Canada, Air Command, *Mess Dinner Procedures* (CFACM 1-900) May 1976, pp. 9-11.

4. Letter to the author from the commanding officer, Royal Canadian Hussars, 10 September 1974.

5. Probably the best known of the Scottish laments is "Flowers of the Forest," a very old melody. The words date from the mid-eighteenth century. Traditionally associated with the Battle of Flodden (1513) near the Scottish border, the "forest" refers to the Peebles-Selkirk district, and the "flowers" are the young men of the district lost in the battle. See Graham, G.F., *The Songs of Scotland*, vol. 1 (Edinburgh: Wood, 1856) pp. 2-5.

6. Farran, Major Roy, *The History of the Calgary Highlanders, 1921-54* (Calgary: Bryant Press, 1954) p. 8.

7. Letter to the author from the commanding officer, Toronto Scottish Regiment, 11 October 1974.

8. Cunningham, A., and MacKay, C., eds., *Burns, Ramsay and the Earlier Poets of Scotland*, vol. 2 (London: Virtue) p. 8.

9. Armstrong, Major W.B., "Customs, Practices and Dress of the Canadian Army," *Canadian Army Journal*, vol. 17, no. 3 (1963) p. 77.

10. Letter to the author from the commanding officer, Toronto Scottish Regiment, 11 October 1974.

11. Letter to the author from the commanding officer, Royal Canadian Hussars, 10 September 1974.

12. *Cent ans d'histoire d'un Régiment canadien — francais*, les Fusiliers Mont-Royal (Montreal: Editions des Jours, 1971) p. 331.

13. *La Sentinelle*, 1975/6, p. 21.

14. Letter to the author from the president, Officers' Mess Committee, CFS Sydney, 12 April 1977.

15. Author's interview with officers of 427 Helicopter Squadron, CFB Petawawa, 7 October 1975.

16. Author's interview with Major W.M. Wolfe, CFB Petawawa, 7 October 1975.

Notes to Chapter 5

1. Lewis, Michael, *The Navy of Britain* (London: Allen & Unwin, 1948) p. 301.

2. Lloyd, Christopher, *The British Seaman, 1200-1860* (London: Collins, 1968) p. 54.

3. Lewis, Michael, *England's Sea Officers* (London: Allen & Unwin, 1939) passim.

4. *Oxford English Dictionary*, vol. 1, under entry "Admiral."

5. Walker, G. Goold, *The Honourable Artillery Company, 1537-1947* (Aldershot, Gale and Polden, 1954) p. 13.

6. Wallace, Colonel R.F.H., "Regimental Routine and Army Administration in North America in 1759," *Journal of the Society for Army Historical Research*, vol. 30 (1952) p. 8 et seq.

7. Nicholson, Colonel G.W.L., *The Fighting Newfoundlander*, Government of Newfoundland, 1965 pp. 17-23.

8. Bridger, W.R.P., "Notes on the Origin and Derivation of Some Military Terms," *Canadian Defence Quarterly*, vol. XII, no. 3 (April 1935) p. 336. See also Langford, Lt.-Col. R.J.S., *Corporal to Field Officer* (Toronto: Copp Clark, 1940) pp. 5-7.

9. Lewis, *England's Sea-Officers*, pp. 235-237.

10. Canada, CFP 152, *Seaman's Handbook*, Ottawa, 1972, pp. 5-10.

11. James, C., *Military Dictionary*, 2 vol. (London: Egerton, 1810).

12. *Canadian Forces Reorganization Act* (15 February 1968). See *The Queen's Regulations and Orders for the Canadian Forces*, vol. II, appendix XI (The National Defence Act — Revised Statutes of Canada, 1970, p. 119).

13. Lewis, *England's Sea-Officers*, pp. 193-9.

14. Author's interview with Major W.J. Bailey, NDHQ, Ottawa, 31 July 1975.

15. Armstrong, Major W.B., "Customs, Practices and Dress of the Canadian Army," *Canadian Army Journal*, vol. 17 (1963) no. 3, p. 76.

16. Fortescue, John, *The Empire and the Army* (London: Cassell, 1930) p. 223.

17. Edwards, Major T.J., *Standards, Guidons and Colours of the Commonwealth Forces* (Aldershot, Gale and Polden 1953) p. 104.

18. Memorandum, Colonel T. deFaye, Director of Administration, to the Adjutant General, Army H.Q., Ottawa, 10 April 1962 (HQ 1935-1).

19. Lewis, *The Navy of Britain*, p. 246 and note.

20. Lewis, *England's Sea Officers*, pp. 199-204.

21. Ibid., pp. 187-191.

22. Beckett, Captain W.N.T., *A Few Naval Customs, Expressions, Traditions and Superstitions* (Portsmouth: Gieves, 1934) p. 44.

23. Fortescue, *The Empire and the Army*, pp. 9-10.

24. Grose, Francis, *Military Antiquities*, vol. 1 (London, 1801) pp. 260-1.

25. Great Britain, Admiralty, *Manual of Seamanship*, vol. 1 (London, H.M.S.O., 1951) p. 81, and Canada, *Queen's Regulations and Orders for the Canadian Forces*, Ottawa, amended to 1975, vol. 1, art. 3 25(2).

26. Bruce, Alexander, *The Institutions of Military Law, &c.* (Edinburgh, 1717) p. 123.

27. Great Britain, Admiralty, *Notes on the Royal Navy* (BR/1868 (50)), (London, 1950) p. 40.

28. Boatner, M.M., *Military Customs and Traditions* (New York: McKay, 1956) p. 33.

29. Fortescue, *The Empire and the Army*, pp. 35-36.

30.   Edwards, Major T.J., *Military Customs* (Aldershot, Gale and Polden, 1950) p. 56.

31.   Fortescue, *The Empire and the Army*, p. 12. See also Boatner, *Military Customs and Traditions*, p. 8.

32.   Kealy, J.D.F., and Russell, E.C., *A History of Canadian Naval Aviation* (Ottawa: Queen's Printer, 1965) pp. 98, 101.

33.   Interview with Mr. P.A.C. Chaplin, Senior Research Officer, Directorate of History, NDHQ, Ottawa, 1 November 1976.

34.   Edwards, *Standards, Guidons and Colours of the Commonwealth Forces*, p. 9.

35.   Moresby, Admiral John, *Two Admirals — A Record of a Hundred Years* (London: Methuen, 1913) p. 122.

36.   May, W.E., letter in *Mariner's Mirror*, vol. 53 (1972) p. 102.

37.   Winter, C.F., "Some Recollections of Service with the Imperials — The Queen's Cocoa," *Canadian Defence Journal*, vol. 4, (1926-7) p. 223.

38.   *Sentinel*, vol. 2 (March 1966) p. 23.

39.   *Journal of the Society for Army Historical Research*, London, vol. 49-51 (1971-73) passim.

40.   Edwards, *Military Customs*, p. 59. See also *A Military Dictionary*, printed for C. Jackson, Dublin, 1780, under entry, "Regiment."

41.   Edwards, *Standards, Guidons and Colours of the Commonwealth Forces*, p. 15.

42.   Canada, *CFP 152, Seaman's Handbook*, Ottawa, 1972, p. 5-5 (502).

43.   *Journal of the Society for Army Historical Research*, vol. II (1932) p. 252.

44.   Walker, G. Goold, *The Honourable Artillery Company 1537-1947* (Aldershot, Gale and Polden, 1954) p. 15.

45.   Field, C., *Old Times under Arms — A Military Garner* (London: Hodge) p. 314.

46.   Stanley, Major G.F.G., "The Canadian Militia During the Ancien Regime," *Journal of the Society for Army Historical Research*, vol. 22 (1943/44) p. 159.

47.   Lewis, *The Navy of Britain,* p. 317.

48.   Grose, *Military Antiquities,* vol. 2, p. 48.

49.   Wolfe, Major-General James, *General Wolfe's Instructions to Young Officers* (London, 1780) p. 75.

50.   Walker, *The Honourable Artillery Company, 1537-1947,* p. 123.

51.   Boatner, *Military Customs and Traditions,* p. 62.

52.   Correspondence in *Journal of the Society of Army Historical Research,* vol. I, no. 6 (1922) pp. 233-234.

53.   Canada, CFP 195, *Basic Officer Training: Military Knowlege Manual,* Ottawa, 1972, Section 1005.

54.   Fortescue, *The Empire and the Army,* p. 12.

55.   "Lower Deck," *The British Navy from Within* (London: Hodder & Stoughton, 1914) p. 129. See also *Sentinel,* vol. 2 (March 1966), p. 23.

56.   James, C., *Military Dictionary,* 2 vols. (London: Egerton, 1810).

57.   Great Britain, Admiralty, *Manual of Seamanship (1937),* amended for Canadian use (Ottawa, King's Printer, 1942) p. 4.

58.   Burney, W., *Falconer's Marine Dictionary* (London, 1815).

59.   Fortescue, *The Empire and the Army,* p. 10.

60.   Ashenhurst, Major J.T., "Barbs, Bullets and Bayonets," *Canadian Army Journal,* vol. 4, no. 5 (1950-51) p. 35.

61.   Canada, *The Canadian Guards — Regimental Standing Orders,* Ottawa, 1962, para. 95.

62.   Laughton, L.G. Carr, *Mariner's Mirror,* vol. 10 (1924) p. 97. See also pp. 206-7.

63.   Moresby, *Two Admirals — A Record of a Hundred Years,* p. 53.

64.   Clowes, W.L., *The Royal Navy,* 7 vols., vol. 2 (London: Sampson Low, Marston, 1897-1903) p. 20.

65.   Pepys, Samuel, *King Charles Preserved (An Account of His Escape after the Battle of Worcester dictated by the King Himself to Samuel Pepys)* (London: Rodale Press, 1956) p. 24.

66.   James, *Military Dictionary.*

67.   Lowry, Lieut. Comdr. R.G., *The Origins of Some Naval Terms and Customs* (London: Sampson Low, Marston, 1930) p. 4.

68.   Hoffman, Captain F., *A Sailor of King George: The Journals of Captain Frederick Hoffman, R.N., 1793-1814* (London: Murray, 1901) pp. 42, 227, 305.

69.   Lewis, *The Navy of Britain,* pp. 93-94.

70.   *The Annual Register of World Events,* 1758-1819, vol. 1 (London: Longmans Green, 1758) pp. 306-307.

71.   *Canadian Forces Administrative Orders,* 3-2 (Annex A) 1974.

72.   Grose, *Military Antiquities,* vol. I, p. 316 (note). See also Gordon, Major L.L., *Military Origins* (London: Kaye and Ward, 1971) pp. 249-250.

73.   Lewis, *The Navy of Britain,* pp. 171-174. See also Lewis, *England's Sea Officers,* pp. 26-27, 32-35, 225-239; and Lloyd, Christopher, *The British Seaman, 1200-1860* (London: Collins, 1968) pp. 232-234.

Notes to Chapter 6

1.   *Journal of the Society of Army Historical Research,* London, vol. 3 (1924) p. 18, citing Public Record Office, War Office Records W.O. 3/1, p. 115.

2.   Canada, CFP 265, *Canadian Forces Dress Manual* (1975) articles 364, 365.

3.   *Journal of the Society of Army Historical Research,* p. 18, citing Public Record Office, War Office Records W.O. 3/1, p. 84.

4.   Gardner, Commander J.A., *Above and Under Hatches* (London: Batchworth Press, 1955) p. 107.

5.   Lloyd, Christopher, *The British Seaman, 1200-1860* (London: Collins, 1968) p. 296.

6.   Stradling, Group Captain A.H., *Customs of the Services* (Aldershot, Gale and Polden, 1962). p. 8.

7.   Fortescue, Sir John W., *The Empire and the Army* (London: Cassell, 1930) p. 11.

8.   *Journal of the Society of Army Historical Research*, vol. 1, no. 4 (June 1922) p. 138, quoted from *Archaeologia: or Miscellaneous Tracts relating to Antiquity*, London (1840) vol. XXVIII, p. 145. See also Field, Colonel Cyril, *Old Times Under Arms: A Military Garner* (London: Hodge, 1939) p. 256.

9.   Air Force Routine Order 151, 8 July 1960, amending CAP 90 *(Manual of Drill for the Royal Canadian Air Force)*.

10.   Beckett, Captain W.N.T., *A Few Naval Customs, Expressions, Traditions and Superstitions* (Portsmouth: Gieves, 1934) p. 42.

11.   Barraclough, E.M.C., ed. *Flags of the World* (London: Warne, 1971) p. 18.

12.   Wolfe, Major-General James, *General Wolfe's Instructions to Young Officers* (London: Millan, 1780) pp. iv, v.

13.   *Mariner's Mirror*, vol. I (1911) and vol. II (1912) passim, and vol. 58 (1972) p. 470.

14.   *Canadian Defence Journal*, vol. 11 (1933-34) pp. 156-8.

15.   Barnard, W.T., *The Queen's Own Rifles of Canada, 1860-1960* (Don Mills: Ontario Publishing, 1960) pp. 131-2.

16.   MacBeth, R.G., *The Making of the Canadian West being the Reminiscences of an Eye-witness* (Toronto: Briggs, 1905) p. 200.

17.   Fortescue, *The Empire and the Army*, pp. 62-63.

18.   *Journal of the Society of Army Historical Research*, London, vol. 4 (1925) p. 19, quoting H.R. Fox Bourne, *Sir Philip Sidney* (London: Putnam, 1891).

19.   Letter to the author from the commanding officer, 12e Régiment Blindé du Canada (Milice), 8 August 1974.

20.   Don, W.G., *Reminiscences of the Baltic Fleet of 1855* (Brechin: Edwards, 1894) p. 51. See also Hall, Captain Basil, *The Log-Book of a Midshipman* (London: Blackie, 1896) pp. 136-144, and Smith, W.E.L., *The Navy Chaplain and his Parish* (Ottawa, Queen's Printer, 1967) p. 39.

21. "Saul" is an oratorio composed by Handel in 1738.

22. "Heart of Oak" was composed by Boyce and first sung in a production called "Harlequin's Invasion," in London in the Year of Victories, 1759. Often erroneously called "Hearts of Oak," even in the eighteenth century, the term refers to the tough, enduring quality of the dark wood in the centre of the oak tree.

23. Quoted in the *Journal of the Society for Army Historical Research,* vol. 3 (1924) p. 66.

24. *Canadian Forces Dress Manual* (CFP 265) para 358(4).

25. Hand-written version as given in the booklet *11th Field Artillery Regiment, Royal Regiment of Canadian Artillery: Centennial Year 1866-1966,* published by the Regiment, 1966, p. 9.

Notes to Chapter 7

1. *Mariner's Mirror,* vol. 13 (1927) p. 378.

2. Moresby, Admiral John, *Two Admirals — A Record of a Hundred Years* (London: Methuen 1913) p. 95.

3. *Sentinel,* September 1971, pp. 35-36.

4. Ibid., 1975/3, pp. 16-18.

5. Burney, W., *Falconer's Marine Dictionary* (London, 1815).

6. Hoffman, Captain F., *A Sailor of King George: The Journals of Captain Frederick Hoffman, RN, 1793-1814* (London: Murray, 1901) p. 7.

7. Admiralty, *Manual of Seamanship,* BR 67 (1/51) vol. I, London, HSMO (1951) p. 262.

8. Beckett, Captain W.N.T., *A Few Naval Customs, Expressions, Traditions and Superstitions* (Portsmouth: Gieves 1934) p. 29.

9. Canada, Maritime Command, Manual of Ceremonial for HMC Ships, Halifax, 3 June 1974, para 305.

10. Irving, Commander John, *Royal Navalese* (London: Arnold, 1946) p. 136.

11. Hoffman, *A Sailor of King George*, p. 231.

12. Lewis, Michael, *England's Sea Officers* (London: Allen & Unwin, 1939) pp. 152-3.

13. Hopwood, Captain R.A., "The Boatswain's Call," *The Old Way and Other Poems* (London: Murray, 1916) pp. 59-63.

14. Nuttall, Z., *New Light on Drake — A Collection of Documents Relating to His Voyage of Circumnavigation, 1577-1580* (London: Hakluyt Society, 1914) p. 157.

15. Booklet: "The Changing of the Guard," Ottawa, published by the Regiment of Canadian Guards between 1967 and 1970, passim.

16. Hodgson, Bryan, "Exploring England's Canals," *National Geographic Magazine*, vol 146, no. 1 (July 1974) p. 84.

17. Smith, Captain George, *An Universal Military Dictionary* (London: Millan, 1779).

18. Raikes, Captain G.A., *The History of the Honourable Artillery Company*, 2 vols. vol. 2 (London: Bentley, 1879) p. 250.

19. Ibid., appendix F.

20. Commission scroll issued to Second Lieutenant Norman Albert Buckingham, the Royal Montreal Regiment (M.G.), signed 10 September 1940.

21. Commission scroll issued to Second Lieutenant Ronald James Gourley, the Corps of Royal Canadian Engineers, signed 2 September 1949.

22. Commission scroll issued to Pilot Officer Ronald James Gourley, Royal Canadian Air Force, signed 1 July 1945.

23. Commission scroll issued to Pilot Officer Tony Hannas, Royal Canadian Air Force, signed 8 February 1950.

24. Fortescue, Sir John, *Six British Soldiers* (London: Williams & Norgate, 1928) pp. 16, 17. See also an exchange of correspondence in *Journal of the Society for Army Historical Research*, vol 38 (1960) pp. 142, 188.

25. Commission scroll issued to Mr. Edward Charles Russell, Sub Lieutenant, Royal Canadian Naval Volunteer Reserve, signed 17 October 1945.

26. Commission scroll issued to Mr John Walter Russell, Lieutenant Commander, Royal Canadian Navy, signed 15 April 1960.

27. Irving, *Royal Navalese*, p. 186.

28. Hoffman, *A Sailor of King George*, pp. 165, 166.

29. Ibid., pp. 14-17.

30. Thompson, Edgar K., in *Mariner's Mirror*, vol. 58 (May 1972) p. 166.

31. Greenhill, Basil, in *Mariner's Mirror*, vol. 55 (August 1969) pp. 289-90.

32. Dyott, William, *Dyott's Diary 1781-1845* (London: Constable, 1907) pp. 87-89.

33. Stevens, G.H., *The Royal Canadian Regiment, 1933-1966* (London: London Printing, 1967) p. 222.

34. *Journal of the Society for Army Historical Research*, vol. 11 (1932) p. 248.

35. Ingram, Bruce S., "The Journal of Francis Rogers (1701-1702)," *Three Sea Journals of Stuart Times* (London: Constable, 1936) p. 152.

36. Author's interview of personnel of CFB Trenton, 22 September 1975, and letter from Mr. S. Rohatinsky, Chief Warrant Officer, CFB Trenton, 20 October 1975.

37. Smyth, Admiral W.W., *The Sailor's Word-Book* (London: Blackie and Son, 1867) p. 292.

38. Surtees, W., *Twenty-five Years in the Rifle Brigade* (London: Muller, 1973) p. 4.

39. Moresby, *Two Admirals — A Record of a Hundred Years*, p. 39.

40. Ibid., p. 265.

41. Barnard, W.T., *The Queen's Own Rifles of Canada, 1860-1960, One Hundred Years of Canada* (Don Mills: Ontario Publishing, 1960) p. 6.

42. Ibid., p. 63.

43. Farran, Major Roy, *The History of the Calgary Highlanders, 1921-1954* (Calgary: Bryant Press, 1954) p. 19.

44. Goodspeed, Major D.J., *Battle Royal: A History of the Royal Regiment of Canada, 1862-1962* (Toronto: the Royal Regiment of Canada Association, 1962) p. 347.

45. Turcotte, Major Lucien, "The Royal 22e Regiment, 1914-1964," *Canadian Army Journal*, vol. 18, no. 2 (1964) p. 22.

46. Mountain, Captain W.G., "In Pace Paratus," *Sentinel*, vol. 6, no. 6 (June 1970) p. 30.

47. *Sentinel*, vol. 8 (January 1972) p. 41.

48. Hering, Squadron Leader P.G., *Customs and Traditions of the Royal Air Force* (Aldershot, Gale and Polden, 1961) pp. 164-167.

49. Charters, Captain A.H., "The Royal Regiment of Canada Celebrates Centennial," *Canadian Army Journal*, vol. 16, no. 2 (1962) p. 53.

50. Williams, Jeffery, *Princess Patricia's Canadian Light Infantry* (London: Cooper, 1972) p. 102.

51. Donkin, Major R., *Military Collections and Remarks* (New York: Gaine, 1777) p. 134.

52. *Journal of the Society for Army Historical Research*, vol. 30 (1952) p. 182, and vol. 32 (1954) p. 184.

53. Bland, Lieutenant General Humphrey, *A Treatise of Military Discipline* (London, 1762) pp. 177-9.

54. *The Gleaner*, Fredericton, 4 June 1973.

55. Willcocks, Lieutenant-Colonel K.D.H., The Hastings and Prince Edward Regiment: Customs and Traditions of the Regiment, Belleville, 1968, p. 15.

56. *The Citizen*, Ottawa, 19 December 1974.

57. "Lower Deck," *The British Navy From Within* (London: Hodder & Stoughton, 1914) p. 136.

58. Edwards, A., and Trystan, B.A., *Three Rows of Tape: A Social Study of the Lower Deck* (London: Heinemann, 1929) p. 40.

59. Author's interview with Lieutenant Commander N.J. Russell, RCN, Ret'd, 11 April 1975.

60. Author's interview with Captain (N) F.J. Mifflin, 3 October 1974.

61. Taylor, Lieutenant Commander A.D., Customs of the Navy, 1956, p. 32. (This was used as a text book in the Leadership School, HMCS *Cornwallis*, during the 1950s).

62. Stevens, G.R., *The Royal Canadian Regiment, 1933-1966* (London: London Printing, 1967) p. 22.

63. Edwards and Trystan, *Three Rows of Tape: A Social Study of the Lower Deck*, p. 71.

64. Lowry, Lieut-Cdr R.G., *The Origins of Some Naval Terms and Customs* (London: Sampson, Low Marston, 1930) p. 34.

65. Smith, P.C.F., ed, *The Journals of Ashley Bowen (1728-1813) of Marblehead*, 2 vols., vol. II (Salem: Peabody Museum, 1973) pp. 83-84.

66. Wolfe, Major-General James, *General Wolfe's Instructions to Young Officers* (London: Millan, 1780) p. 15.

67. Canada, *The King's Regulations and Orders for the Royal Canadian Air Force* (Ottawa: King's Printer, 1924) art. 1068A.

68. Canada, *Regimental Standing Orders for The Queen's Own Rifles of Canada*, 1965, article 2.14.

69. Canada, *The RCEME School Precis 7-9-1: Guide to Young Officers Commissioned into The Corps of Royal Canadian Electrical and Mechanical Engineers*, Ottawa, p. 51.

70. Author's interview with personnel of the Second Regiment, RCHA, CFB Petawawa, 7 October 1975.

71. Goodspeed, *Battle Royal*, pp. 132-3.

72. Barnard, W.T., *The Queen's Own Rifles of Canada, 1860-1960, One Hundred Years of Canada* (Don Mills: Ontario Publishing, 1960) p. 185.

73. Bruce, Alexander, *The Institutions of Military Law &c.* (Edinburgh, 1717) pp. 69-70.

74. Ibid. See also Adye, S. Payne, *A Treatise on Courts Martial, also an Essay on Military Punishments and Rewards* (London, 1805) p. 240.

75. Great Britain, War Office, *Manual of Military Law* (London, HMSO, 1929,reprinted 1940) p. 215.

76. Bruce, *The Institutions of Military Law &c.*, pp. 102-103.

77. Great Britain, War Office, *General Regulations and Orders for the Conduct of His Majesty's Forces in Great Britain* (Whitehall, 1799) p. 113.

78. Dyott, *Dyott's Diary, 1781-1845*, vol. 1, p. 30.

79. Author's interview with Colonel Strome Galloway, 25 November 1974.

80. Canada, *Manual of RCAF Drill and Ceremonial*, Ottawa, 1941, CAP, 90, Sec. 126(6). In a letter to the author dated 17 May 1977, Air Commodore W.I. Clements, RCAF (Ret'd), stated that, in the RCAF, promenading "goes back to at least 1930 and probably back to the early 1920s."

81. "Oh, How I Hate to Get Up in the Morning," Irving Berlin, 1917.

82. Simcoe, Elizabeth Posthuma, *Mrs. Simcoe's Diary*, Mary Quayle Innis, ed. (Toronto: Macmillan, 1965) p. 91.

83. Stevens, G.R., *The Royal Canadian Regiment, 1933-1966* (London: London Printing, 1967) p. 222.

84. Worthington, L., *The Spur and the Sprocket — The Story of the Royal Canadian Dragoons* (Kitchener: published by the Regiment, 1968) pp. 30-31.

85. Barnard, *The Queen's Own Rifles of Canada*, p. 193.

86. Goodspeed, *Battle Royal*, p. 36.

87. Farran, Major Roy, *The History of the Calgary Highlanders, 1921-54* (Calgary: Bryant Press, 1954) p. 24.

88. Davies, John, *Lower Deck* (New York: Macmillan, 1945) p. 47.

89.   MacBeth, R.G., *The Making of the Canadian West, being the Reminiscences of an Eye-witness* (Toronto: Briggs, 1905) p. 161.

90.   Author's interview with Squadron Leader W.T. Osborne, RCAF (Ret'd), Ottawa, 2 October 1975.

91.   *Sentinel*, 1975/1, p. 19.

92.   *Journal of the Society of Army Historical Research*, vol. 6 (1927) pp. 118, 181.

93.   Smith, *An Universal Military Dictionary.*

94.   Bland, *A Treatise of Military Discipline*, p. 216.

95.   Fortescue, Sir John W., *The Empire and the Army* (London: Cassell, 1930) p. 161.

96.   Willock, Roger, "Green Jackets on the Red River," *Canadian Army Journal*, vol. 13, no. 1 (1959) p. 31.

97.   *Regimental Standing Orders for the Queen's Own Rifles of Canada* (1965) Annex A, p. 8.

98.   Smyth, *The Sailor's Word Book*, p. 581.

99.   *Journal of the Society for Army Historical Research*, vol. 12 (1933) p. 58.

100. Author's interview with personnel of the Royal Canadian Regiment, Wolseley Barracks, London, 22 October 1974.

101. Author's interview with Captain (N) F.J. Mifflin, NDHQ, 3 October 1974.

102. Denison, Captain F.C., *Historical Record of the Governor-General's Body Guard* (Toronto: Hunter, Rose & Co., 1876) p. 83.

103. *Advice to the Officers of the British Army: with the Addition of some Hints to the Drummer and Private-Soldier* (London: printed for G. Kearsley, 1783) pp. 9, 20. According to R.D. Heinl's *Dictionary of Military and Naval Quotations* (Annapolis: USNI, 1967) p. 187, this work was written by the well known military writer, Francis Grose.

104. Admiralty, *Manual of Seamanship* (BR67), 1937, (Reproduced as amended in Canada, 1942, for the exclusive use of His Majesty's Canadian Naval Forces) pp. 428, 432.

105. Nuttall, *New Light on Drake*, p. 59.

106. Ingram, "The Diary of Dawtrey Cooper," *Three Sea Journals of Stuart Times*, p. xx.

107. Moresby, *Two Admirals — A Record of a Hundred Years*, p. 24.

108. Teonge, Henry, *The Diary of Henry Teonge, Chaplain on Board H.M.'s Ships Assistance, Bristol and Royal Oak, 1675-1679* (London: Routledge, 1927) pp. 35, 248.

109. Smith, Waldo E.L., *The Navy Chaplain and His Parish* (Ottawa: Queen's Printer, 1967) p. 193.

110. Canadian Forces Administrative Order (CFAO) 36-35 (1976).

111. Wolfe, *General Wolfe's Instructions to Young Officers*, p. 76 (Order issued at Point Orleans, New France, July 2 1759).

112. Worthington, L., *The Spur and the Sprocket* (Kitchener: Reeve Press, 1968) p. 23.

113. CFAO 36-35 (1976).

114. *Nautical Magazine*, vol. 209, no. 5 (May 1973) p. 303.

115. Author's interview with the officers of HMC submarine *Okanagan*, Halifax, 25 October 1976.

116. Canada, CFP 201, *Manual of Drill and Ceremonial* (1969) art. 2404.

117. Fortescue, *The Empire and the Army*, p. 66.

118. Bland, *A Treatise of Military Discipline*, p. 206.

119. Wolfe, *General Wolfe's Instructions to Young Officers*, pp. 11-12.

120. Letter, E. Boscawen, Admiral, to the commanding officer of His Majesty's Troops on board the *Two Brothers*, transport, 12 May 1758. Document in the possession of Hugh F. Pullen, Rear Admiral, Royal Canadian Navy, (Ret'd).

121. How, Douglas, *The 8th Hussars, A History of the Regiment* (Sussex, N.B.: Maritime Publishing, 1964) p. 61.

122. *Journal of the Society for Army Historical Research*, vol. 19 (1940) p. 248. The significance of first and last post in beating the tattoo is also described in a letter from the adjutant general (Major-General Letson) to the district officer commanding, military district no. 10, Winnipeg HQ, 420-18-11 dated 31 August 1943, quoting *The King's Regulations and Orders for the Canadian Army 1939* (Ottawa). See also *The King's Regulations and Orders for the Royal Canadian Air Force* (Ottawa: King's Printer, 1924) articles 934, 935.

123. This point is ably discussed in H.G. Farmer's article "The Retreat: A Suggested Origin of the Modern Ceremony," *Journal of the Society for Army Historical Research*, vol. 23 (1945) pp. 119-120.

124. Smith, *An Universal Military Dictionary*.

125. Moresby, *Two Admirals — A record of a Hundred Years*, p. 53.

126. Lanctot, Gustave, *Montreal under Maisonneuve, 1642-1665* (Toronto: Clark Irwin, 1969) p. 94.

127. Bland, *A Treatise of Military Discipline*, p. 203.

128. Author's interviews of personnel at CFB Trenton, 22 September 1975, and of CFB North Bay and 414 Squadron, 8 October 1975.

129. Canada, *Canadian Forces Dress Manual* (CFP 265), NDHQ, Ottawa, 1977, para 204, 1(4).

130. Canada, *Regulations and Instructions for the Clothing of the Royal Canadian Air Force* (CAP No 9), RCAFHQ, Ottawa, 1927 (reprinted 1937) p. 38, amendment No 47 (1941).

131. *Journal of the Society for Army Historical Research*, vol. 21 (1942) p. 108, and vol. 25 (1947) p. 188. See also Barnes, Major R. Money, *Military Uniforms of Britain & the Empire, 1742 to the Present Time* (London: Seeley, 1960) pp. 166 and 236.

132. Norris, Geoffrey, *The Royal Flying Corps: A History* (London: Muller, 1965) passim. See also Saunders, H. St. G., *Per Ardua: The Rise of British Air Power, 1911-1939* (London: Oxford University Press, 1944).

Notes to Chapter 8

1. *Sentinel*, 1974/9, p. 19.

2. Ibid., 1974/6, p. 29.

3. Canada, BRCN 150, E.C. Russell, ed., *Badges, Battle Honours and Mottoes, Royal Canadian Navy*, 4 vols., vol 2 (Ottawa: Naval Headquarters, 1964) "Fraser."

4. Ibid., vol 4, "Terra Nova." See also *Sentinel*, vol. 9, 1973/10, pp. 13-14.

5. Willcocks, Lt-Col. K.D.H., The Hastings and Prince Edward Regiment: Customs and Traditions of the Regiment, Belleville, 1968, p. 17.

6. Letter to the author from the commanding officer, CFB Edmonton, 27 April 1977.

7. *Roundel*, vol. 9, no. 2 (March 1957) p. 3.

8. Donkin, Major R., *Military Collections and Remarks* (New York: Gaine, 1777) p. 133.

9. "Troop Transport in Canada, 1843," *Canadian Army Journal*, vol 10, no. 4 (1956) pp. 100-101.

10. *Journal of the Society for Army Historical Research*, vol. 25 (1947) p. 46. The antics of Jacob the Goose of the Coldstream are described in detail in General Sir Daniel Lysons, *Early Reminiscenses* (London, 1896).

11. Worthington, L., *The Spur and the Sprocket* (Kitchener: Reeve Press, 1968) pp. 69, 71.

12. Nicholson, Colonel G.W.L., *The Fighting Newfoundlander: A History of the Royal Newfoundland Regiment* (St. John's: Government of Newfoundland, 1965) pp. 219-220.

13. Farran, Major Roy, *The History of the Calgary Highlanders, 1921-54* (Calgary: Bryant Press, 1954) p. 50.

14. *8th Canadian Hussars . . . Regimental Précis no. 4*, CFB Petawawa, 1975.

15. *8th Canadian Hussars (Princess Louise's) Regimental Standing Orders*, 1974. See also *Sentinel*, vol. 6 (March 1970) and vol. 9 (July 1973) and How, Douglas, *The 8th Hussars, A History of the Regiment* (Sussex, N.B.: Maritime Publishing, 1964) p. 271.

16. Thorgrimsson, T., and Russell, E.C., *Canadian Naval Operations in Korean Waters, 1950-1955* (Ottawa: Queen's Printer, 1965) p. 74.

17.   *Sentinel*, vol. 9 (February 1973).

18.   Stevens, G.R., *A City Goes to War* (Edmonton, published by the regiment, 1964) passim.

19.   *Roundel*, vol 9, no. 7 (September 1957).

20.   For an account of the sending of one of Queen Victoria's goats to the Royal Welch Fusiliers in 1844, when that regiment was on garrison duty in Canada, see Broughton-Mainwaring, Major R., *Historical Record of the Royal Welch Fusiliers* (London: Hatchard's, 1889) p. 160.

21.   *Canadian Army Journal*, vol. 10, no. 1 (1956).

Notes to Chapter 9

1.   Canada, Commander Maritime Command, *Manual of Ceremonial for HMC Ships* (draft, 3 June 1974) Halifax, art. 316-318.

2.   Canada, Naval Staff, "Sketch History of HMCS Assiniboine," Naval Historical Section Papers (1 May 1961) and "Brief History of HMCS *Assiniboine*, Second of Name," ibid., 24 September, 1963.

3.   Bell, F.J., *Room to Swing a Cat* (New York: Longmans, Green, 1938) pp. 206-7. See also *Imperial Oil Fleet News*, Summer 1975, and *The Compass*, Jan/Feb, 1959.

4.   Clowes, Sir W.L., *The Royal Navy*, 7 vols., vol. 1 (London: Sampson Low, Marston, 1898-1903) p. 342, and vol. 7, p. 73.

5.   Webster, J.C., ed. *Journal of Jeffrey Amherst, 1756-63* (Toronto, 1931) p. 174.

6.   Ibid., p. 223. A snow was square-rigged on the fore and mainmasts, and had in addition a stumpy mizzen-mast stepped close abaft the mainmast on which was set a fore-and-aft trysail, and, in this way, differed from a brig.

7.   Lovette, Vice Admiral L.P., *Naval Customs Traditions & Usage* (Annapolis, Md.: United States Naval Institute, 1959) p. 47.

8.   Beckett, Captain W.N.T., *A Few Naval Customs, Expressions, Traditions and Superstitions* (Portsmouth: Gieves, 1934) p. 52. See also Admiralty, *Manual of Seamanship*, vol. 1, BR67(1/51) (London, HMSO, 1951) p. 264.

9. For an appreciation of the many frustrations facing a captain engaged in preparing for the commissioning of an eighteenth century frigate, see Grice, Lieutenant-Commander H.R.C., "HMS *Daedalus,*" *Naval Electrical Review,* vol 22, no. 4 (1969).

10. Russell, E.C., "The Cook, a Mighty Man Was He," *The Crowsnest,* January, 1960, p. 19.

11. Booklet: "The Commissioning of HMCS *Athabaskan,*" 30 September 1972.

Notes to Chapter 10

1. The badges of HMC ships may be seen in colour in the limited edition of BRCN 150, E.C. Russell, ed., *Badges, Battle Honours and Mottoes, Royal Canadian Navy,* 4 vols. (Ottawa: Naval Headquarters, 1964) Black and white reproductions of regimental badges are in volume I of the *Canadian Army List, The Regiments and Corps of The Canadian Army,* compiled by Lieutenant Colonel Alice Sorby, CWAC, (Ret'd) (Ottawa: Queen's Printer, 1964). See also Canadian Forces Publication (CFP) 267, illustrating and describing the unit, ship, station, base, formation and command badges current in the Canadian Forces today.

2. Hering, Sqn. Ldr. P.G., *Customs and Traditions of the Royal Air Force* (Aldershot, Gale and Polden, 1961) pp. 131-132.

3. *Roundel,* vol. 14, no 1, (Jan/Feb 1962) p. 6.

4. *Sentinel,* vol. 6 (April, 1970) p. 47.

5. Canada, Maritime Command Manual of Ceremonial for HMC Ships (draft), Halifax, 3 June, 1974, para 403.

6. Letter from Mr. Joseph Stephenson, ex-Royal Naval Canadian Volunteer Reserve, *Crowsnest,* June 1957, pp. 15-16, and Mr. A.J.A. Bell, ex-R.N.C.V.R., *Crowsnest,* December 1957, p. 3.

7. *Sentinel,* April 1973, pp. 24-25.

8. The whole story of the RCAF and RAF eagle vs. albatross controversy is given in *Sentinel,* April 1968, p. 47.

9. The air historian, Wing Commander F.H. Hitchins, researched this matter and placed his findings in "The Great Eagle — Albatross Controversy," *Roundel,* vol. 1, no 10 (August, 1949) pp. 13-14. For a description of the badge of the Royal Air Force, see Hering, *Customs and Traditions of the Royal Air Force,* p. 77.

10. Letter to the author from the commanding officer, the Grey and Simcoe Foresters, 11 October 1974.

11. Memorandum, Director of Ceremonial to Chief of Air Operations, NDHQ, 18 August 1975.

12. Millan J., *Signals for the Royal Navy and Ships under Convoy* (London, 1778) p. 4.

13. *Mariner's Mirror*, vol. 8 (1922) p. 222.

14. For information regarding the original Astral Crown, designed for the Royal Air Force, see Scott-Giles, C.W., *Boutell's Heraldry* (London: Warne) p. 187, and Gerald W. Wollaston "Heraldry and the Badges of the Royal Air Forces," *Roundel*, vol. 3 (1950-51) pp. 29-31, originally published in a RAF pamphlet in 1944.

15. Smyth, Admiral W.W., *The Sailor's Word-Book* (London: Blackie & Son, 1867) p. 319.

16. Moll, Dr F., "The History of the Anchor," *Mariner's Mirror*, vol. 13, no 4 (October, 1927) p. 293. See also letters in vol. 5, no. 6 (December 1919) p. 189; vol. 6, no. 8 (August 1920) p. 253 and no. 10 (October 1920) p. 316; vol. 7, no. 3 (March 1921) p. 88; vol. 9, no. 4 (April 1923) p. 127.

17. CFP 267, *The Badges of the Canadian Forces* (Ottawa, 1977) chapter 1.

18. Memorandum dated 22 November 1951; draft Canadian Army Order, 3 April 1959; and memoranda dated 27 February and 31 May 1963, all on file 5250-28-10 — Canadian Army Badge.

Notes to Chapter 11

1. Grose, Francis, *Military Antiquities*, 2 vols., vol. 2 (London, 1801) p. 41.

2. Smith, Captain George, *An Universal Military Dictionary* (London: Millan, 1779).

3. From *Thomas Ainslie's Journal* quoted in the *Journal of the Society for Army Historical Research*, vol. 20 (1941) p. 103. See also Stanley, G.F.G., *Canada Invaded, 1775-1776* (Toronto: Hakkert, 1973) p. 96.

4. Hoffman, Captain F., *A Sailor of King George: the Journals of Captain Frederick Hoffman, RN, 1793-1814* (London: Murray, 1901) p. 113.

5. Nicholson, Colonel C.W.L., *The Fighting Newfoundlander: A History of the Royal Newfoundland Regiment*, Government of Newfoundland, 1965, pp. 6-7.

6. Lloyd, Christopher, *The British Seaman, 1200-1860* (London: Collins, 1968) pp. 83, 85.

7. Webster, J.C., ed., *The Siege of Beauséjour in 1755, A journal of the Attack on Beauséjour* . . . (Saint John: New Brunswick Museum, 1936) pp. 33-34.

8. Downey, Fairfax, *Louisbourg: Key to a Continent* (Englewood Cliffs, New Jersey: Prentice Hall, 1965) pp. 73, 103. See also McLennan, J.S., *Louisbourg from its Foundation to its Fall* (London: Macmillan, 1918) pp. 178-180.

9. Hart-McHarg, W., *From Quebec to Pretoria* (Toronto: Briggs, 1902) pp. 222-223.

10. From the Rodgers and Hammerstein musical, *Oklahoma* (1943).

11. Kealy, J.D.F. and Russell, E.C., *A History of Canadian Naval Aviation, 1918-1962* (Ottawa: Queen's Printer, 1965) p. 97.

12. Winstock, Lewis, *Songs and Music of the Redcoats* (London: Cooper, 1970) p. 67. See also, Edwards, Major T.J., *Military Customs* (Aldershot, Gale and Polden, 1950) p. 15.

13. *Canadian Defence Journal*, vol. 7 (1929-30) p. 491. The diarist, a Channel Islander named Lieutenant John Le Couteur, not only took liberties with the song's title, but also the instrument. It was probably a fife, for it is said that the bugle, being a valveless instrument, cannot produce the notes of "The Girl I Left Behind Me." For a more detailed account, see Squires, W. Austin, *The 104th Regiment of Foot (The New Brunswick Regiment) 1803-1817* (Fredericton: Brunswick Press, 1962) pp. 118-136.

14. Adam, F., *The Clans, Septs and Regiments of the Scottish Highlands,* (Edinburgh: Johnston and Bacon, 1960) p. 418. See also MacNeill, Seumas, *Piobaireachd: Classical Music of the Highland Bagpipe* (Edinburgh: British Broadcasting Corporation, 1968) pp. 1-9.

15. Nicholson, Colonel G.W.L., *Canadian Expeditionary Force, 1914-1919* (Ottawa: Queen's Printer, 1962) pp. 184-185.

16. Binns, Lt-Col. P.L., *A Hundred Years of Military Music* (Gillingham, Dorset: Blackmore Press, 1959) p. 14 et seq. See also Grose, *Military Antiquities*, vol. 2, page 41 et seq.

17. Adkins, Lieut-Col. H.E., *Treatise on the Military Band* (London: Boosey, 1958) pp. 1-9.

18. Officially approved marches are listed in Canadian Forces Administrative Order 32-3, Annex A.

19. Wood, Walter, *The Romance of Regimental Marches* (London: Clowes, 1932) pp. 76-77.

20. "Soldiers of the Queen" was written by one, Thomas A. Barrett (1866-1928), known professionally as Leslie Stuart.

21. Wood, *The Romance of Regimental Marches*, p. 27.

22. Farmer, H.G., "Our Bands in the Napoleonic Wars," *Journal of the Society for Army Historical Research*, vol. 40 (1962) p. 33.

23. Edwards, *Military Customs*, p. 23.

24. Scholes, Percy A. *The Oxford Companion to Music* (London: Oxford University Press, 1950) p. 420. See also Firth, C.H., *Naval Songs and Ballads*, vol. 33 (London: Navy Records Society) p. 220.

25. Hering, Squadron Leader P.G., *Customs and Traditions of the Royal Air Force* (Aldershot, Gale & Polden, 1961) pp. 181-185.

26. Message 1015Z April (date, time group mutilated) from ministry of defence, United Kingdom (Air) to British Defence Liaison Staff (Air), Ottawa, received in Ottawa 5 April 1972.

27. Canada, Department of National Defence, *Divine Service Book for The Armed Forces*, Ottawa, 1950, hymn 158.

28. Lovette, Vice Admiral L.P., *Naval Customs, Traditions & Usage* (Annapolis: United States Naval Institute, 1959) appendix K.

29. Smith, W.E.L., *The Navy and Its Chaplains in the Days of Sail* (Toronto: Ryerson, 1961) p. 197.

30. Canada, *Divine Service Book for The Armed Forces*, hymn 159.

31. *Regimental Standing Orders*, 8th Canadian Hussars (Princess Louise's), 1974, page xi.

32.   *Regimental Standing Orders*, The Queen's Own Rifles of Canada, 1965, Section 9 (1.20).

33.   Royal Canadian Air Force press release No. 558, 17 January 1942. "High Flight" has been set to music by Dr. Lloyd Pfautsch, composer and conductor of choral music, for use at the United States Air Force Academy, Colorado Springs.

Notes to Chapter 12

1.   Smith, Whitney, *Flags Through the Ages and Across the World* (New York: McGraw-Hill, 1975) pp. 64-65. See also Barraclough, E.M.C., ed., *Flags of the World* (London: Warne, 1972) p. 123.

2.   Canada, Secretary of State, *The National Flag of Canada* (Ottawa: Queen's Printer, 1966) pp. 19, 20.

3.   Author's interview with cadets and staff, Royal Military College of Canada, Kingston, 23 September 1975.

4.   Author's interview with personnel of 427 (Helicopter) Squadron, CFB Petawawa, 7 October 1975.

5.   Teonge, Henry, *The Diary of Henry Teonge, Chaplain on Board H.M.'s Ships Assistance, Bristol and Royal Oak, 1675-1679* (London: Routledge 1927) p. 128.

6.   Moresby, Admiral John, *Two Admirals — A Record of a Hundred Years* (London: Methuen, 1913) p. 51.

7.   Canada, Maritime Command, Manual of Ceremonial for HMC Ships, Halifax, 1974, para 207.

8.   Admiralty, *Manual of Seamanship*, vol. 1 (London: HMSO, 1951) p. 258. See also *Mariner's Mirror*, vol 9 (1923) p. 64, and *Sentinel*, vol. 6, no. 8 (September 1970) p. 45.

9.   Barraclough, *Flags of the World*, p. 35.

10.   Davies, John, *Lower Deck* (New York: Macmillan, 1945) p. 92.

11.   NDHQ message to Maritime Command, Halifax, 121730Z November 1975.

12.   Lowry, Lieut. Comdr. R.G., *The Origins of Some Naval Terms and Customs* (London: Sampson Low, Marston, 1930) pp. 52-53. See also Barraclough, *Flags of the World*, pp. 12-13.

13.   Cumberland, Barlow, *History of the Union Jack* (Toronto: Briggs, 1900) pp. 36-45.

14.   Edwards, Major T.J., *Standards, Guidons and Colours of the Commonwealth Forces* (Aldershot, Gale and Polden, 1953) p. 25 and appendix A.

15.   Admiralty Fleet Order 1057/1924, 25 April 1924. See also Edwards, *Standards, Guidons and Colours of the Commonwealth Forces*, pp. 145-146.

16.   British Government Despatch No 156, 31 March 1925, and telegram 14 April, 1925, file NSC 1460-25 vol 1.

17.   Message 231807Z OCT 59 COMBRAX HALIFAX to CANAVHED, file NSC 1460-25 vol 2.

18.   Address of Her Majesty the Queen to the Royal Canadian Navy, enclosure to flag officer, Atlantic Coast letter to naval secretary, Naval Headquarters, Ottawa AC 1225-41, 29 May 1959, confirmed in AC 1460-1, 28 October 1959.

19.   *Roundel*, vol 2, no. 8 (1949/50).

20.   Department of national defence press release, June 28 1968.

21.   Edwards, *Standards, Guidons and Colours of the Commonwealth Forces*, appendix A.

22.   Ibid.

23.   Field, Cyril, *Old Times Under Arms — A Military Garner* (London: Hodge, 1939) p. 446.

24.   Bell, G., *Rough Notes of an Old Soldier*, 2 vols., vol. 1 (London: Day, 1867) p. 15.

25.   Edwards, *Standards, Guidons and Colours of the Commonwealth Forces*, p. 25.

26.   Grose, Francis, *Military Antiquities*, 2 vols., vol. 2 (London, 1801) p. 51.

27.   Edwards, *Standards, Guidons and Colours of the Commonwealth Forces*, pp. 170-172. See also Lehman, J.H., *The First Boer War* (London: Cape, 1972) p. 151.

28.   Letter by Brigadier R.O. Alexander, *Journal of the Society of Army Historical Research*, vol. 14 (1935) p. 185.

29.   Ibid.

30.   Williams, Jeffrey, *Princess Patricia's Canadian Light Infantry* (London: Cooper, 1972) pp. 5, 30-31. See also *Sentinel*, 1975/2.

31.   Final stanza of song, "The Ric-A-Dam-Doo," *Song Book* (Edmonton: The Loyal Edmonton Regiment, 3 PPCLI n/d) p. 1.

32.   Jackson, C., *A Military Dictionary* (Dublin, 1780).

33.   Edwards, *Standards, Guidons and Colours of the Commonwealth Forces*, p. 26.

34.   Canadian Forces Administrative Order (CFAO) 62-5.

35.   Hering, Sqn. Ldr. P.G., *Customs and Traditions of the Royal Air Force* (Aldershot, Gale and Polden, 1961) pp. 59-60.

36.   *Roundel*, vol. 14, no. 5 (June 1962) p. 30.

37.   Canada, Department of National Defence, Director of Artillery, *Standing Orders for the Royal Regiment of Canadian Artillery*, Don Mills, 1963, paras 161-163. See also Edwards, *Standards, Guidons and Colours of the Commonwealth Forces*, p. 34 (fn); Edwards, *Military Customs*, p. 103; Fortescue, Sir John W., *The Empire and the Army* (London: Cassell, 1930) pp. 68-69. For an interesting account of the guns as colours over a century of service, see booklet, "Centennial Year 1866-1966," 11th Field Artillery Regiment, Royal Regiment of Canadian Artillery, Guelph, 1966, p. 11.

38.   Regimental Standing Orders for The Queen's Own Rifles of Canada, 1965, pp. 8-10.

39.   Author's interview with the commanding officer, the Algonquin Regiment, North Bay, 8 October 1975.

40.   Fetherstonhaugh, R.C. *The Royal Canadian Regiment, 1883-1933* (Montreal: Gazette Printing, 1936) p. 164.

41.   Willcocks, Lt. Col. K.D.H., Customs and Traditions of the Regiment, Belleville, The Hastings and Prince Edward Regiment, 1968, p. 13.

42.   Booklet: "The Colours of the Queen's Rangers: The Story of the Return of The

Colours to The Queen's York Rangers (1st American Regiment)," Toronto, The Queen's York Rangers, 1975, pp. 7-11.

43.   Brochure, *Presentation of Colours to the Governor General's Foot Guards*, Parliament Hill, 1 July 1972.

44.   Nicholson, Colonel G.W.L., *The Fighting Newfoundlander: A History of the Royal Newfoundland Regiment*, Government of Newfoundland, 1965, p. 2.

45.   Broughton-Mainwaring, Major R., *Historical Record of the Royal Welch Fusiliers* (London: Hatchard's, 1889) p. 163.

46.   Ibid., pp. 163, 165.

47.   Boissonault, C-M., *Histoire du Royal 22e Régiment*, 2 vols., vol. 2 (Québec: Pélican, 1964) frontispiece.

48.   Letter to the author from the commanding officer, the Queen's Own Cameron Highlanders of Canada, Winnipeg, 12 November 1974.

49.   Canadian Forces Administrative Order (CFAO) 62-5 (1976), (23 and 24).

50.   *Journal of the Society for Army Historical Research*, vol. 23 (1945) p. 130.

51.   *Sentinel*, Nov/Dec 1969, p. 40.

52.   Galloway, Colonel Strome, "The Canadian Guards," *Sentinel*, vol. 6, no. 8 (September 1970) pp. 22-23. For more on the colours of the Canadian Guards, see booklet "The Changing of the Guard," published by the Regiment of Canadian Guards, circa 1967-70.

53.   Farran, Major Roy, *The History of the Calgary Highlanders* (Calgary: Bryant Press, 1954) p. 37.

54.   Gordon, Major L.L., *Military Origins* (London: Kaye and Ward, 1971) p. 38.

55.   Hering, *Customs and Traditions of the Royal Air Force*, pp. 57-58. For a detailed, scholarly treatment of this subject see Edwards, *Standards, Guidons and Colours of the Commonwealth Forces*, pp. 118-122.

56.   Smith, Captain George, *An Universal Military Dictionary* (London: Millan, 1779) under the entry "Drum."

57. Letter, commanding officer, 48th Highlanders of Canada, to the author, 18 October 1974.

58. Letter, commanding officer, the British Columbia Dragoons, to the author, 5 December 1974.

59. Letter, commanding officer, Royal Montreal Regiment, to the author, 15 October 1974.

Index